Irish Hearts

Caress Across The Ocean

©

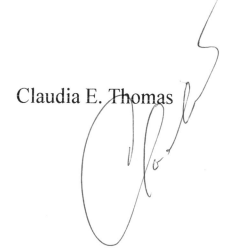

Claudia E. Thomas

Blaze Books ◆ Helena, Montana

To the dear friends and family that supported me! With special thanks to Judy, Stacie, Brenda, Beth, Heather, Fritz, Steve, Harry and Hall. To Michael, poet, editor, and friend...who put the "very" into my writing...you know what I mean! Last, but most certainly not least, to my children, who I am completely devoted to and grateful for - they give me courage and dignity. Thank you all for loving me.

Aflame in Twilight's Blaze

Quiver of arrows pierced my heart,
Cupid's spray sets well apart.
In spring's still quiet thus he lays,
make lovers' fools on which he preys.

And he fell upon us both it seems,
where in sweet solace of our dreams.
He assaults our minds, our souls and hearts,
entangled ecstasy he thus imparts.

Our deep desires his game he plays,
we hold no power over fiery days.
We have fallen victim his dearest flare,
now in each other's eyes we stare.

He retreats us now, his deed well done,
new devoted fools he thus will run.
And frolic in the dewdrop's haze,
set lovers' aflame in twilight's blaze.

CONTENTS

Chapter 1
The End

It was an unseasonably warm October day, especially for this part of the country. The rain at first appeared to hold itself back, that is, until the burial service started. But now, it was as if God Himself were crying tears for her.

"...what can I possibly add about the passing of one who had such a zest for life. A woman who gave her life completely to her community, friends and family. As when the sun shines down its warmth on us, so she too shined her light with uncomplicated simplicity and love. Mother, grandmother and friend, Colleen Keating will be missed by all that knew her. She wanted us not to gather in grief, but in celebration for the life to come and her belief that she will again one day be joined by all of you in paradise."

It now seemed that the cloudburst and the pastor's eulogy were simultaneously concluding. It appeared the angels themselves were parting the clouds to allow glimmering beams of sunlight to illuminate the flag draped coffin. The flag was removed, folded in military style by six uniformed fire department pall bearers, and as she had requested, presented to my Uncle Jim. The sunbeams looked like fairies dancing upon the finely polished casket as it was gently lowered into the ground to the music of Amazing Grace, played softly by the bagpiper in the background.

"Mother, grandmother and friend." How inadequate the words. What did that really say about this woman whose shell of a body was lying in the grave, but whose spirit now soared freely with the angels she so deeply believed in. A double rainbow pushed back the stubborn clouds even further, every color of its prism enhanced as the last remnants of the early morning downpour turned the silver-lined clouds into castles and sea creatures.

My mind drifted to an earlier time when we went

cloud dreaming. I could hear her voice say, "Do you see it, Caetlin?"

"Yes! Yes, I see it, Grandma. The dark knight is killing the dragon. But what is that?"

"Why it's only the fair maiden Aurorame waiting to receive the kiss of the dark knight."

"Does she love him do you think, Grandma?"

As if a secret for just we two, she whispered, "Oh yes, she's been waiting for him all her life. She has dreamed of this moment and made up her mind years ago she would settle for nothing less than his true love."

How I will miss this grand lady. Her and all her wonderment and mystery. Sometimes it seemed she were the child and I the grandmother. She was young at heart stirring my imagination with her stories and her kindness to me.

"Gave her life completely to her community," the words hardly expressed her dedication to community work. She shared with me many accounts of being the first woman volunteer firefighter and emergency medical technician in this small western town. Grandma also worked with various other community groups. When I asked her how she dealt with the anxiety and stress of her emergency work she said, "Why Caetlin, dear, I travel!" And how she loved to travel! Of all the countries she knew, there was no place in the world that made her eyes sparkle quite the way they did when she spoke of her Ireland. As a child, I was spellbound at her every word while curled up in her lap in the overstuffed chair near the fireplace. Through her eyes, which were the color of her beloved Ireland, emeralds and topaz, I gained an insight of the world that would have otherwise been lost to me. Her world seemed full of quests, yet I don't believe that I ever really understood even a fraction of why she was who she was.

"Uncomplicated simplicity and love." Yes, I can see why the pastor would say that. Yet I could not help but think her life more complex than what people perceived it to be.

I glanced back over my shoulder at her grave as I made my way to the car. I could almost hear her voice saying, "The skies were gray when I first saw the shoreline from the plane window with hints of blue and gold sunbeams peeking through to the fields below. As the clouds parted, I could make out the most lovely cherubs, and see the green paddocks and babbling brookes as we continued our descent," she said. "It's so green there even the water is green! You must see it someday, mo grah!"

Angel

There's a cherub over emerald isles,
bestowing frolic and bantering smiles.
The angel fills all hearts with love,
as descends he the heavens from above.

He touches me also with brush of wings,
cheerful heart and songs he sings.
He steals away all souls turned cold,
and places in them sweet golden mold.

I'm sure, 'tis Ireland where he dwells,
lighting hearts with his magic spells.
For no other place is near as grand,
as precious a sight as that dear land.

I watched in quiet amazement as the parade of people returned to their cars, fire trucks, ambulances and police cruisers. The procession had stretched along the entire length of Main Street, Grandmother's coffin carried on the vintage 1941 Chevy fire truck at the head of the line. She had wanted to be buried back here in Montana and we naturally respected her wishes. I would return in a few days to the cottage in New England which she had willed to me, where she had spent much of her life.

The small cemetery had been overflowing with mourners who were now all headed to the bar to have a bite to eat and, what Grandmother would have deemed a "true Irish wake!"

"No I don't want a lot of grieving and sniffling. Death is a natural process and a time for celebration. No, Caetlin, do not grieve my passing for I will see you again. Besides, I want people to share a grand time together." She had told me, "Not all the stories they tell will be lauding my innocence, but I'm hopeful they will be, at least, interesting. Don't forget to take the case of Paddy's Whiskey from the basement! It will help loosen their tongues, they'll cry and, I hope, mostly laugh, and I promise I will be watching it all from above."

Riding with my mother and Uncle Jim, who had flown in from his military post in Germany, we arrived at Murphy's Pub just behind the brunt of the crowd. It was a fair-sized bar in the center of town and was one of my grandmother's favorite watering holes. "It's a grand Irish pub," she would say. "No finer in all of Montana, though don't let them hear you say that in Butte, for they'd never believe you."

There were so many people there many I knew, and many more I did not. The former Chief of the fire department, John Stiger, walked over to us as we entered saying, "She was a very special woman. I remember when she joined the department."

"It was very difficult for her when she joined," my mother said.

"It was a different time then," he said. "We never had a woman before...she wasn't wanted and she knew it. Still, she stuck out all the hard times and gained the respect and admiration of all the men."

John was a large man, over six feet tall with a more than slightly noticeable beer belly. He was balding, only a hint of blonde fuzz circled his head like a crown. He'd lived in this town all his life and was active, not only on the fire department, but on the town council and other community organizations.

"She spoke many times about your support, John," my mother added.

"Ah, I have to admit, I was one of them who didn't find having a woman doing a man's work a pleasant prospect either," he said. "But she was no-nonsense...did her job and then some. I wish half of the members would have even a small portion of the sense of commitment that Colleen did."

His eyes filled with a reflective gaze as he told us, "I remember the time when the Jones' home was on fire, and there went Colleen, caution to the wind, running inside and pulling out old man Jones. He was none too happy about it either as all he had on was his jockies and it was about ten below outside. But she grabbed a blanket and stuffed him in the police car. All the time with him complaining and carrying on. But I watched her take his hand in hers and, she didn't say a word, just grinned. She melted his angry facade with her smile and then he smiled too. Funny, the way she could talk to people with nothing more than a smile."

"But God help the one who got on her bad side," Jim stated. "Not that she would hold a grudge. Like she used to say, 'I may forgive, but I can't forget.'"

"I don't know how she kept up with it all at times," mother added. "But she loved being on the department."

"Is it true she went parachute jumping?" I did not need an answer for I had come to know my grandmother's adventuresome spirit and held no doubt that she had. But it created some small way of joining in the conversation and the opportunity for yet another tale.

"Oh yes," Uncle Jim said. "I remember watching her. Half the family turned out to see it. Her and my Uncle Wade had decided to join forces for the experience. They jumped from such a small run-down Cessna that, when climbed aboard, they were relieved to have parachutes on. Wade jumped first with her not far behind. Mom said it was the quietest and most wonderful sensation in the world...until she landed that is. With an 'Oh shit', she lay back on her chute bag knowing she had fractured her ankle. I'm sure I still have the video somewhere."

"Mom didn't even complain of the pain," my mother added. "She just asked for a cigarette and relaxed while one of the men splinted her...said she was much too 'high' on the experience to let a small thing like a broken ankle ruin it."

"Small thing," Jim said, "broke both bones clean through...even had several pins and screws put in there."

"I remember," mom said, "she said how it would get sore whenever the weather turned cold."

"Wade said she held some sort of death wish because she wasn't at all nervous getting on the plane," Jim added. "But I think it was just her sense of pursuit. She wanted to experience as much of this world as she could. She was fearless at times."

"Yet she was a sensitive woman in many ways, it seemed that she..." John started to say.

"Who's that man over there?" I interrupted pointing to a stranger who had just walked in. But no one recognized him.

"He must be one of your grandmother's out-of-town friends," John concluded.

At that moment, the loud squeal of radio pagers sounded. The room fell quiet as everyone listened for the call and where to respond. "This is the last page for Colleen Keating...a dedicated firefighter and EMT. Repeat, this is the final page for Colleen Keating. She will be dearly missed," the voice said.

I could hardly hold back the tears. "This one's for Colleen," someone at the bar shouted, "A fine woman and one damn fine firefighter!"

"We all cared about her very much," John said.

"I can see that," I said, fighting back the tears as John put his massive arm around my shoulder.

"You can be very proud of her," he said. I excused myself to the privacy of the ladies room to allow my tears an opportunity to run freely.

After a while, refreshed and ready for my own sip of Paddys, I walked out of the ladies room. My mother and Uncle Jim had moved to one of the tables to visit with some friends. The stranger I had asked them about earlier was now looking through Grandmother's photograph albums that had been neatly spread out on a table at the back of the room. He was a handsome man, standing six feet tall with shoulder length hair the color of moon-streaked midnight. A man of Grandmother's years, I had noticed him earlier at the church.

He flipped through the pages, stopped a moment to smile to himself, then continued to examine each picture as if he knew all the players. I stood watching for several minutes before I finally built up the courage to approach him. "Hello, you must have been a friend of my grandmother?" I asked.

"Oh, yes, a good friend, a very good friend," he replied, still partially distracted by the photo albums.

I introduced myself. His voice was pleasant and held a ringing that only his lovely Irish brogue could sound.

"She was a fine figure of a woman," he said continuing to flip pages before turning his full attention to me. "Oh, I'm sorry, I didn't mean to be rude. I was caught up in the pictures. Here," he drew my attention to one of the prints, and said in an endearing, childlike manner, "look here, that's me with Colleen in Eire. It was many years ago."

The pictures showed my grandmother in various stages of her life. She never seemed to age much at all until the last ten years or so. The photographs of her in high school looked only slightly different from pictures of her in her

thirties. She was an attractive woman who stood barely five
foot three inches, with golden bronze tones in her hair. I
remember she told me that her pregnancies had "sucked the
platinum blonde" right out of her hair. She was plump in a
most pleasant way and I thought she had a sensuousness to
her - full hips and well-endowed breasts - a true hour-glass
figure, not attributes I inherited, unfortunately. I was five foot
eight inches and as flat chested as I was lacking in hips, often
likening myself to Olive Oil of Popeye fame with Olive's
same straight black hair, only much longer. I think I had
grown my hair to hip length because my grandmother loved
it so. She had told me on several occasions, "Caetlin, a
woman's hair is a crown of glory...and besides, most men find
it alluring!"

"How did you meet her?" I asked the mysterious
stranger.

"We met during one of her trips to Ireland," he said.

"Grandmother spoke of Ireland so often and always
with such fondness," I told him as he continued to look
through the yellowing pages.

"Muckross Gardens...she said I looked like an elf next
to those giant leaves," he said as he pointed out the enormous
plants looming over him in the picture. He looked up at me
once again saying, "you have her same beautiful eyes."

I shyly smiled at the compliment.

"And the same lovely smile too!"

I was glad to have this chance to meet one of her
friends from Ireland. She had talked of them all quite often.
How many times had I looked through the pictures with her
and watched as she gazed longingly at her "Eire," as she
fondly called it by its Irish name.

"Caetlin, dear, I'm so sorry for your loss." My
thoughts were again disrupted just as I was about to ask my
grandmother's handsome friend his name. "She was a fine
woman and a good friend. I will miss her so very much,"

Mary Gifford told me as the tears welled up in her eyes and she sipped on her Irish whiskey.

"Mary, I'd like you to meet a friend of Grandmother's...I'm sorry, I didn't get your name."

"Kelly. Ciaran Kelly." He said taking Mary's hand cupping it between his two. "Ah, so you were a friend of Colleen's?"

"Oh, yes," Mary replied with more than a hint of a flirtatious slur that obviously was the whiskey settling in. "Old and dear friends, old and dear...excuse me, there's Hank, I must go after him before he finishes every drop in the bar." With this she sped off across the room, with the speed of a woman half her age, to keep a watchful eye over her husband.

Many people shared stories with me about my grandmother's firefighting, medical, and active community service experiences, but their stories lacked a sense of personalness that I was longing to explore. I wanted to know more about this woman who had affected my life so deeply. Why did she shut herself off from the world in her later years? I so needed to know why she was who she was. Perhaps Ciaran could help.

I started to return to our conversation when another of Grandmother's friends approached me. It was her good friend George Carlson, who I knew well. I remember him visiting her on several occasions at her New England cottage. They were traveling companions and had covered much of Europe together in their younger years. He was a soft- spoken man in his mid seventies with a full head of salt and pepper hair. "Hello Caetlin, it's so good to see you again," he said as he embraced me. "I'm so very sorry...you know how much I cared for Colleen."

"She spoke of you often. I know she cared for you too," I reassured him. "George, I understand you both were very close and this may sound silly, but sometimes I feel I never knew her at all. She seemed so road weary and withdrawn at times from the rest of the world. Yet at other times, she was as outspoken as a television comedian."

"She often said of herself that she had the mouth of a truck driver," George said laughing at the thought, "and believe me, I can attest to that."

He continued, "I'll tell you a story about your grandmother you may not have heard before and may help you understand the kind of woman she was. She and I worked as emergency dispatchers together, did you know that?"

"Yes, Grandmother told me that was how you met."

"Well, one evening she received the 911 call that she, or any dispatcher for that matter, most dreaded ever having to handle. The caller told her there was a raging house fire on the outskirts of town with people still in the home. The neighbor who had placed the call was naturally emotional. The mother and one of the children who escaped the burning house had gone to the neighbor asking her to call us. There were still five people inside the inferno; two of them were small children. Your grandmother reacted appropriately by paging out the city fire department. Luckily, one of the rural fire departments was not far behind them as the city department was about out of water, with no hydrants available to them. The rural department showed up with water tenders, which quickly helped to douse the flames. Meanwhile, however, the same caller had once again phoned dispatch and asked if Colleen could try to get in touch with the father, who was not living with the family at the time."

"In between Colleen's trying to find the dad, she was handling radio traffic to all the responding agencies including sheriff's deputies, city police, fire and medical personnel. Over all these distractions, she clearly heard one of the firefighters yell over the radio, warning that the fire was blowing out the back. She told me how the panic in his voice made her feel that a flashover had taken place and she well knew what a deadly proposition that could prove to be. A few moments later, she received a call for help over the radio saying, "we need all the EMTs we can get out here!" She wasn't clear whose voice it was as many of the responders were stepping on each other; talking at the same time over the radio. She couldn't help but imagine some of the firefighters, her friends, must have been injured. She made the necessary decision to call out her own neighboring city's fire department which she knew had more medically trained personnel than any other in the county. This naturally placed additional stress on her; worrying about her "guys" as she called them, being involved in such a horrific scene, on top of making a decision normally out of the scope of our positions as dispatchers."

I fell silent at his story, taking in each syllable with deep concern and interest. I could visualize the blaze from his detailed account and tried to relate to the chaotic situation and how grandmother must have been affected by it.

"A third call from the same woman came in while Colleen was paging out command staff personnel, in addition to having to immediately meet and react to the needs of the responders on scene over the radio. This time, as they spoke, the woman started tearfully telling how she was watching the lifeless bodies of the children being carried out from the structure. Your grandmother might as well have been there in person, with hands tied, forced to watch all that was taking place. She felt helpless and it was very hard on her wondering if she had performed properly, along with her concern about the guys at the scene."

"There was no greater nightmare for her. As a firefighter and EMT she had always said two situations she never wanted to be involved with were a fatal fire or an incident where a child could be seriously injured. Now, as a dispatcher, imprisoned behind a radio with confused communication of what was actually going on, she was dealing with both. Sometimes the mind's eye can be more graphic than the real world, but not this time. They took five bodies out of the structure that day. Two of them children of five and six years old."

"I never saw Colleen closer to going over the edge as I did a few days later when she told me about the call. Her confidence was at an all time low. Our supervisor gave her a copy of the incident tape which she had asked to take home so she could listen to it alone. I offered to listen to it with her several weeks later; we did. What I heard was a calm and collected Colleen taking command of the situation, but she didn't see it that way for quite some time. She told me that after listening to it several times she did feel somewhat better, but needed to dissect her performance and all that had taken place in order to get control of it. She continued to have problems, however, with all the classic signs of stress apparent in every aspect of her life. Her thoughts were confused, she was irritable, she was not eating, and a deep depression clasped her soul. I always admired her strength. That made it especially hard to see her that way. She started talking about quitting all her emergency services work - not from a lack of loving it or helping others - but because of her low self-esteem. She felt she had somehow failed and was incapable of working a scene again. All I could do was tell her to hang in there, which as a woman of fortitude, she did. She refused to give in to the stress completely, but the situation was wearing her out emotionally."

"What did she do?" I asked.

"A month or so after the incident, she responded to a burn victim call with her own fire department. At the scene, some of the guys who worked with the victim had already stripped him down to his underwear and were applying bottled water over his burns. Riding in the ambulance with him to the hospital, she recognized he was burned over eighty percent of his body, which meant he would have to fight against nearly impossible odds of surviving. She told me how she took his blood pressure and saw his skin peel away from the reddened under-layer into her hands and how she laughed and joked with him, trying to make the ride in as comfortable as possible. And, most remarkably, how her intuition told her that he was going to be all right. It seemed to me after this call she overcame her past experience with the fatal fire. She finally felt back in control again."

"And was he all right?" I asked.

"Oh yes. It was a miracle for sure. That's him over there," he said pointing to a heavy-set gentleman near the edge of the brass railed bar.

"He looks fine." I said with amazement.

"He had very good care," George said. "Try to understand, it's not that she was a control freak, Caetlin. She was a sensitive, caring woman who would have laid down her life for anyone. She was also an 'action' person and slept well most nights after dealing with an on the scene call. You can be proud of her," he concluded. "Are you continuing with medical school?"

"Yes, just about over with my senior year," I told him.

"You know, she saw a lot of herself in you and was so very proud of you."

I was grateful for this insight into my grandmother. I too knew her to be a special and willing person who would take risks for the safety of others. It was good of him to reinforce my feelings. She usually did not reveal herself freely but had found a true friend in George and, as I well knew, had opened herself up to him. I even thought at one time they must have had more than a simple friendship, but recognized the special nature of their platonic relationship. She was sincere and considerate to others, yet would retreat into herself when any conversation of her personal life came up. She was a living paradox, placing her hopes in the nature of people yet holding back her deepest thoughts from most.

There was a lack of trust of others that must have come from years of betrayal. Grandma was a proud and private woman who had tucked herself and her thoughts away in her cottage by the sea. She had chosen to live out her later years as a recluse, allowing only a few into the private domain known as self. Yet she had always told me, "don't be afraid to tell someone you love them, Caetlin. Better to be a fool for love than to find that person suddenly gone and living a lifetime of emptiness and regret from not having said the words. Even if they betray you in the end, you can walk with your head held high."

Yes, it seemed Colleen Keating was a woman of many contradictions. Yet she always freely gave her wisdom and love to me; this was evident in her smile. What was it she told me once? I remember, it was "Never hold back your love from people, but keep your secrets to yourself. Many a friendship has been lost through good intentions and loose lips."

I had been so lost in my memories of her that I hadn't noticed when her Irish friend, Ciaran Kelly, slipped out the door.

Chapter 2
From East to West

"That's it! I'm going to take a vacation. I've talked about it for years and I've made up my mind, I'm going to Ireland," I suddenly announced to my friend and co-worker, George Carlson.

"Well, good for you Colleen! You and Kent will love it there. Will you be taking the kids?" George asked.

"No way," I quickly said. "This is my own private vacation and, since Kent hates to travel, I will selfishly take myself to new heights of adventure without him. It's worse than a trip to the dentist to drag him along anyway. He'd only spend most of the time sleeping. He'll understand. You know how it's been for us. He probably won't even notice when I'm gone. The kids, on the other hand, won't exactly be happy campers, but I really need to do this. Besides they'll be out of the house in just a few years and able to spread their own travel wings! You know how stressed out I've been this last year and the time off to myself will do me good. Yes, this will serve as my solitary little getaway. No husband, no kids, no work!" Just the thought of getting away made my mouth water.

"Well, I know you've been stressed out lately and you deserve the break, Kiddo," he said, supporting me. "It's been way too long since I've been to Europe and, if I wouldn't be intruding, perhaps we could meet up over there and split some of the expenses. That is, if you think that would fly with Kent?"

"You know there's no problem where Kent's concerned. He's used to my independent nature; we've been living separate lives for years. He has his annual trek to Tahoe without wanting me along. Never mind that; our meeting over there is a great idea...as long as you promise not to sleep the whole time! Where would you want to go?" I asked.

"Actually, I've never spent any time in Ireland. So

that would be great. We could buy Eurail passes and hit the Continent. I know Germany, France and Spain like the back of my hand. I'd be glad to show you around there," George replied with growing excitement. "How would you feel about hitting England?"

"I have quite a bit of ancestry I'd like to check out in Wales, England, and Scotland," I said contemplating. "And I could sure accomplish a lot more by expanding the trip. What are...what were they...Eurail passes?"

"They're a special pass for traveling the trains and ferries in the Republic of Ireland and the Continent. You can travel as much and as far as you want within a twenty-four hour period and use up just one day of the pass," he explained. "It's been a while since I looked into them. As I remember, you can buy as many days as you need. They used to be quite reasonably priced, but I don't know how much they would be now. We should check it out, that could save us quite a bit and let us see a lot more."

What a great opportunity. George had the know how to make this trip an enjoyable experience. I knew deep inside I would feel safer and prefer his company to traveling alone. He clearly understood that we would maintain the platonic relationship we had already established, even though my marriage has been on its last legs for some time. We could split some of the costs and I'd have an opportunity to see more than I would if I were to travel alone. "Sounds great! Let's see, it's September now..." I said looking at my pocket calendar. "I can't go until next May. I'll need the time to budget and have the vacation time earned at my full-time job."

"That'll work out great for me, Kiddo. I'll arrange an Army flight over and meet you wherever you think will work best for you," he replied.

"Must be nice traveling for free," I kidded. "I'll call home and ask Kent to drop off my atlas. We can get a feel for where we might want to go."

I called Kent and told him I decided to finally take the vacation in Ireland I had always wanted and that George would meet me to be my traveling companion part of the time. I told him how George and I would be splitting the expenses and how much safer I would feel with him along. I asked Kent to drop off the atlas at work so George and I could take a look at it. Without hesitation he agreed to drop off the book.

"We've had an unusual set-up," I thought. "Married for over twelve years; the last seven being mostly miserable. At least we never held silly jealousies between us. I always found jealousy to be such a destructive emotion. And, after all, when we first met, I was still married to my first husband. Kent and I had many opportunities to fall into lust-filled nights, but resisted the temptations, holding firm to our Christian beliefs, which didn't make allowances for such a thing. Our background certainly built up trust in one another. Our beliefs didn't make allowances for fornication either, but after my divorce we didn't let that stop us from filling the lonely nights in each others arms.

I later suspected he may have taken a lover, as he hadn't approached me sexually in years. We were now at a point in our relationship where I didn't really care.

Comments from friends also reinforced my feelings that Kent and I had the somewhat unique relationship. Most of my friends seemed forced to ask permission of their spouses to get out for a night on the town. With Kent, who didn't drink, dance, or socialize outside his circle, I had always found I had to entertain myself. If I wanted to go dancing I would get together with some lady friends and we would go out together, simply letting Kent know I wouldn't be home until late. As my friends married off, it didn't take long to see they didn't have the same freedom I had, so I found myself venturing out more and more on my own. I've always chalked up my relationship with Kent to both the individuality that was so predominant in both of us and, the fact we married because I was pregnant with Angel.

I had only been divorced a few weeks when we had taken our mutual loneliness to a physical plane. Kent was a svelte six feet three inches tall and attractive, in a cowboyish way, with blue eyes, mustache and Viking ancestry. The items that first attracted me to him was that he had the most wonderful hands, slender with long fingers and the perfect A-frame shoulders. Our lust relationship, which we mistook for love, had gone on for several months. Suddenly, one of the rubbers broke and bang! Pregnant. Marriage was, after all, the right thing to do at the time and seemed the only solution.

I had told him I wasn't ready to marry again so soon and he offered me the options; even went so far as to drive me to an out-of-town clinic to end it. As I waited for the doctor at the clinic, I looked around at the books on Bible stories and watched the glowing mothers walk in, doting over their new-born infants. I knew I couldn't go through with it. I walked up to the receptionist's desk and, in tears, told the nurse of my change of heart. I had just turned to leave when she came running over to give my money back. She was openly happy that I had changed my mind. That helped to reinforce the idea I was making the right decision. Still, I was concerned in that I already had one child. How in the world would I be able to support a second one on my own?

As I rode the elevator to the main floor, I thought about my options. I could marry Kent and hope for a Donna Reed household with the white picket fence or I could always move back East to my mother's home. As independent as I believed myself to be, I knew that the only sensible option was to marry Kent. I moved to Montana in 1977 with my first husband who then moved out of state after our divorce in 1982. So here I was with a three year old son, pregnant and about to be laid-off my job as an office manager. I felt lonely and Kent was feeling the same way. It had been so natural in the beginning for us to come together. There was no way I could now bring myself to move back to New Jersey. I hated it there, not that I was completely in love with Montana, but it was my home now, the place where my son was born, and I was determined to keep distance between my past life and present.

With tears still welling up inside me, I told Kent, who had been waiting at the car for me, that I couldn't go through with it. He didn't 'seem' to mind and I felt that he really didn't want me to have the 'procedure' in the first place. He asked me again to marry him. "We can head for Coeur d'Alene right now," he told me. Coeur d'Alene was, and is, the hot spot for quick marriages in this area. Couples go there, as in Vegas, and could get married the same day, compared to waiting over ten days for the license in Montana. I declined the quickie wedding, stating that I still didn't think I was ready for a permanent commitment...it was too soon after my divorce. However, we later agreed to make the commitment for our unborn child and if things didn't work out, no problem. We would go our separate ways while maintaining parental involvement. Kent didn't seem ready for marriage either and was quite content with this idea, as it gave us both an easy out. Within three weeks, we held the ceremony of commitment with all our friends and his family in attendance. Most of them knew I was pregnant, a not so uncommon condition at most weddings those days. Several people came up to me at the wedding to tell me that I was the best thing to happen for Kent...that maybe he would settle down now. He had never been married before and had spent much of his years as an active alcoholic. He quit drinking just a year or so before I met him and this also concerned me, as my first husband was also an active alcoholic. I didn't want to go through that again.

Just over six months later, Angel was born. I was

elated with my decision not to end her life. In truth, I don't think my conscience could have handled it. I was, after all, a Christian, a believer in life and had always stood against abortion. But now I had an aching personal understanding of the desperation a woman must experience when she feels the act is the only way out. As I watched my beautiful little girl grow through the years, I could hardly believe that the thought had even entered my mind. But the hopelessness of a single parent barely able to care for herself and son could give rise to thoughts that went beyond the imagination, or belief system, of a professed Christian. We had already broken the rule against fornication.   I had thought at the time, condemning myself by my own actions, "sin is sin". "Oh, God," I thought, "thank you for not letting me add to my sins by taking my daughter's life."

Kent and I had remained together as a matter of convienence all these years. But I thought it better to stay with him for both Angel and Jimmy. Jimmy's father, Matt, had seemingly dropped off the face of the earth after our divorce, making the way easy for Jimmy to accept Kent into his life as his dad.

Matt and I had been the best of friends in New Jersey. He was five foot eight with features and coloring similar to my own. So much so that in Montana, people often times mistook us for siblings, instead of lovers. He had received a settlement from a car accident and had spent most of it traveling from New Jersey to the South America, and then to Montana where he decided to settle. We had always stayed in touch, spending hours on the phone keeping each other up to date on what was going on in our lives. He returned to New Jersey when his father died and we naturally got together for long visits. He was a good man who was one of my best friends.   We ruined our friendship by getting married... something I've noticed in too many marriages. He never got over the partying side of his life and I did.

At the time I decided to move with Matt to Montana, I had been engaged to every woman's dream man. Don was Italian, successful, handsome, drank only occasionally, and was a lover who enjoyed pleasing a woman. He had moved to America only a few years before we met and already secured a good job with a substantial savings account. He was my first.

"I've never done it before," I said, "you'll need to teach me."

"Don't worry, I'll be gentle," Don assured me.

He could not have been more gentle. He understood my virgin modesty as we lay on the living room floor of my apartment. He slowly unzipped the back of my dress and slid it down my shoulders, running tender kisses along his way. His hands felt warm and his body was eager as he lifted me to my feet to move into the bedroom. We stood at the foot of my bed for many long leisurely minutes as he stroked my neck with his kisses. I then allowed my dress to slide fully off my shoulders to the floor. He lifted me into his arms, placed me gently on the pillows, and fondled my nipples with his mustache and lips. Following his instruction, I returned his kisses along a similar route but shyly held back my affections towards his now hard member. He did not force me but simply placed his body on top of mine. It was a mixed blessing of pain and ecstasy as he penetrated my never-before fulfilled region. He retreated from me before he began to flow as we had no form of birth control available at the moment. I was surprised at how little time it took for him to climax and thought it should have taken longer.

I don't think he truly believed I was a virgin until after a visit to the doctor two days later when the physician told us I had torn slightly from the experience and should refrain from any more encounters for a week or so.

I thought I was in love with Don and found myself staying with him almost three years. I was the one who had originally wanted a more permanent relationship. When he finally did start talking marriage; however, he told me how I would never have to work because he wanted me to stay home and raise our ten or so children. He also told me he wouldn't accept my having any male friends, such as Matt, hanging around.

I was an independent woman even then, having moved out on my own when I turned eighteen, and wasn't interested in spending the rest of my life barefoot and pregnant. In addition, I had mostly male friends, as women's friendship never much interested me at that time. I found most women intrusive and argumentative, whereas men were comfortable for me to talk to. I needed time to think about my future and being "stuck" in New Jersey with Don.

The one person, in retrospect, I believe was most responsible for my wanting to escape the Jersey rut was my friend Luke Longfellow. When I was in high school, and he just entering college, we used to spend hours together waiting out back of the police station for our fathers to get off duty. His dad was the Police Commissioner and mine a rookie. We reached a spiritual type of understanding and trust during our philosophical talks and felt a mutual attraction. He even promised me once that when I was old enough, he would take me out on a date. I did have a bit of a crush on him and was sure he did on me. After I had moved out on my own, I didn't see him much. But, when I was fortunate enough to run into him, he was always cheerful and joking around. Sweet, dear Luke: he could always put a smile on my most depressed moods.

Luke tried for over two years to get on one of the local police departments. Dedicated to getting his body into shape, he lost fifty pounds putting himself through the rigorous training of the police academy. The first time I saw him after academy I hardly recognized him. He was now a 'lean, mean, fighting machine' compared to his former chunky self. He loved law enforcement, but I always felt his gentle nature wasn't really cut out for it.

One Sunday afternoon, when I was out using my learner's permit driving at one of the oversized corporate parking lots in town, he rolled into the lot to check out who the crazy woman behind the wheel must be. When he noticed it was me, he placed the passenger side of his patrol car about two inches from my driver's side door. His partner and I had been looking at each other when I said to Luke, "Damn you pigs, always harassing the tax-paying citizen."

I thought his partner was about to pull his gun on me when Luke started returning the banter, "You aren't old enough to be a tax paying citizen." I don't think I had ever seen someone's ears turn so red with anger as those of his partner who obviously still hadn't caught on to the fact Luke and I were friends.

"Oh sure, and I suppose you'll want to take me off to some dark alley to practice some police brutality now!" I responded.

"It's a thought," he said barely able to hold back the laughter. With this he turned on the lights and sirens and drove in circles around my car, then roared off to his patrol.

The last time I saw him was at one of the local diners. Don and I were sitting at one of the clean Formica-topped tables waiting for our meal when Luke walked in. He came over and sat down beside me and I was appalled at how unfriendly Don was being. He didn't even offer to shake hands with Luke when I introduced him. I noticed immediately that Luke was not acting his usual outgoing and fun-loving self. He was distant and not exhibiting his typical ball-busting with me. Something I shook off because we were not comfortable visiting together with Don present. He politely made an excuse and made his way to the front counter. I trailed behind him and promised I would call him sometime in the next couple of weeks.

Less than ten days later, I received the call from my mother.   She told me that Luke had taken his .38 Police Special, put it to his head and pulled the trigger.   He was twenty-five years old.

I knew Luke was having some problems, yet I never found the time to call him.   "Time," I told myself, "what could I have been thinking?   Did I ever tell him how special he was to me?"   The thoughts were agonizing.   "My friend needed me and I wasn't there for him."   His father was being investigated for inappropriateness on the job and possible mob connections and his brother had been in trouble with the law for some drug deal gone sour.   On top of all this, Luke had been involved in a shooting that resulted in the death of a local prominent business man.   The man's wife had called the police and told the radio operator that her husband had a gun.   He was going to kill her.   When Luke and his partner arrived on scene, the man came running from the house pointing the weapon at them, threatening to shoot.   They had no choice but to protect themselves.   Luke might have accepted this simple fact after finding out the suspect's gun was empty except that the wife lodged a complaint against him and his partner for negligence.   I also heard he was having problems with his girlfriend.   It was just too much for his sensitive nature to handle.   He had taken what he thought was the easy way out and I resented him for that.

My guilt combined with anger as I approached the open casket.   The aroma of the room filled with flowers would have overwhelmed anyone with even a little sense of smell, yet I noticed them not at all.   I touched the sleeve of his blue uniform and broke into tears of hysteria.   No one, including my mother who accompanied me, could understand my loss of control.   Luke's father didn't even recognize me - he thought I was Luke's girlfriend.   "You must be Linda," he said.   I was hardly able to say a word as my eyes filled with quivering tears and my throat constricted in anger.   This seemingly innocent comment of his only increased my anger. I wanted to shout, "You never even knew anything about him," but struggled to hold the thought to myself.

In retrospect I knew his death was a primary reason for my compulsion to run away. "I'll wind up doing the same thing one day if I don't get out of here," I told myself.

I was the one who had approached Matt to ask if I could drive him back to Montana. I explained my frustrations and need for a change without really revealing the totality of my reasoning at the time. I asked if he would put me up for a few months at his trailer in exchange for my covering the expense of the trip. He was more than agreeable to the idea. I gave notice to my boss, kissed my parents, friends and Don goodbye and packed up my belongings, leaving most of them on the sidewalk next to the apartment building. I was on my way within two weeks.

Matt was such a free spirit...too much so, perhaps. We had taken over a month crossing country to reach Montana and visited with friends along the way. I was never the type to hop into bed with just anyone and had, in fact, made a conscious decision to lose my virginity with Don. I had felt like a prudish freak turning down Don's advances. Now, falling into lust sometime about halfway into the trip with Matt, I knew I wanted to experience more than one man. Somewhere in Vegas, I fulfilled that desire. It hadn't proved to be the pleasant experience I had with Don...more along the line of "let's get naked." But it was different.

When we arrived in Montana, I had spent my entire savings and had only forty-two dollars in my pocket.

"I don't know how to tell you this, but I lied," Matt said as he pulled my car over to the side of the road just miles before our final destination where his trailer would give us a place to stay and his savings in the bank would pay me back for the extra money I had loaned him along the way through Vegas and Reno. "I have no money left and lost my trailer gambling. I've been trying to tell you...I don't blame you if you head back to Jersey right now."

"That's the last thing I want to do. It's okay," I (the eternal optimist) said. "We'll manage somehow. After all, we have other friends who live here. Perhaps they could put us up until we could find work."

As things have a habit of doing, all worked out well. I found a job and Matt started working part-time as a mason with one of our mutual friends. We soon purchased the trailer we were renting and I settled into my new life in Montana.

I still don't know why, but we decided to marry less than six months after our arrival. I wasn't pregnant or even in love with him. I still don't know exactly what was going through my mind but it seemed the best choice at the time. Maybe it was the "nice girls don't sleep around, they get married" cliche.

We returned to New Jersey for the church wedding that our parents had arranged. My friend and bridesmaid, Toni, drove me to the church. I told her I felt this was a mistake and I didn't want to go through with the wedding. Toni was a live wire, a beautiful young woman with black hair and a John Lennon smile. She and I were so completely opposite, we complimented each other perfectly. I was the prudy one and she had the devil-may-care attitude I envied at times. She told me sometimes women have to provide for their own orgasms and even explained how to achieve that goal. She lit up a joint and told me I shouldn't waste a good party. "After all you can always get a divorce in a few months."

On the plane ride back to Montana my new husband told me how he spent part of the evening before our wedding getting a blow-job from a prostitute in New York City. "Some things are better kept to yourself," I thought. Whether it was my old-fashioned outlook on life or too much Ozzie and Harriet, I had decided to try my best to make the marriage work. Six months later I was pregnant with Jimmy. After three more years I could no longer take Matt's alcoholism nor the dry drunk he experienced during the one year he quit drinking. He told me that by quitting drinking for a year he proved he was not an alcoholic, then conveniently went back to his nightly twelve pack of beer the moment the year was over. He hardly remember a family birth date, but he sure did remember, down to the minute, when he allowed himself to start drinking again. Of course, his drinking was "all my fault," especially after I told him I was discontented with our relationship and asked him for a separation.

We tried separation on three different occasions, the third was the last. I returned from work one evening to find him passed out on the sofa holding the remains of a cigarette which had burned down to his fingers. Our three year old son slept in the next room. I refused to consider staying with a man who had endangered his own child. Alcohol did not allow him to think clearly but this act of irresponsibility made it clear to me that had to go. We divorced after a short battle and he skipped the state, leaving me to raise our son alone. Jimmy was the best thing to come out of that relationship, as children often are. A sweet and happy child, he was every mother's dream.

I was already working with Kent when my divorce was final. I'm convinced Kent and I both thought our relationship a mistake; it seemed we were just going with the flow aspiring to the 50s ideal of the house and picket fence. He even mentioned several years later that he knew it was a mistake and he wasn't sure that he loved me. Many were the harsh and unforgettable words that passed between us over the years. Yet we weren't overly argumentative, just settled into a loveless relationship in which communication and affection were only meaningless words spoken by television evangelists and shrinks. This was a marriage in name only, and only because of the children. I had, however, come to the realization that perhaps it wasn't really "for the sake of the children," since they were growing up in a dysfunctional household with parents who held no affection for each other. Although they were exceptionably well behaved children most of the time, both had problems dealing with school and personal relationships. Regardless of their parents' "separate lives", there was much love and affection rained upon them both. Alas, the effects of living with estranged parents under the same roof eventually hurt the kids which was obvious and shown in their outbursts of frustration.

It was now 1994 -- I felt a new sliver of hope and goal-setting by planning my trip abroad. George would be a great traveling companion and we both felt this would our ultimate trip. He was just a few years older than me and had already retired from the Army. I found him fascinating especially when he talked about his adventures in Germany and other foreign lands. In addition, when he talked about one of his four prior marriages, I felt empathy instead of disdain. He was quite a free spirit and a native Montanan. He worked diligently at remodeling his own house which sat next door to his parent's home. I sensed of his longing for a new love in his life. This feeling was magnified when he shared the story of his attraction to a woman he met while camping in Oregon. He planned to meet her again during the next summer. I so hoped this would be a positive relationship for him and that he would find the love so elusive to him. He believed that love had a beginning and an end, according to George, there was no such thing as a "forever" kind of love and living for the moment seemed his primary objective in life...mainly consisting of several short-term marriages.

The months flew by as we got together occasionally to plan our trip. I'd fly into Gatwick, one of the London airports and he would meet me there. We would be as spontaneous as possible as we planned on seeing Wales, Scotland, and Ireland. From Ireland we would ferry to Paris and travel by

Eurail pass to visit the perfume factories of France, the ruins of ancient Rome, and take in all the sites in between and beyond. We would have three weeks for this grand excursion and I relished every moment of the planning.

After one of George's visits to my house, Jimmy mentioned that his sister told him she thought George and I were having an affair. "Television is ruining the world. Too much 90210," I thought to myself. But, I could not let her go on thinking I was capable of such a thing. When I asked her about her feelings, my shy, yet outspoken eleven year-old stormed out of the room and refused to talk about it.

Angel was a stunningly beautiful young lady, this child of mine. Her long light blonde hair cascaded just beyond her shoulders and her dark brown eyes could melt the ice in coldest heart. Yet, she was as stubborn and strong-willed as a person could be. She had a most wonderful, sensitive side to her nature when she chose to reveal it. I understood how she tried to protect that sensitive side by closing herself off to conflict and frustrations by allowing the stubborn streak to stonewall me and everyone else.

Determined in my belief that I had to make Angel understand George was nothing more than a friend and that I had no intention of cheating on her dad, I decided to do what seems best for a mother and daughter to do...go shopping. We stopped at the local Wal-Mart where we picked out a new outfit for her. Angel gave me ideas for what to bring her back from my trip. I then allowed her the choice of eating establishments and we naturally wound up at McDonalds...where else would an eleven year old want to have lunch?

I told her that we could no longer avoid talking about my going to Europe with George. Whether it was the shopping or the Big Mac, she finally opened up to my plea for communication. "Angel, you have a lot of friends don't you?" I started.

"Yes, mom," she shyly replied.

"And many of your friends are boys, right?"

"Well, yes." She answered with a knowledgeable smirk as she realized where I was headed.

"Do you make 'kissy face' with all the boys you play with?" She smiled shyly at this thought and vehemently denied making kissy face with any of the boys. "Why is that?"

"Because they're just friends, mom, not boyfriends!"

"Well, that is what George is to me. You know how dad hates to travel and this is something I've wanted to do for a long time. I would never hurt your dad. Do you understand?" I was hopeful my clumsy analogy would somehow sink in. Voila! She smiled, said she understood and told me that she loved me. Mother and daughter had somehow come to an understanding that mom needed to explore the world. Someday Angel too would need to do the same thing and understand that not all the men in our lives would turn into lovers. We finished our burgers and enjoyed additional conversation mainly about her suggestions about what I was to bring her back from my trip.

Jimmy was always more understanding of his mother's excursions than my Angel. I had taken him back to New Jersey a few years earlier and he was used to my taking a weekend here and there to visit a friend in California or Wyoming. But, this was going to be a long trip without family and I was concerned he also had negative images about it. When I returned home I thanked him for telling me how his sister felt as it gave me the opportunity to straighten things out with her. It was just two weeks before I was to leave and I sure didn't want to take off with the children thinking their mom was some sort of floozie. I asked Jimmy if he felt the same way and he stated, "No". He knew his mom, as he put it, was "different"! A typical insight I suppose, from a fifteen year old. He then told me how he wanted a flag from every country I visited and he would never forgive me if I let him down.

Jimmy was a bright and handsome young man, with a mane of thick blonde hair and the bluest eyes this side of Robert Redford. He easily won people over with his charming personality and personal salesmanship. I thought he would most likely wind up a politician someday. His bedroom eyes easily won over every woman's heart. He held a deep respect for women and I was pleased about that. The only time he ever threw a blow at someone, it was in defense of a girl whose boyfriend was about to pummel her. He stated quite emphatically he would hold onto his virginity until he was married someday...maybe more than a politician...a preacher! Lord only knows how my children held fast to such old- fashioned morality. I was proud of this attribute, as well as many other things about them. Since AIDS and the drug culture were fully entrenched in our society, I was thankful God and all his angels had touched my children's hearts with wisdom and love. How much more could a mother want for her children!

It wasn't until Angel was almost five and Jimmy nine that I joined the local fire department. Two of the firefighters had come to my home one evening asking if I would sign a petition for the department to be absorbed into an adjacent district's department. I gladly signed as I struck up a conversation with them. "I've wanted to join your department for quite some time, but my kids have been too young for me to make that commitment." In addition to the age of the children, the truth was, that at least Kent wasn't actively drinking and careless as Matt had been. It wouldn't be such a problem for me to fulfill this life-long dream of being a firefighter now since I wouldn't have to worry about my house burning down from a drunk's discarded cigarette, while I was off putting out a fire.

They said they would be happy to have me join and I

felt I had made two new friends in Ryan and Joe. Ryan was originally from the East Coast and had moved to Montana over a decade before. Without him, the fire department that protected our small sub-division would not have existed. He, with the help of his close friend Joe, had built the station and allocated money from the county for equipment. He put many years of hard work into the department and was openly proud of his accomplishments. Joe was the quieter of the two, hardly speaking a word, letting Ryan talk for both of them.

Joe was a native Montanan who, oddly enough, didn't mind us out-of-staters as many Montanans seem to. Many natives believe that anyone moving into the state has devil's horns and a mind-set to destroy the pristine beauty of the parks and streams, in addition to eating their children. They brag about how their ancestors came from the "old country" and settled in Montana in the late 1800s; this supposedly gave them more right to live here than the rest of us foreigners. I enjoyed pointing out to them that my family came to this country in the 1600s, settling in Maryland. "Why, I'm even part Cherokee on my father's side and 'relatively certain' the Cherokees were here before any white folks showed up. Yup, I figure I'm as much an American as the next person and have a right to live anywhere I want." This argument would leave them speechless and I felt full of myself, having given them something to think about.

Ryan and Joe had no problem with a woman joining the department. I wish I could say the same for the rest of the men as it didn't take long to recognize that I wasn't wanted. The only other woman who had ever been a member on this department lasted six short months. One of the men told me she appeared to be out to catch a husband rather than fight fires. Not knowing the lady he spoke of, I could draw no opposing conclusion.

It didn't take long to experience sexual harassment. I've never understood how some men could behave so ignorantly treating women with slight regard. After all, their moms, sisters, wives and girlfriends are women. I guess I shouldn't be too surprised, as everyone seems to want to be superior to someone else. If it's not women, then it's Blacks, Jews, Indians, Poles, or anyone different from themselves. I will never understand how learned hate fills our hearts toward others.

During one of my first training drills, I was handed a near empty air bottle and sent into a smoke-filled room. When the warning bell sounded I was about to run out of air, just a minute or two after I reached the basement. I quickly pointed out to my partner that we needed to exit. I waited for him, as protocol dictates, and followed the hose line to the exit. I was completely out of air when we reached the outside door and quickly pulled off the face mask to take in several deep breaths of fresh air. The responsible parties found this very amusing and had quite the laugh at my expense. I didn't find out until several years later their prank was done on purpose to discourage me from remaining on the department. Other trying incidents took place throughout my years as a firefighter, but I would not let them get the best of me.

Eventually, I even became their Training Officer, albeit for a short time. The membership recognized the need for someone to take over training as it had been poorly executed during the past several years. After a long discussion with the Chief, when I pointed out my experience and the fact I was not about to let him place some rookie in the position, he reluctantly agreed to give me a try. I was pleasantly surprised in that I received many compliments over the next year because the new training program I had implemented was the best training the department ever had.

Some time later, I heard that one of the men, who also served as a trustee, had told the others upon hearing of my new position, that he "wouldn't take orders from no fuckin' woman!" I had expected no less, especially from this jerk, as he had physically tried shoving me into a tree at one of our fires. He had consistently criticized my driving, hose handling, and other tasks performed in the field. I did nothing right in his eyes and never would. I had no doubt that he spent his nights beating up the wife and kids while guzzling beer and watching the football game -- all at the same time.

I had however grown close to one of the guys, Ray, who, in addition to his membership on the valley department, was a paid firefighter and emergency medical technician. When I was a rookie, at one of the training drills for the valley, he placed the side of his body against my back to give me added support for handling the two and a half-inch line. I found his kindness very reassuring and the position comfortable as it relieved the stress on my back from the force of the hose. Shortly after he left for the night, one of the guys in charge of training told me to pick up another line for practice. What I didn't know was he told the engineer to pump up the pounds per square inch up to two hundred. Most stout men could not handle a line with that kind of pressure by themselves, but I had one of the other rookies standing behind me to assist. Just before the water started to flow, the rookie disappeared. He was told by the man in charge to step back from the line leaving me struggling to hold down the snaking nozzle. When the water was shut off, I asked why I was left alone with the hose. The laughing trainer said, "Just wanted to see if you'd be able hold it back from breaking your jaw."

"What a great and safe way to train," I sarcastically remarked. "Let's see who we can injure!"

He responded, "Yeah, and I suppose that Ray 'butting' up against you before was better!"

"He was relieving the stress on my back," I answered. "Why, do you have a problem with that?"

He smugly implied that Ray and I must have achieved some sexual gratification from the procedure. Fat chance!

We both had forty pounds of full turn-out gear on at the time - not much of a turn- on for anyone! Reacting to the trainer's ignorance wasn't worth my time, so I walked away without allowing him the satisfaction of a rebuttal.

Ray was the one responsible for sparking my interest in medical response. Although the valley department didn't respond to medical emergencies, he was always available when we were called to vehicle accidents that many times required his additional expertise. I admired the way he took charge of victim's medical needs and hoped I could get into this field. But, it was unlikely the valley trustees would expand our services to include medical response.

After six years on the valley department, I moved into a house within the city limits and decided to apply for membership on the city fire department.

Ray continued to be a good friend. He warned me when I joined the city department that the chief of this department had told him they were looking for any excuse to get rid of me. It crushed me to think I would experience the "same shit, different day" attitude since I was so hopeful for a new start. His revelation gave me an opportunity to confront the individual and straighten things out right from the beginning.

I asked the Chief at that time during the next meeting, "Jack, would you step outside for a minute?" He shuffled his oversized feet and let me know what a bother I was, but joined me outside the glass bay door. "Jack," I said, "I heard a rumor. I know a person can't ever take a rumor as fact, but I heard that one of the guys on the department was looking for any excuse to get rid of me."

He stammered and said, "You'll be treated the same as anyone else on this department!"

"I'm really glad to hear that," I told him.

"You'll be treated the same..."

"I can't tell you how happy I am to hear that. It's

better to put my mind at ease than pay attention to some stupid rumor."

Again, as if he couldn't say anything else, he stated, "You'll be treated the same as anyone else."

"Thanks a lot, Jack; coming from you that makes me especially comfortable..."

"...the same," he started once again.

"Especially since I heard you were the one to say you were looking for any excuse to get rid of me," I told him. He fell silent at the sound of truth ringing in the air, but once again, after a short gasping pause, assured me I would be 'treated the same as anyone else on the department'!

Things were running along relatively smoothly with the new department, but I did get a taste of the old double standard when Jack told me to climb a ladder to the roof of the station during a drill. I refused, saying, "I'm not climbing any ladder with these boots...it's not safe." I had told him months before that the boots I was issued were three times my size and that my feet slipped out of them. He had ignored my request to get a pair that fit, saying we didn't have the money in the budget.

"Well, you want to be a real god-damned fireman, don't you?" Egging me on. "Or maybe you're just afraid of heights!"

I replied, "I have no problem climbing a ladder or with heights." I found his challenge particularly annoying as he knew I had been parachute jumping just prior to joining the department - not a sport for someone suffering from vertigo. "But I'll be damned if I'll do it in unsafe equipment," I retorted. With this, I slipped my street shoes back on and shimmied up the ladder.

He finally, reluctantly, agreed to pay for new boots and told me to go ahead and order them. When they arrived, he denied having approved my purchase, leaving me to pay the bill out of my pocket.

When word got around of my out-of-pocket expense, there was quite a heated discussion at one of our monthly business meetings. The vote was twenty-seven to one that night in favor of reimbursing me for the necessary equipment. The added comment by one of my buds was, "After all, she can't help it if she's got itty-bitty pussy feet." This brought on hearty laughter from the rest of the members.

Ray passed away at the age of thirty-three from a form of lymphoma.

The Firefighter

Attack again the living flame,
save a life, a face, no name.
The blaze is seen against night skies,
"Save my child!," the mother cries.

Then breath of life and a parent's smile,
make the risks and tears all worthwhile.
To follow this life is what I chose,
where it may lead, no one knows.

But destiny's lot or wisdom's fate,
the mystery leads to Heaven's gate.
Where before the throne of God I stand,
and take my rest in His loving hand.

****

The differences between the city and valley departments was like comparing day to night. The guys at the city made it obvious they didn't want a woman on their department from the moment I turned in my application. But at least they weren't underhanded in their prejudice. A few women had made application through the years without success; I was the first woman to join. Once I was on, they treated me like any other rookie, teaching me things I never learned on the rural department. "Have you ever used a hose clamp before?" the training officer, Rick, asked me.

"No," I somewhat timidly replied. I was still full of trepidation that this would be a repeat of the other department and I was about to get hurt.

The clamp squeezed the hose together holding the water back until connections could be made at the truck. Rick took me over to the hose clamp and had me push down on the large metal handle against the force of the partially filled hose. I was very proud of my accomplishment. When he told me to release it, he stopped me as I straddled the clamp, ready to let it go. He told me, "Now, if you were a man, I'd warn you that you may hurt your family jewels straddling it that way; but since you're a woman, I'll just tell you to stand to the side as it may pop up at you causing serious injury." We both laughed at his attempt to be politically correct but I quickly moved to the side of the clamp and allowed the water to run free from the hydrant to the pumper.

One of the main concerns I heard from several of the men was how I could be expected to pull a three-hundred pound person out of a burning structure. Since we worked in teams, I told them it shouldn't matter much since I didn't believe any one of them could pull a three-hundred pound person out on their own either. "When the adrenaline pumps, it's amazing what we're capable of," I reassured them. "If any of you can do it, then so shall I. I'll never leave one of you behind!"

I didn't find their humor offensive. I believe a woman needs to maintain a sense of humor and that part of the problem with a woman joining an all men's organization is we are too quick to cry wolf at nothing more than an off-colored joke. During the local rodeo, the local bars hold various contests. During our business meeting, under "Good

of the Order", one of the guys made a motion, "I move that
Colleen represent the department...in the wet tee shirt contest
at the Kick Ass bar." The laughter was roaring...thinking I
would turn red and hide. However, I came back at him with,
"That's only because you know I'd win!" To another round
of hearty belly-laughs. It was these harmless exchanges that
helped them to feel relaxed around me. I never had one of
them put their hands where they shouldn't and the newly
elected Chief, John Stiger, even removed the "girlie" calendar
from the wall upon hearing I didn't appreciate it being there.

No, these guys were nothing like those on the other
department. They may not have liked my being in their
formerly all men's club, but they accepted me. I wouldn't
have to be concerned about my physical safety nor the other
side of the spectrum -- receiving special treatment. I knew I
could trust any one of them to back me in a bad situation and
they slowly started to believe it of me also.

Within a year after joining the city department, I
completed a first responder medical course which allowed me
to assist on medical calls. This department had well-
established themselves in medical response and was one of
the first in the state to have a quick response unit. It wasn't
long before I expanded my training and became an
Emergency Medical Technician, then a training coordinator
for medical services and CPR instructor. I came to
completely enjoy this aspect of the fire department and
couldn't imagine not serving in this capacity. It is a valuable
service to the community and I never understood why the
valley department chose not to serve its district this way.

I was extremely active on the city department, serving
on various committees. In the fall I taught children fire
prevention, while in the spring I organized fund raisers. I
served as department representative to local organizations
located in the county. In addition, I taught various training
segments,   including   wildland   firefighting,   arson

investigations and communications. The list went on and on. All my activity helped me to accept leaving the valley department that I had invested so much time and energy in. "Why cast pearls before swine," I told myself, "when I have oysters right before my eyes!"

I had wanted to be a firefighter since I was a young child watching the guys at the station next to my house. Now, here I was living out my dream and enjoying every minute of it.

I had come to know myself here in the West and imagined myself living out my years under the Big Sky.

The weekend before I was to leave for Europe, we held our annual fire school. We began on Wednesday night with training on Self-Contained Breathing Apparatus (SCBA). The maze of the smoke filled room, coupled with the duck-taped face masks, gave the illusion of realism necessary to prepare for the actual event. Thursday night we watched videos on confined space rescues with proper hose handling practicals not far behind. Friday evening we worked a live burn on an old garage donated for this purpose by one of the local residents. Each evening's training would culminate in most of the members patronizing the three local bars, "to show our support." The first year I was on the department, I gladly traipsed along with the others; but, now that I was older and wiser, I chose to make my evenings end early lest I try to manipulate the powerful and dangerous deluge nozzle with a hangover the next day.

Saturday was the climax of training. Starting at six in the morning, we gathered for breakfast. Then on to reviewing all we had learned over the past three nights. After giving the station its annual cleaning, the retired members would join us for lunch. We watched a video put together from old thirty-five millimeter films from '55 and '56 when most of those guys were active. As we all enjoyed the video, the 'old-timers' reminisced about their experiences and the 'right' way to do things.

I retreated home to try to catch a nap before rejoining the throng for our annual banquet which started at six that night. I was exhausted, but looked forward to the evening out.

John Stiger had asked me to make the twenty-year membership award's presentation and I looked forward to paying homage to our recently retired members. After all the presentations were completed, including the prestigious "Firefighter of the Year" award (given to Pete this year), we moved the tables to the back of the room allowing space for the band to set up.

This was when Kent made his annual exit. Even at the prodding from several of the wives, he would never stay to enjoy the night. Left alone, many of the fellows would take their turns dancing with me...in between filling up a glass from the open bar we had set up. As we danced, now after four years with them, they started to tell me how I had been misjudged and that they truly respected me.

After I sang the closing song, Amazing Grace, with the band, one of the guys who hadn't said a word to me in over two years came up to me saying, "Colleen, I must apologize. I know I haven't treated you well. Can you forgive me? I hope we can be friends."

Yes, I could crash and die on the plane content tomorrow knowing my "brothers" cared about me. I had to be at the airport by six in the morning in order to catch my seven o'clock flight. "The alcohol will help me sleep throughout the sixteen hour flight," I told myself as I packed my toiletries and prepared to go.

Chapter 3
The Trip

I landed at Gatwick airport, London, England, Monday, May 8, 1995. George met me at the airport and then walked me to the motel room he had secured the night before. It gave me an opportunity to wash up after the sixteen hour flight and I was very thankful. After I completed my relaxing, hot shower; we examined our map and decided where to sojourn first. London was the obvious choice so we walked back to the airport to catch a shuttle bus to Victoria Station where, as promised in George's handy European guidebook, there were several bed and breakfasts from which we could choose. On the short trip to Victoria Station, we continued to lay out our plans. When we got there, we found a bed and breakfast where we shared a room to save money. I could already see that London was going to be an expensive proposition. The room cost us over fifty pounds each, eighty-dollars American. George asked if I'd like to take a nap before we went out, but I declined any thought of resting. I was too excited to hold back from taking on London: it was the experience of a lifetime.

We were surprised to find it was V-E day. We couldn't have planned it any better. Fifty years after the war, here was London, in all its glory, celebrating Victory in Europe day. What good fortune! We walked to Buckingham Palace where the Queen was delivering a message of peace and hope that the days of WWII would never return again. She had invited local handicapped children to tea and we watched as the kiddy parade entered through the enormous palace gates. It was so crowded that it was impossible to get close but were still able to observe much of the festivities from our location at the top of a grassy park. A fly-by of vintage aircraft soared above our heads as the crowd cheered. I had never seen fireworks in the daylight and I felt like a child taking in every precious moment for the first time. We walked around the merchants' stands, purchased several V-E

Day commemorative books which outlined the celebration and the assorted events. After walking what seemed like a "bazillion" miles, we returned to our room. I was so exhausted as George and I talked, laying out our plans for the evening, I fell asleep in mid-sentence. George went off on his own to enjoy the London nightlife while I slept to overcome jet-lag.

The next morning, realizing that London was too expensive for our meager budgets, we made plans to head on to Scotland that same day. First, we retraced our steps from the day before, but this time took in an additional sight we hadn't previously had time for, George's personal favorite, Big Ben. Westminster Abbey is just across the street, so we spent some time walking around this wonderful stone structure. The Cathedral's boys' choir was practicing inside and I sat for some time listening to them sing, I then walked through the stone halls where headstone plaques dating back centuries lined the walls. We returned by way of the hilly park near Buckingham Palace where we had perched the day before. The lack of crowds allowed us to examine the ornate golden gates at close range. They were massive; we felt dwarfed beneath their filigree. We took a few memorable photos, leisurely stopping at various shops along the way.

At the Queen's Bookshop, I noticed a book listing all the castles of Great Britain. I knew that my ancestor, Sir Rhys ap Thomas, had a castle named Carew, but I hadn't any idea where in Wales it was located. To my delight, Carew Castle was listed in the book; four miles from Pembroke, Wales. I pointed this out to George and wrote down the name of the town. I asked if he would like to travel on to Pembroke to see what remnants of the castle, if any, still existed. He was more than open to the idea. After returning to our room to pick up our belongings, we walked to Victoria Station to catch the next bus to Pembroke.

It was quite a ride. Night had fallen by the time we

pulled into the town of Pembroke Castle at eight o'clock. I again felt the fatigue of jet lag setting in and hoped we could find a place quickly to rest our weary bodies. Fortunately, just a block or so from the bus stop we found the most lovely bed and breakfast that we ever could have hoped for. It was less than half the price of the place where we stayed in London and had twice the ambiance. The kind lady of the house, Annie, came to the door cascading friendly affection upon these two weary road warriors. She told us how she enjoyed "backpackers" and showed us to a most beautiful room embellished with antiques, a four poster bed and a large bay window. George, anticipating my fantasy, had already laid his luggage on the smaller bed near the door. "Go ahead, Kiddo, this is your heritage. Feel like a princess and the next place we stay, I'll take the bigger bed."

I decided it was only right to enjoy a bubble bath in the spacious bathroom just down the hall from our room. Laying back in the rose-scented water, I found myself day-dreaming of knights on great stallions rescuing maidens from fire-breathing dragons. This joy lasted nearly an hour until I forced myself from my bath and returned to my room a new woman - refreshed and rarin' to go. We decided to take the quickest possible path through the town as it was near ten p.m. and the bars closed at eleven. There was a mill pond, the size of a small lake, just below the bed and breakfast. We walked along the pathway to a pub named The Watermans just a half mile away. The reflection of The Watermans' lights looked inviting in the pool of calm water.

We went inside and enjoyed some croquettes, a delicacy to be sure...mashed potatoes rolled in hot dog fashion in a batter of bread crumbs and fried to perfection. This in addition to sampling some of the local beers, including my personal favorite, Woodpecker Cider!

The next morning we asked Annie the best way to get to Carew Castle. A short bus ride later we were at the home of my ancestors. I knew little about them other than their names on sheets of paper found through my research at churches and libraries back home. Again, our luck was incredible. Here before us, stood not just a remnant of a wall or two from hundreds of years ago, but a full blown castle almost a thousand years old. As we entered the main gateway, a pole bearing the family crest of three ravens towered over our heads. Missing its original wooden floors and beams, but complete in so many other ways, it was in the process of being refurbished to much of its original splendor. It was easy to imagine living in the year 1485 and enjoying the last Great Tournament of Great Britain that Sir Rhys held here. The tour guide made the history of the place come alive as he talked about the Tournament and the hundreds of knights that attended the feast, enjoying the merriment. The guide spoke with great enthusiasm as if he had lived those times himself, telling us how Sir Rhys was reportedly the one responsible for killing the evil King Richard III (a.k.a., The Boar), in battle. In slaying Richard, he saved his cousin Henry Tudor's life and helped place him on the throne of England. Without Sir Rhys' support and influence over the tribes of Wales, Henry might not have been successful in his campaign. It seemed certain, according to the tour guide and poets of old, that Sir Rhys was one of the most powerful men of his times. Henry VII affectionately referred to him after that as "Father Rhys", an endearment of great respect. The guide went on to tell us how Rhys was a Knight of the Garter and Governor of all Wales. Sir Rhys owned many castles throughout Wales, but Carew Castle was one of his favorite residences. He spoke of Rhys' grandson, who was beheaded by Henry VIII for being a traitor. It was discovered later to be a false accusation, but that was of no help to Rhys' headless grandson.

Carew

On a sojourn I traveled to the Castle Carew.
Where I pondered my lifelines and my heart did renew.

And I thought of Sir Rhys, great, mighty and strong.
His jousting and merriment filled me with song.

I wandered the fields with the sheep meek and mild.
Kissed the sweet cross and felt as a child.

Old matters stand past, and things yet are new.
Still strong the reminder from the Castle Carew.

It was like walking through a dream. Black-faced sheep grazed contently on the grounds and sipped from the river surrounding the castle. The green rolling hills that could be seen for miles gave me a feel for days long ago when King Arthur and his knights gathered at the Round Table. This vision was more than apt in Sir Rhys' family ancestry; he claimed descent from Sir Urien Rhygard, a Knight of King Arthur's Round Table. A prophesy had been spoken over Sir Urien by Merlin who said the Raven would fall a king of England. This was fulfilled by Rhys hundreds of years later. I purchased some historical biographies, an incredible history of prominent people, and felt I was about to clean out the gift shop when we fortunately decided it was time to return to Pembroke Castle for dinner.

We returned to our fairy tale room to freshen up. Then it was off to The Watermans again for an evening of relaxation. We had already decided to leave in the morning for Paisley, Scotland in an attempt to track down some family history information on my maternal side. We stopped in another pub along the way to The Watermans where we met several local firefighters. Pembroke Castle was an oil town and they had many a tale of spectacular oil fires, including several stories of being bombed during WWII. They stated that they used to call themselves "firemen" before the ladies joined and seemed to have no problem with female firefighters, stating quite succinctly that the women were as well adapted to firefighting as the men. They asked how it fared for me in America as a woman firefighter. I told them I was the first to join my town's department and I was not a welcome addition in the beginning. However, after four years of being on the department, I felt most of the men had come to accept me. They were very kind and enjoyed hearing about American firefighting techniques and equipment. They left us with a Welsh toast, "yichyda," meaning "good health".

Continuing on to our now familiar Watermans, we ate our fill of croquettes and drank sweet apple cider beer, deciding to make an early night of it in order to catch our bus in the morning. When we returned to our room and were already dressing down for bed, I realized we had left The Watermans without paying for the croquettes. I did not want to leave these kind people with the impression that a couple of Americans just ripped them off. Since we planned on leaving town before the Watermans would open in the morning, I told George, as I grabbed my clothes to get dressed, I needed to run back down before they closed for the evening. George seemed happy at the prospect of returning for one last night cap and joined me as we walked again the millpond path. Stepping inside, we saw the bartender we had briefly talked with earlier in the evening. I confessed to my "criminal activity" and he laughed heartily at my sense of humor. He said they had realized it just after we left but hadn't planned on calling the police out after us just yet for ninety-five pence. It proved to be worthwhile to return as I knew we made a dear friend in Tripp Tristan the bartender.

Charming Annie, to whom we brought a bouquet of flowers earlier in the day met us at the door. We told her we would not be around for breakfast in the morning because the bus arrived at eight. She said she would gladly wake up early to feed us before we'd have to leave on the long bus ride. Her kind gesture of rising early to take care of our needs went well beyond anything we ever expected. Early the next morning, we ate in the oak and pine finished dining room. The adjacent room held a small antique billiard table with netted pockets for guests' enjoyment and a bay window to view the main street. It was difficult to leave Pembroke but we had so much more to do and see. We were only three days into our adventure and I was feeling like a princess walking through a fairy-tale story-land.

Wales

Wales, prize of my fathers, full of beauty and grace.
With friends newly found, great and wonderful place.

Like a princess I feel, in castles so vast.
Home far from home, in your mold I am cast.

The Raven on black stallion, and I on white steed.
Fourteen generations have passed since the Boar took heed.

These roots I hold sacred to my heart dear and true.
To your shores I'll again travel, sweet glistening dew.

And I will hold up the goblet, "yichyda" and good cheer.
Have me a pint of sweet cider, and you the stout beer.

The ride to Glasgow, Scotland was long and arduous. We arrived almost twelve hours after we left Wales. It was dark but, with our luck holding firm, we easily found a bed and breakfast near by to spend the evening. It was quite run down in comparison to the splendor of Annie's place in Wales. But it had a bath tub and a clean bed at which I looked longingly after the long drive. We decided we couldn't just call it a night and so walked down the steep hill behind us to visit one of the Scottish pubs. It was almost empty. There were, however, a few die-hard Scots enjoying their whiskey and rye and singing their hearts out. I never heard so many Elvis Presley songs in all my life, sung with an accent that would charm the angels of heaven. They knew every word to each song and I found myself merely sitting back enjoying the entertainment. After a short time, a woman walked into the pub selling long-stemmed roses and I remember thinking they even have Moonies here in Scotland! One of the men at the bar purchased two of the flowers, presenting one to the lady they were harmonizing with. He then stepped over to my table and graciously handed a long-stemmed rose to me saying he wanted to be sure that I had a enjoyable experience in Scotland and would think well of the Scottish people. Pleasantly surprised by his grand gesture, I thanked him and, indeed, left Scotland with a great memory of the Scots.

The next day found us riding the top of a double decker bus to Paisley, an experience I would recommend to everyone. One of the sights that stuck most in my mind as we took the short trip to Paisley was the wonderful red-brown stonework that most of the buildings are constructed of. I hadn't seen anything like it anywhere before and I'm sure it is a stone unique to the region. I was without success in finding any information on my Scottish ancestor as his name is too common and I knew too little about him. A gentleman at the local library told me that the name McDonald was a highland name and that many of them immigrated to Nova Scotia, Canada and America in the 1800s to escape the tyranny of English rule. I found the Scots as wonderful and friendly as the Welsh and could hardly imagine what the land of Ireland would bring, as I'd heard it was the friendliest place on earth. How much more kindness could someone experience without having it bring out the kind side of our own natures long ago forgotten?

We decided to continue on that night and made our way to Stanraer, taking the ferry to Larne, Northern Ireland. We arrived just after midnight. George asked directions from one of the stewards where we could camp for the night and we quickly sought out his recommendation upon landing. The weather had worsened and it appeared that we would be caught in a downpour by morning. George, camp man that he is, had brought a blue tarp to help protect us against the elements. We spread out the tarp with our suitcases and backpacks placed in the center and rolled the end around us. I was neatly tucked in the fold, completely protected from the elements while George took the open end, not fairing as well during the downpour.

Next thing I knew George was asking me if I was wet, to which I said "No, I'm high and dry, but need to pee."   He was soaked clear through and didn't appear to have caught much more than a nap in the hours that had passed since our arrival.

After taking care of my "business," with no real plan in mind and still beguiled by the pathways of my ancestry, we decided to catch a train to Belfast.   We had plans of continuing on that night to Dublin, where my Irish ancestor was born.   We walked over to the deserted train station, praying that we wouldn't have to sit around long waiting for the next train.   As George started walking down the road to see if anyone could tell us when the next train was due, the train pulled up to the station.   I yelled to George to hurry back.   Trying to juggle our belongings, I ran up to catch the train which already started pulling away.   The conductor peeked his head out of one of the windows and yelled to me in the most endearing Irish accent, "Did you want to ride?" I happily yelled back, "Yes!"   I could hardly believe that this wonderful man actually stopped the train to give George and me time to board. Wonderful people, these Irish!   If we were in the States, they would have closed the door on us and flipped us off as the train pulled away with our coats stuck inside the electric doors.

We took advantage of the short trip to Belfast where we would change trains for Dublin, to take a well-deserved nap. The train to Dublin seemed to be waiting for us as we pulled into the station; we hopped aboard like the world travelers we were becoming. While George peacefully slept, I met a wonderful lady who was on her way to Dublin to speak to a group of lay people of the Franciscan Order. She had been involved with the Franciscans for many years and I totally enjoyed the opportunity to speak with her. I asked about the "troubles" of Ireland. When I brought up the subject, she looked all around with fear in her eyes. She said it still was not a good idea to talk of such things. She explained when I told her I was Protestant, that the argument was not so much a religious issue as it was a political one. We talked briefly about some of the history of Ireland as George continued in dreamland, lulled by the rhythmic sway of train against rails.

Suddenly, I felt something hard land on top of my head. The next thing I knew, there was blood streaming down my forehead. The warm sticky fluid seemed never-ending. The woman sitting across from me seemed horrified that the item, a hard-plastic map-tube, which had fallen from the top rack, belonged to her. She pulled out some tissue and said I was lucky she had some medical training. She also said that I must have remained so calm due to my background in emergency medical treatment, stories I had just been sharing with her. We both applied direct pressure to stop the bleeding. Bleeding from a head wound usually looks a lot worse than it is although I must admit that I was quite light-headed the rest of our trip that day. I think I felt worse about how this poor lady was feeling than the pain from the accident.

Dublin is a large city, full of shops and protestors. It was a good time to be in Ireland. The cease-fire had been in effect for several months and protests against English rule were peaceful. We walked the Dublin streets which boasted one-quarter of the entire Irish population. I stopped briefly at a local library to research my Irish roots. My ancestor had been born in Dublin in 1633 and if I had had more time, I'm confident I would have found her listed somewhere in one of the thousands of manuscripts available. The security at the library was more intense than that of the White House in Washington. I had to have my picture taken and be given an identification card before the very efficient guard would allow me entrance to the inner sanctum. I found the people helpful and full of information, but time ran short and I decided I would need to return to Ireland in the future to spend a few weeks at the Dublin library alone.

We were trying to decide what to do next. We felt that our best option would be to travel on to Cork City, near Kinsale, home to my Irish ancestor's family, for the evening as it would most likely be less expensive than staying in a city the size of Dublin. The truth was, we were having a bit of a hard time finding a place to stay there. We did some shopping and I found myself a cart to help get my ever-bulging suitcase around more easily. George purchased a new backpack: I was amazed at how he managed it along with all his other items of travel. But George is a man who actually owned a jacket which turned into a sleeping bag and back into a jacket again. He was extremely resourceful and I was grateful for the opportunity to get to know him better. We talked endlessly about our common interests as emergency 911 dispatchers and how wonderful it felt to be away from the stress. He was always the perfect gentleman, helping me with my load, on top of his own. But he was looking a bit haggard by now and I thought he must be quite ready for a good night's sleep. We found a local tourist information center and asked them to book us a room in Cork City as we knew we would be late in arriving and neither of us were much in the mood for going door to door from the bus station to look for a place. So with the name of a bed and breakfast near to the Cork City bus depot and reservations made, we bused to Cork.

The drive was beautiful. The weather cleared enough to see the castles and green hills overflowing with grazing sheep, divided off by well manicured hedgerows. The bus driver was the typical Irishman, small in stature and driving about a million miles an hour.   We stopped for an unscheduled break at Murphy's pub in Cashel. We hadn't thought there were any stops between Dublin and Cork City and so were caught off guard when the driver pulled off near the pub and announced we would be taking a fifteen minute break. We both welcomed the opportunity to stretch. I was wearing one of my fire department insignia shirts. As George and I stepped off the bus the burly, huggable pub owner, Paul Murphy by name, noticed my shirt and zoomed in on us. "Montana," he said. "Montana is where me mother was born. Butte, Montana. Do you live near there?" I told him that I lived only about an hour away, near the capital city of Helena and that I knew Butte well.   It is a well known Irish community, filled with pubs and proud Irish descendants. We talked at length about Montana and I found that our break was passing along much too quickly. He mentioned several names of relatives still living in Butte and I said I would try to look them up for him when I returned.   He explained his grandmother had decided to return to Eire after years in America.

I mentioned my friend back home who was somehow related to the Smithwicks of Irish beer-making fame. I explained how I had promised her I would bring something back with the Smithwick logo on it for her. He quickly took me by the arm and ushered me into the pub where he told the bartender to find some Smithwick's beer mats for me. The bartender gave me a handful and Paul then instructed him to go to the basement to find some of the special Guinness mats that were stored away. If I hadn't stopped him, I think I would have walked out with every beer mat in the place. His friendly disposition and generosity were customary of these grand people. I don't think I ever felt more at home anywhere else in the world.

We loaded ourselves back onto the bus and continued to Cork City. It was dark as we pulled into the Cork depot. With directions to the bed and breakfast in hand, we went on our way.

With little trouble, we found the place about a mile from the bus depot which put poor George into the "I don't want to move" stance. We carried our luggage up the two flights of stairs to our room after conversing with a rosy-cheeked lady who I thought would never stop asking questions. She went on talking to us about anything and everything under the sun. This friendly woman was named Aileen; she left us with the line to "have a good crack" while there. George and I glanced sideways at each other to her closing remark. Less than a minute later, she returned to the room to clarify that she didn't mean "crack" the drug like we use the word in America, but the craic of a joke and good time. We all laughed and I added, "like cracking up." She said she didn't want us to think they were all some kind of drug addicts.

George was exhausted and had a terrible heat rash that had spread to cover both his inner thighs. We had a very nice room with two beds and he stated in no uncertain, and pain-filled, terms that he wasn't going to move a muscle for the rest of the night. I told him it was his turn to take the large double bed and I would be content with the smaller single. Seeing him uncomfortable, yet being excited at the prospect of finally being in Ireland, I decided to venture out on my own to seek out one of the local pubs.

Just across the street from the bed and breakfast, I spotted what looked to be a small pub. It was difficult to tell as the windows were all dark and there was no light was coming out from inside at all. The front door however was open and I therefore ventured inside. The small hallway led to another glass door which revealed patrons inside.

So, taking a deep breath, I entered the traditional Irish pub called McNamaras. I shyly walked up to the bar, my hair still wet from my shower, and asked for a glass of Baileys. I couldn't have my first drink in Ireland without having my favorite of all drinks, Irish cream. I was astonished at the mostly ice-filled glass, with a touch of cream, that was handed to me. I decided then and there that I would need to stick to the less expensive apple cider beers (maybe stout) or I'd have no money left to continue on to France in a few days.

Many of the pubs in Ireland have low-set tables, surrounded by benches and stools. The people join around them in conversation, song, and a game or two of cards. I noticed an empty stool near two woman and asked if they would mind if I sat down. They were quite gracious and quickly introduced themselves. They wanted to know all about me and what I thought of Ireland and where in America I was from. After describing the Rocky Mountains and my location near the Canadian border, I excused myself to get a beer. When I returned to the table, the ladies mentioned that they were going to head to another bar just down the road. I couldn't help thinking that "just down the road" could mean several miles and did not feel the stamina built up for such a walk. The lure of my bed just across the street was too inviting to risk a long walk back alone. I thanked them for the invitation but explained that I was going to finish my beer then return to my room to get some rest.

No time had passed at all after the ladies left when a very handsome man and his friend literally hopped into the bench seat the ladies had emptied. "Hello," the dark haired stranger said.

"Hello," I replied.

"You're from America are you?"

"Yes, Montana...are you familiar with it?"

"Whereabouts is that?"

"It's near the Canadian border in the Western part of the United States."

"Do they have horses there?"

"Oh, yes, we're part of the old West, we have cowboys and Indians and plenty of horses there," I told him. I asked him his name and he told me it was Patrick and introduced his friend as Edward.

"You see, I am only drinking some apple juice, no Guinness for me tonight," he said with a broad grin gesturing towards his beer. We talked at length about the various apple juices available as I purchased a round for us. Edward was a short, unattractive man, boisterously bragging about his being from Kerry. I found him very friendly, as well as entertaining. He struck me as one of the fighting Irish and even resembled the logo of Notre Dame College. While I enjoyed his company, my attention was drawn to the more gentle-spoken Patrick.

"Will you be staying in Cork for long?" Patrick asked.

"Just a few days I think. I'm here with a friend and I'm not sure how long we'll stay. We have plans to go on to France next." I told him.

I explained our trip so far and that George was my traveling companion, that he was not feeling well and that was how I wound out on my own.

"How old are you?" interrupted Edward.

"That's no sort of question to be asking a lady!" Patrick jumped in.

"Fuckin' cunt, it's just a question," Edward stated. I

heard this expression endless times during my visit and while
I found the term offensive at first, it flowed so naturally from
so many Irish with no intent to offend that I found myself not
even noticing after a while.

"And watch your language too. You don't go on
talkin' that way in front of a lady." Patrick was insistent they
mind their manners around me. His accent was gentle and I
could tell he was making a special effort, but every now and
then he would slip into the faster and harsher sounding Cork
sound.

Getting back to Edward's question, I asked, "How old
do you think I am?" Edward guessed around twenty-five and
Patrick said closer to twenty-seven. "How old are you?" I
asked.

Patrick stated he was twenty-nine, but closer to thirty,
although I would have guessed nearer thirty-five and Edward
seemed to be distracted by a pretty little thing that just entered
the door. "I'm thirty-nine," I told him.

"You certainly don't look it," he said. "What is it that
you do back in America?"

I explained that I worked at the police department as
an emergency dispatcher. "A guarda," Patrick exclaimed with
a great sense of humor. "Oh, no she's going to get out the
cuffs and take me off to the gaol." With this he held out his
arms as if waiting to be cuffed and I had to explain that
dispatchers were not police officers, but handled radio and
telephone communications for law enforcement, medical
responders, and fire departments in the area.

"However, I'd be happy to cuff you if I had some with
me," I told him, playfully returning his flirtation.

The tone of the conversation seemed to turn and I
could not put my finger on what transpired or why the subject
had come up. But, Patrick asked me why I thought children
suffered. I explained that I didn't have the answer to such a
question, but that I believed in a God who loved children and

didn't want to see any of them harmed. It was the fall of mankind that began the suffering of the human race. I continued by telling him that I believed there is a place to which we will go after death where there is no more pain or suffering and this place was where God dwelled. He seemed quite taken with my speech. I told him how, the summer before, I had lost a niece to an extremely rare genetic disorder and watched her go through the dying process for over seven months. I told him this experience enabled my sister and brother-in-law to eventually part with her. I went on to explain how we cherished little Darla during the short time she was with us. He confided to me he had a son who was killed and couldn't understand the attitudes he encountered as the boy lay in a hospital for almost two years paralyzed from the neck down. I got the distinct impression he was somehow blaming himself for his child's demise and could see the pain in his eyes and hear it in his cracking voice. I thought this must have been some recent occurrence for him to be so clearly touched in telling the tale.

He then quickly turned the conversation around stating he didn't want to talk about it anymore. We joked and laughed and the next thing I knew the bartender, a dear man by the name of Michael, was announcing that everyone needed to leave the bar. I went to pick up my drink, finish it off and leave, when Patrick touched my arm and told me not to go. "No, no, he'll go on like that for a time, you're fine, you're fine, enjoy your cider."

And sure enough, it must have been over half an hour before most of the people finally cleared out. We were the last to leave as I bid Patrick and Edward goodbye. "Wait, I'll walk you out," Patrick called to me. He and Edward walked me to the outer door when I noticed Patrick gesturing to Edward to get lost and leave us to ourselves.

I told Patrick I was only staying across the street and that it wasn't necessary for him to walk me. But he insisted and we took the sixty second walk across to my bed and breakfast. We stood for a few minutes talking when he reached his hands out, tenderly holding my face, and planted the deepest, wettest kiss on my lips that I think I had ever felt. "We can't do this, Patrick," I said, trying half-heartedly to pull away from his embrace. "I'm married and not free. I'm sorry, I didn't mean to lead you on." He seemed to ignore what I was telling him and kissed me again but this time I pulled free. "I can't," I told him repeatedly. We talked for several more minutes when he reached out to kiss me again, taking me in his arms tenderly, yet with a strength I found myself longing to embrace. I discovered myself starting to give in to his charm but with a final insistence, pulled away and bade him goodnight. He kissed me again, quickly this time, and said goodbye. I walked up to the door, head hanging, with the taste of him on my lips and burning within my soul.

The next morning, George seemed to be feeling much better. We met downstairs in the dining room to enjoy Aileen's home cooking and friendly manner. There is no comparison of the Stateside hotels to staying at a bed and breakfast in Ireland. There are all the advantages of feeling like you are living in a home, rather than a hotel. The morning meal, included in the price, includes several eggs, bacon, a basket of toast, coffee and juice. Certainly more than adequate to get one going in the morning, not to mention the rest of the day. The hospitality that comes with the meal cannot be equaled. The dining room had several tables splashed with soft white Irish linen and the aroma of coffee and bacon circling the senses.

"And what did you do last night?" Aileen inquired of George who explained his heat rash and that he decided to stay in and take advantage of a good night's rest. They spoke at length about the home cures he could use to help him through his pain when she turned her curiosity on me and asked what I did the evening before.

"Oh, I ventured out on my own. I didn't want to wait to experience an Irish pub and felt too much energy to stay in," I told her.

"Grand," she said, "and where did you venture to?"

"To the little pub just across the street."

"Oh dear God," she exclaimed, "if only I had known, I would have warned you of the place. It is no place for anyone, full of drug addicts and gypsies."

"I found it quite pleasant and the people were very friendly," I responded.

"Oh sure, they'll be that way, looking for a free drink and a craic. They latched on to one of our regular guests a while back. They were always over here expecting him to go to the pub and supply the rounds for the night. He went along with it and I must admit I don't understand why. But, dear, you don't want to be going into that place...it's much too dangerous. Oh, if only I had known I would have warned you beforehand. I feel terrible, I should have said something to you last night but I never expected you'd think to go to that place. But then how would you know any better? You must try Jackie's down the road; it's a nice pub and the people are a better crowd. Why, I go there myself, but you'd never catch me in that place across the way." She was sincere in her regrets for not warning me about the place and genuinely concerned for my welfare.

"The owner seemed like a very nice man." I told her trying to persuade her, and especially George, that it wasn't all that bad. Michael was a retired gentleman who seemed to have purchased the bar to give him something to do, rather than to provide an income. He had worked for Ford Motor Company in Cork for over 25 years, retired, and had run several pubs in the area before purchasing McNamaras.

"Oh my yes, he's a dear. But there's no accounting for the sort that hang around in there," she reiterated. "I hold nothing against him, but take my word, it's a bad place to be going, especially for a woman alone." I explained to George it was true the bar appeared a bit of a dive, but I had felt safe and secure in the warmth of the people I met.

She retreated into the kitchen to attend to two new guests who had just seated themselves in the dining room. It seemed each time Aileen walked in and out of the room that she would stop by us with some comment about McNamaras. "Oh, McNamaras, I can't believe it, such a place." Then finally asking, "and what are you both up to today?"

We told her we had no definite plans and she happily informed us of at least a dozen places to go and of course, the one place not to go.

George seemed to take her every word as gospel and stated I was pretty lucky that nothing happened to me the night before. I explained to him over and over that I found the people most kind and friendly and even if they were drug addicts and gypsies, they treated me well and seemed not to expect anything from me other than conversation. He was not convinced and felt safer in holding to Aileen's word as to the state of the place.

Thanks of course, to Aileen's tour guide information, we decided to go to Cobh for the day. She told us of a new business providing boat rides, saying it would be much more enjoyable than riding the train or bus, and pointed us in the right direction to find the boat on the Lee River. It sounded like a good plan to us. So, after devouring our breakfast and trying to soak in all Aileen's ideas for places to go, we set out for a day on the River.

The boat ride was wonderful and at only five pounds return (meaning round-trip), a budgetary delight. I must give Aileen credit for knowing all the best things for a tourist. The ride to Cobh took about an hour. George and I were two of only five passengers. The captain and his mate gave an informational session about the history of the area. The mate talked about several points of interest, such as Black Rock Castle and the old shipyards. Evidently when the shipyards closed, over two thousand people lost their jobs. This and the closure of the Ford factory had raised the unemployment in the area to over twenty percent.

The Captain, Sean, had spent some time in America. I found this out after mentioning to him he had a very mild accent for Cork. We arrived at Cobh Harbor early in the afternoon. With the warmth of the summer sun, the cold of the water was quickly taken from us.

We walked to the nearby museum stopping to admire a beautiful bronze statute at the entrance which faced America. It commemorated the first Irish immigrant to sail for Ellis Island. The plaque stated that there was an identical statute at Ellis Island facing towards Ireland. Somewhere in my memory, I thought the statute of Annie Moore and her two brothers looked familiar. We went inside and purchased post cards and something to drink, enjoying the passers-by as we wrote out the usual one-liners: "having a wonderful time" and "wish you were here." We still had time before our return to Cork, we spent it window shopping. The streets were winding and the buildings colorful with many small shops along the way.

The return to Cork was equally as pleasant as the way out. I spent most of the time visiting with Sean and telling him about a boat tour service at Gates of the Mountains near Helena, Montana. He was quite interested in the set-up as he had just started the tour business and was looking for any ideas that would help him launch it successfully. I asked for his address and promised to send him some photographs and brochures of the Gates boat tours.

We returned to the bed and breakfast and relaxed for a short while, reexamining our booty from the day's shopping and trying to decide how to spend the evening. George, completely brainwashed by Aileen's words about

McNamaras, felt it best to try out the spot she had
recommended, Jackies, and to stay clear of the seedy "other
pub". Again, I tried to convince him that it wasn't as she said
and I felt we would have a wonderful time there, but I could
not persuade him. "Oh, it may be safe for you Kiddo, but
sometimes it doesn't fare so well for a man. Best we try out
this Jackies and see what it's like." I was open to anything,
but was deep inside my thoughts with regard to the dark,
handsome Patrick; I wanted to see him again. Convincing
myself this was stupid thinking, that I was a married woman,
howbeit unhappy, and it would be senseless to put my
emotions through hopeless romantic daydreams, I reluctantly
agreed to go to the "good pub".

It was just after nine when we walked into Jackies. It
was a clean place, about twice the size of McNamaras, with
the traditional bench, table and stool set-up. I noticed
immediately when we walked in every face in the pub turned
to check out who the strangers were, not unlike many of the
small town bars back home. They picked no bones about it,
simply stared at us, then returned to their conversations and
card playing. George and I purchased a couple of beers and
sat at one of the benches. No one intruded on us. No friendly
conversation was forced on us by the locals. We simply sat
and talked to each other about the trip so far and some of our
plans for ferrying to France. We agreed we were in no hurry
and needed to spend a few days in one place.

After finishing off the first round, I stepped up to the
bar to order us another. While waiting for the order to be
filled, a well-dressed man of around thirty-five walked up to
me and asked where I was from. I told him that I was from
America, to which he belligerently stated, "I knew that, where
there are you from?" I explained I was from Montana and
tried to maintain some semblance of courtesy even though he
was obviously looking for an argument and did not project the
friendly hospitality that I was getting used to. He kept

badgering me about America and stated I felt it was better than Ireland. I told him that was not how I felt and that both places had fine points. I further told him how much I was enjoying Ireland and how beautiful it was. He persisted in trying to tell me how I thought, when luckily a woman walked up, helping to draw his attention away from me and towards her.

I picked up the beers from the bar when the man to the left of me asked, "Annoying isn't he?"

I replied, "No doubt." We both laughed. The belligerent one looked disappointed at not being able to continue his interrogation of me since I had returned to my table.

I told George what had happened. He had been observing the encounter and I explained to him that I hadn't found this attitude from any of the people at McNamaras. I noticed the stranger looking at me continuously as we sipped on our new round. When he took a flash photograph in the bar of his lady friend, I blinked. He stated quite loudly, "Oh, didn't mean to bother the tourists." At that, I told George I was ready to call it a night; we returned to the bed and breakfast.

I knew there was no use in asking George if he'd like to try out McNamaras so didn't pursue the point. However, after returning to our room and knowing the pubs were still open for a short while, I decided to go over to McNamaras on my own for a nightcap.

When I walked in I could not help but wander my eyes in looking for Patrick. There he was, sitting at one of the benches with two young girls, each barely twenty, if a day. They were laughing and having a good time. He smiled at me but did not approach as I sat there sipping my cider. I noticed he got up to go outside and I heard the bartender, Maggie, call out to him, "Goodnight, Ciaran." He replied he would be right back. Maggie and I had been talking for several minutes as I sat at the bar. A very fine looking woman in her mid twenties with lovely, thick, long blonde hair. She explained she was Michael's daughter and helped out a couple of nights a week tending the bar.

After I heard her call Patrick, "Ciaran," I was baffled. "What   is   his   name?"   I   inquired.

"Why, that's Ciaran Kelly," she replied. "He comes in here all the time."

"Are you sure his name isn't Patrick?"

"Oh no, I know him quite well, his name is Ciaran."

"I must have been mistaken." Anger was welling up inside me. "Why would he lie to me about his name?" I thought. I knew he was just looking for a good time the night before but felt betrayed having been somewhat seduced by a man who would lie about his own name to me. I felt hurt, yet remained sitting at the bar thinking that I needed to say something to him about his deception.

I had just finished my cider and was about to leave when he walked back into the pub. I don't know what moved me, but I could not just let it lie to have played the American fool for him. I walked over to where he was entertaining the two girls, leaned over and whispered in his ear, "You should not have lied to me about your name."

He didn't say a word but simply looked up at me with a puzzled look on his face. I smiled and left the bar thinking "good riddance to bad news," yet still with a longing to be wrapped by his arms once again, whatever his name might be.

I had been in such a miserable marriage for so many years that perhaps it was just the prospect of someone finding me attractive. I had grown fat the last few years and while I never lacked receiving propositions back home, hadn't felt appealing in a very long time. American men seemed to want their women tall and slender in addition to just wanting to get laid but, then apparently the Irish did too...wanted to get laid, that is. Men are men world-wide, I suppose. What it was that drew me to this man and not others who had approached me I couldn't explain. Perhaps it was the fact that my husband, on the rare occasions he was home, had parked himself on the living room sofa for almost four years. He hadn't touched me or shown any affection for so long that I had resigned myself to living like this "for the sake of the children" and financial stability.

Perhaps it was due to the fact that my self esteem had hit a new low. It's not healthy for a woman, nor a man, to feel ugly and unwanted. There was a time when I fancied myself to be somewhat sensuous. It was always my thought to leave a relationship gone sour; I would gladly let a man out of my life if he wanted it that way. But, this marriage tied me down and I was settling for the day-to-day rather than experiencing all I could be. Being married made me believe I could feel free to enjoy our European adventure and not fall victim to another man's advances. I felt safe with George, who was the perfect gentleman and never made a pass at me. Patrick, along with the people here, were friendly and I felt they were bringing out a side in me that I hadn't known for years. Now I felt I was more myself than I had ever been in my life. Perhaps it was his dark hair, soft eyes and charm that made me feel I melted under his gaze.

When I returned to the room, I woke George and told him all about Ciaran, a.k.a. Patrick, the experience I had the night before and then tonight in learning his true name. I told him of my desire to be with this man, but that I couldn't break my marriage vows, even if the marriage was dead. George, being the new-age man that he is, told me to "go for it" and enjoy life. He earnestly encouraged me to hook up with Ciaran and put some passion in my life. It was fun talking with George. He was so open and honest and held the philosophy that life is what you make it; you should love and be loved whenever it makes you feel good. After four marriages of his own, he believed that love wasn't forever, but a person fell in and out of it with various people throughout their lives and shouldn't ever feel saddled by an unhappy relationship. It was hard to ignore his rationalization and I found myself agreeing with much of what he was saying, yet still holding fast to my belief that love should be forever and that a contract commitment was to be kept. Kent was not necessarily a bad man, he was a fair provider and a good father. He fell short in being a husband however, and had left me feeling inadequate, alone and neglected.

The night brought fantasies of being embraced by my handsome stranger - long, lingering kisses passionately streaming over every part of me. When I woke up in the morning he was deeply embedded on my mind and I prayed silently that I would have the strength to resist his advances if they were to come again. And, somehow I knew they would indeed come again.

George and I washed up, and went to breakfast. Aileen, with the dearest of politeness, asked about our day out. We told her how much we enjoyed the boat ride and Cobh and were planning to kiss the Blarney Stone this afternoon. We told her about the incident at Jackies and she was very apologetic that things worked out that way but repeated her feelings that it was a fine place where people generally left you alone. I told George later that I didn't want to be left alone, I wanted to talk to the locals and soak up everything they said and did. Aileen enjoyed the idea we were headed to the Blarney Stone and told us how it really was just an old latrine that the tourists were taken in by.

I had always imagined the Blarney Stone to be some massive boulder the size of a small semi-truck. I was surprised after climbing the five stories to the top of the castle to find it was simply an outside wall. A gentleman sat near the place to hold onto us turkeys as we bent over backwards with lips becoming one with the outer wall of the castle for a brief moment. There was quite a gap between the outer wall and the inner and I asked the "holder" if he had ever lost anyone yet. I'm sure this was not an original question, but he laughed and stated it had been some time since one got away. With this I told him I trusted him and bent back to attain the gift of eloquence.

The rolling fields and rich green grounds of Blarney Castle were an enjoyable way to spend the afternoon. After kissing the stone, George and I walked down to the Woollen Mills where fine handmade wool sweaters and scarves were sold. We spent several hours wandering the store, filling our bags to capacity with doilies, sweaters and bric a brac of Eire. There was some time remaining before we'd need to catch the bus back to Cork; consequently we fell into one of the pubs, where we enjoyed some Guinness. The child tending bar, and I do mean child, could be no more than fourteen and had pixie-like features. She attended the patrons like an expert well beyond her years and the other children sitting around were instructed by her on their behavior as she poured them their colas. One boy flirted with her but she kept to her business, leaving him sitting disappointedly near the bar. Barely able to reach over the edge of the high standing bar, I thought she must have been a member of the family that owned the pub to be working here at all.

It was my last night in Cork and on the bus ride back from Blarney, George and I decided we would go our own ways that night. He held no interest in getting into a bar room brawl at McNamaras (which he felt would inevitably happen) and neither of us wanted to go back to Jackies. He said he hoped to meet some sweet colleen and create some memories. Far be it from me to cramp his style! I welcomed the chance to go off on my own. It seemed that as a couple, people were less apt to chit chat with us. We found that even riding the buses, that if we separated, we would be more likely to sample the best of the people who were so willing to share their thoughts with us as individuals.

Spiffied up and wearing my best pair of jeans, (my last clean pair, at that) I headed over to McNamaras. I did not see Ciaran there when I arrived, so I sat visiting with Maggie, who again was tending bar. Many of the other locals started up conversations with me. I met another fellow named Tom who I had noticed the night before and we talked at length, enjoying our surroundings and sharing stories about both Ireland and America.

About an hour later Ciaran walked into the bar. "Obviously a popular guy," I thought, as it was clear he was a regular patron and well liked by the people in the pub. He came over to me, smiled, and entered into conversation with Tom as he ordered his Guinness from Maggie. Another fellow, a rather happy sort who'd had his fill of stout already, came over visiting with us asking questions about Montana. He was a bit slobbery and I kept placing Ciaran between us to help keep him at bay. Ciaran seemed to thoroughly enjoy playing my protector and we had many a craic at the expense of the drunken benefactor who happily purchased several more rounds for us. He kept asking me if I rode horses in Montana to which I constantly answered, "Yes." He asked if I rode bare back and I told him "no". After he asked me this for about the twentieth time, I replied, "I ride their backs and I ride them bare!" Ciaran laughed hysterically and Tom equally enjoyed my exasperated humor.

We closed down the pub that night with both Tom and Ciaran walking me out the front door. Ciaran gestured to Tom that he would catch up with him later and Tom stated how it was fine, he'd wait for him. Ciaran gave him a look which Tom seemed to understand as, "You can leave now." Tom instantly disappeared up the road headed towards his home.

Ciaran wasted no time in taking me, more forcibly this time, in his arms. "I love you," he said as he bent down to meet my lips with his.

"Love me?" I said, "you don't even know me."

"I knew it the minute I saw you," was his reply.

"Knew what? What could you possibly know, you don't love me and you don't know me, but I will tell you that I'm very much attracted to you," I told him. "What's my name?"

He thought for a minute then spoke the proper response to my question.

He melted me with his kisses and I found it impossible to hold back, I didn't want to hold back, I wanted him and was having a hard time refusing his advances.

He looked deep in my eyes and I knew I was losing all power to him.

"I knew it the minute I laid eyes on you." Ciaran, gently this time, wrapped his arms around me bending down to draw me close to his chest. My heart was pounding wildly and I found myself melting, swaying into his body. The instinct to go off with him, as he kept asking me to do, became overpowering, yet I still knew I must resist. I slowly pulled away from him and told him that we couldn't continue. "I'm married and this wouldn't be right."

"Come with me, I have a place just up the road," he said as he lightly tugged at my arm.

"No, I can't do that, Ciaran. As much as I'm tempted, I can't do that," I told him. "Can we sit a while and just talk?"

"Why, of course."

"Why did you lie to me about your name, Ciaran?"

"I didn't know who you were," he said. "You could be a guarda. I'm the biggest gangster in all of Cork and I couldn't take a chance on not knowing who you were. It meant nothing. Just an Irish name like Paddy or Michael. You could have been there to arrest me, I didn't know if I could trust you or not."

"Oh, so you're the biggest gangster in all Cork, are

you?" I teased. "Do you think you can trust me now?" I looked deep into his eyes for the answer to my inquiry.

"It would be lovely to be cuffed by you and taken away," he joked. "Yes, I trust you."

We moved a few yards down the sidewalk to sit on the small stone retaining wall that ran along the curb. He placed his arm around me and kissed me again.

"Ciaran, you must understand, I've never done anything like this before. I can't be with you. I'm sorry. I want to, but I can't."

Again he asked me to go to his place and again I told him I couldn't.

"I know what will happen if I go with you, Ciaran, and I dare not. If I were to give in to my desire, I would never forgive myself. I must stay true to my marriage vows, even if my marriage has been in name only for many years now." I tried my best to explain that even though I suspected Kent of having numerous affairs throughout the years, I was not the type to go against the grain of my beliefs and had remained completely faithful to him. "Please try to understand, I'd be likely to put a bullet through my brain from the guilt. Please try to understand this." It was as if I were begging him to be strong for both of us - he picked up on this quickly.

"I love you," he said again with the deepest of sincerity.

"There's no such thing as love at first sight."

We continued talking and holding hands as the evening passed.

"I'm leaving in the morning, Ciaran. I'll always remember you fondly," I told him.

He walked me back to the door of the bed and breakfast and again gently, yet with a simple strength, kissed me, said goodbye and that he loved me. "I knew it the minute I saw you," he said again.

"I love you, too, Ciaran," I whispered as I watched

him disappear from my sight even though I didn't believe the words coming from either of us were literally true.

I went back to the bed and breakfast feeling my heart broken and wishing that things could have worked out differently. If I weren't married, I could easily fall into his arms and let him take me anywhere.

George was awake as I entered the room. "How was your night, Kiddo," he said.

"Oh, it was grand, simply grand," I answered with a bit of a brogue. "What about you, did you get lucky tonight?"

"No, there were a few prospects, and I met two very nice ladies, but couldn't seem to get them led to the Streams of George," he said disappointedly.

He told me he had gone to the other side of town, did some dancing and met two beautiful specimens of Irish womanhood. I told him how I saw Ciaran and the difficult time I had in maintaining my values. He told me he was sympathetic, but "perhaps it was for the best." Then he added, he thought I would have had a wonderful time if I would have given in and it was too bad I held back because of my old world mentality since my marriage was already dead. He slept like a baby. but I spent my last night in Cork sitting in the window sill, thinking about my dear Irishman and how I would never see him again.

Chapter 4
France

George and I woke early the next morning to catch the bus to Rosslare Harbor.

From the bed and breakfast we made the trek back to the Cork City bus depot. Again the travel gods smiled upon us, as we practically stepped right onto the bus as we arrived. It was a long ride to Rosslare Harbor, taking us through Waterford, where we had a two hour wait for our connection. George took advantage of the time while I kept an eye on his gear at the depot. He took off for the crystal factory. While he was gone, I met some very kind elderly ladies who helped me pass the time by showing me their own booty of crystal and linens they had purchased along the way. George returned in plenty of time to catch our bus, clutching a beautiful Waterford crystal clock he purchased as a gift for his mother. He had it engraved at the factory and was childlike when he showed it to me and the other ladies. With the utmost care, he then tucked it inside several layers of clothing secure inside his knapsack.

We boarded the bus in anticipation of the next part of our journey. The bus took us through Wexford, then on to the Harbor where the ferry was readying to leave. It was a twenty-two hour boat ride across the "ocean" to LeHavre, France.

Irish Ferries is a very organized operation, providing an enjoyable voyage across the seas. The ferries are clean and more like cruise liners than any ferry I remember during my time growing up near New York City when I rode the Circle Line tours around the Hudson River.

George and I had sailed with Irish Ferries from Scotland to Northern Ireland and were ready for this next sojourn across the water. We decided, due to the length of the trip, to secure a stateroom which had a shower and four bunks in it. We could have opted to sleep in one of the reclining chairs for five pounds or share a cabin in the bowels of the boat for the same price. We decided to treat ourselves and proceeded to drop off our weighty baggage in our room.

It was nearly four in the afternoon when the ferry pulled away from the harbor. I found myself watching Ireland slip from my sight with a heart heavier than any luggage could ever possibly be. My thoughts turned to Ciaran and how much I wished I could still be with him. I kept thinking that if there were some way to jump ship and run back to his arms, I would. Not a bright idea for someone who can't swim! I stood at the railing for what seemed to be hours and remained long enough to watch the sun set over my beloved Eire and on my longing for what could not be.

I returned to our room to freshen up after a brief stop at the duty free shop to purchase some tee shirts, cigarettes, and a bottle of Cream. George returned shortly after I arrived and we shared stories over a glass or two or three. He told me he had his eye on a French lady whom he had struck up a conversation earlier. I enjoyed listening to what his wandering eyes had seen. It seemed that almost everywhere we were, he found some sweet little thing who drew his attention. We laid our plans out in case he got lucky and wanted to use the room for some privacy. We decided we'd hang the "do not disturb" sign on the door handle should one of his new found prizes decide to join him for a nightcap. We finished our Cream, then went our separate ways, walking around the decks of the Ferry Killian.

I explored the ferry knowing I was not in the mood to visit with anyone. I needed to spend time with my thoughts and confusion. I tried to make sense of it all, but found myself staring at the sea from the upper deck, wanting nothing else but to return to Ireland...to him.

I heard some music coming from the other side of the ship and decided to investigate.

Here two fellows with acoustical guitars were playing traditional Irish tunes. I struck up a conversation with them during one of their breaks. They told me how they were headed to Germany for a gig. I sang a tune or two with them. They played a song for me that they said was American although it was unfamiliar to me. It was a beautiful tune and we all exclaimed, with great pride, how much influence the Irish had in American folk music.

Before I returned to the room, I stopped once again to gaze at the full moon lying low in the sky and wondered if I could talk George into returning to Eire. "At least they speak English there," I thought, even if the Cork accent is thick and sounds foreign at times. When I returned to the room George was there, having not gotten lucky after all, drinking a bit of the Cream and feeling a tad sorry for himself. I started to believe my thoughts of returning to Ireland silly and didn't broach the subject with him.

The gentle rolling motion of the ship combined with the effects of the Cream lulled us both into a deep sleep. My dreams were filled with Ciaran and I could not, as much as I tried, clear him or his touch from my heart.

We landed in France on schedule. I mentioned to George how I wished I were back in Ireland. We then caught the shuttle bus to the train depot and laid out our plans. When we arrived at the train station, George went into one of the tourist information centers to get copies of schedules to help us decide on where we would go. Italy, perhaps or maybe Spain - all depending on the schedule. George came out of the office with a hand full of brochures and talking a mile a minute about his ideas of what we could do next. There was a young Spanish woman there, dark and beautiful, who came over to ask us questions about the next train to Spain. As George stood eagerly explaining the schedule, I found myself making up my mind once and for all that I wanted to be nowhere other than where my heart was. I turned to George and told him I'd rather be in Ireland to which he sweetly replied, "Go for it Kiddo, enjoy yourself, but be careful."

I had just enough time to catch a cab back to the ferry in order to make the next trip back to Eire. In order to help ease my guilty conscience for leaving George, I quickly handed over two of the three rental car coupons that had come with our passes to him and took one for myself that I could use in Ireland. He helped me run to catch a cab, gave me a big hug and told me again to be careful. "You can't ever go back, you know Kiddo. Be careful with that heart of yours but go for it and be happy. I'll see you back in the States."

I asked him what he was going to do and he said he thought he might follow this new interest to Spain and see how things worked out. I wished him luck and quickly jumped in the cab with only fifteen minutes left to catch the ferry. The cab driver was quick - dropped me at the dock with time to spare. I found out as we drove up to the dock that the ferry left according to Irish time (an hour later than France) so I had plenty of cushion to stand around and get checked in. While taking a place to stand in line I accidentally brushed my suitcase up against a woman, obviously American, who acted as though I had just punched her in the face. If looks could kill I would have dropped dead instantly from this wench's cold stare. I apologized twice but, her attitude remained unforgiving as I proceeded to the end of the line. While waiting to board I kept repeating to myself I was crazy for returning. "What in the world are you doing, Colleen? This is wrong." But it was too late now to try to meet back up with George. His train had been due to leave already and I would have been in a terrible state of mind trying to get around in a non-English speaking country alone for the next week. So, with this rationalization in mind, I continued to convince myself returning was the right thing to do. After all, I didn't have to return to Cork...to him. Ireland was a big enough country and I could go anywhere. I had less than a week left and would have to return to France once more in order to connect in Frankfort for my return flight to

America. I almost had my mind made up to head to Dublin or Killarney or anyplace other than Cork, when the line started moving and I boarded for the long journey back to Eire.

I didn't want to go to the expense of securing an entire room to myself and the prospect of sleeping in one of the recliners was not a happy one. I decided to share one of the rooms in the hold of the ship with three other women. I was the first in the room and chose one of the bottom bunks for myself. I laid my items on the blankets to safeguard it from being taken by one of the others who would soon descend upon the room. "I can put up with anything for a night," I thought to myself. "Just my luck the wench from the lobby will wind up in here with me." Shuddering from that thought and the idea no shower came with this room, I canvased the ferry to see if another shower would be available for in the morning. I hated the prospect of continuing on any trip without having the wake-up call of a fresh cup of coffee and a shower. Simple needs really, considering I was about to spend the night with what could prove to be a thief or murderess or two or three.

I went up the four flights of stairs to one of the upper decks and watched France disappear. I felt elated to watch it go and knew in my heart that a strong longing for Eire had been in me for many years.

In a high school production of Finian's Rainbow, a wonderful musical about an Irish immigrant and his daughter played by Fred Astair and Petula Clark in the movie version, I acted the part of Finian's daughter, Sharon. The play projected a passion about civil rights mixed with the magic of Irish folk lore. Finian and Sharon had immigrated to America after Finian had stolen a pot of gold from a leprechaun. The daughter naturally fell in love with a handsome farm boy and the father got off the hook with Og, the leprechaun who followed them trying to regain his pot of gold. Og fell in love with the handsome farm boy's mute sister, and everyone lived happily ever after. I so enjoyed the part finding that the Irish brogue came quite naturally to me. I received many standing ovations that night. There is no feeling in the world like performing in front of a live audience and knowing they enjoy the performance so much.

I remembered even earlier, as a child, I was always inquisitive about Ireland and it's people. Yet, I had learned little about it through the years other than being proud of my Irish roots, wishing I knew more. My best friend in the world, a very attractive woman of Italian and Russian decent, had enjoyed teasing me about my "Mick" heritage and I would return the ball-busting in kind about her "Wop" roots. Layla was a great and generous friend who was there for me over the past thirty years. I had phoned to tell her of my plans for a trip to Europe and had promised to send her a post card from Italy...but I guess that wouldn't happen now...she'll just have to do with one from Ireland instead. Most people talk about having best friends who actually turn out to be either fair-weather friends or betrayers of inner thoughts. This is a lesson I learned early on. But Layla was different. I could tell her anything and trust it to stay with her alone. We had disagreements through the years, but always returned to our loving relationship built on trust and support. I never felt I was near as good a friend to her as she was to me. She had pretty much adopted me into her family as a young child, before my mother remarried. Her dad was my dad and her mom was my second mother. We did everything together including one of our most favorite pass times, meeting boys at Palisades Amusement Park which was just a few blocks from where we lived. We did crazy things at a very early age. By the time we were eight years old we'd head over to Greenwich Village to watch the hippies and gypsies hang out selling their wares. By nine, I tried my first joint; it was given to me by one of our mutual friends, a gypsy who lived in an old Victorian-style home down one of the side streets.

I remember how upset my grandmother was when she found out we were hanging around with Joan. "Dirty gypsies," she would say, "you can't trust them and I don't want you around them anymore." Funny, Aileen seemed to have this same distrust of gypsies and I couldn't relate to that at all. Joan's home was always clean; our smoking pot had nothing to do with her heritage. It was more due to the 1960s and we were all old beyond our years, eager to experience anything different laid out before us, gypsy or not. We were invincible and nothing would harm us. Joan was twelve going on twenty and I enjoyed every minute with her. Besides, she had a couple of cute brothers Layla and I had our eyes on.

No, Layla would understand why I chose to return to Ireland and by-pass Italy. I knew I could never tell her what I knew would take place. Not that she wouldn't understand, but I was about to go against everything I believed in. I didn't want to prove such a bad witness against Christianity by revealing this new, darker side of my spirit.

What was this longing inside me? I knew I was lonely, but I had always exhibited better than average self-control over my emotions. What would I do when I returned to Eire? I decided it best for my own mental health to think along the same lines as Margaret Mitchells' Scarlet O'Hara...to worry about it later, because...'after all, tomorrow is another day'. "Oh well", I thought, "I'll just deal with it when I get there".

I returned to my room to find all three previously empty bunks now had suitcases and back packs on them. It was going to be a full room that evening - I hoped that they wouldn't want to spend half the night up talking. I was emotionally drained and looked forward to a good night's sleep. I sipped on the remainder of the Irish Cream and sat back, looking over the map of Ireland. The door opened and a woman in her mid-twenties entered the room. Behind her walked in another woman, an American, who was absolutely stunning and unfortunately, knew it. Her typical "princess attitude" turned me off immediately as she whined about feeling sick, yet stuffed her face with a Snickers bar and seemed to bitch about any subject that came up. The first woman, however was quite pleasant. She was from New Zealand and was traveling on her own for the last eight weeks. She was in the bottom bed across from me, the Princess was bunking over her head. A few minutes later my premonition realized came the wench from the lobby, still scowling. All I wanted to do was either hit her or roll over and sleep until morning. She stood at the foot of my bunk talking with the others whom she seemed to already have gotten to know. She didn't say anything to me but gave me another of her looks. Trying to lighten things up, I jokingly said, "I knew somehow it was destiny for us to wind up together."

She eased up a little but acted as if I should give up my bottom bunk to her just because she was complaining about trying to climb into the upper one. Had she been kinder toward me, I would have volunteered just that, but she had an obvious chip on her shoulder and I felt the brunt of it. I got the impression she felt the world and everyone in it owed her something.

When she and the Princess left the room for a while, I told the New Zealand woman, Nikki, of my experience back at the lobby. "Oh, I wondered what was going on," she said. "It seemed a bit frosty in here."

We talked until the others returned exchanging information on our home countries, work, and other interests. She told me of her travels and how she had just a few more weeks left before she would have to return home. She told me that the wench did indeed have a chip on her shoulder. Evidently several years earlier, she had treated her son to a trip by chartered plane which unfortunately crashed, killing everyone on board. She blamed herself and in her misery appeared to want to make everyone around her miserable too. "Everyone has had some tragedy in their lives," I told Nikki. "But, it's no excuse to treat other people poorly."

The Princess and the wench returned to the room and announced their plans. The wench was headed for Cork and the Princess for Dublin. The Princess crawled back up in her bunk, looked at me and snottily stated, "If you snore I'm going to throw something at you to wake you up, I hope you know that."

Tired and grouchy, I replied, "If you value your long bleached blonde hair, I wouldn't try it if I were you." I decided to make myself perfectly clear in not putting up with her hoity toity attitude.   This proved effective as she immediately backed off.

Nikki was oblivious to it all. She seemed impervious to these two and their snottiness, yet was not ignorant of her instincts either. She started telling me about her "popple," a semi-stuffed toy that had been her traveling companion. She commented on how it was now showing the wear and tear of the long trip. She was sweet and childlike in the way she curled the popple up under her head and told the tale of their travels together. The princess then in all her rudeness said, "How old are you anyway?"

This too went over the dear Nikki's head who simply stated, "Twenty-six, how old are you?"

I watched as the Princess in all her exasperation at not being able to ruffle the feathers of the New Zealander replied, "Twenty-two."

I envied Nikki's enthusiasm and fortune at taking such a long trip on her own. Single and pretty much unattached, she told me she planned on going to Cork for a couple of days before returning to Wales and England. We decided to join forces and travel to Cork together excluding the others. I think she was growing vaguely uncomfortable with them and their stuck-up, obnoxious American attitudes. At some point, when they both left the room a short while, I explained to her the sarcasm behind the Princess asking her age. She had been indeed naive about it and shrugged it off as if it were yesterday's bad news. Yet, I could see the hurt in her eyes and wished I hadn't mentioned it at all. I had only wanted her to be careful of her backside around these two and didn't want her to think they represented all Americans.

The morning came quickly and if anyone was snoring it was the Princess. I felt like yanking her off the bunk by her scrawny legs and stuffing her out one of the port holes. Must have forgot to have my saucer of milk that morning to even think such a thing.

I quickly retreated from the room before anyone else. Nikki joined me shortly after in the lobby where we made our plans for catching the train since we both had Eurail passes which covered train travel, but not the bus. My budget had dwindled much faster than I had anticipated and I didn't want to get any more than I had to from my credit card.

Nikki truly was a dear girl with a sweet disposition, I couldn't help but enjoy her company. She told me about her boyfriend back in New Zealand but, how she had met a man, a grave-digger, in Wales to which she had succumbed to without any sense of guilt. What an old-fashioned morality I held! I knew that I was trapped within this ancient mind of mine and yearned to break free, even if only for a short time. We had fun talking about her grave-digger and how she planned on returning to see him again in a few days. She couldn't help herself any more than I could and she was clear she didn't want it any other way. Her longing seemed to be more physical than emotional and I felt mine much too spiritual and already deeply heartfelt. "Is it possible to really fall in love so quickly," I ran the question around and around my mind, over and over again.

We returned to Rosslare to catch the train to Cork. It was almost dark now and we wouldn't arrive until nearly midnight. We settled into our seats and sipped a fresh bottle of Irish Cream which I had purchased along the way, continuing to exchange stories of love, romance and lust. Figuring this girl didn't know me from Eve and I would never see her again, I found myself openly telling her of my purpose for returning to Cork. After all, I was acting like a school girl, why not talk like one too. She seemed as happy for me as George had been and I felt like a high school virgin with a crush on the handsome football quarterback. We spent the entire journey talking and drinking, and started to feel quite 'pissed' (Irish for "drunk"), when we pulled into Cork. I asked if she would mind if we stopped by McNamaras to see if Ciaran were there. McNamaras was just a block or so up from the train station and she had no problem with our giving it try. I had to knock as the door was locked but, I hoped the patrons would still be sipping on the last call of the night. Michael came to the door and said Ciaran wasn't there and that everyone had left.

We walked down to one of the local youth hostels on the main avenue and booked a couple of beds for the night. Before turning in, I decided to take a cab to the address Ciaran had given me to write to him. I found that this was his x-wife's home who, at one o'clock in the morning, told me that he didn't live there and didn't expect to see him. "He just picks up his mail here," she said. I gave up any hope of finding him for the night and resigned myself to staying at the hostel in the filled-to-capacity, twenty bunk room.

I crawled up on the only open top bunk and immediately smelled body odor, old body odor at that. I decided then and there I would need to come up with somewhere else to spend my nights after this. It may be cheap and I don't consider myself a prig but there's something about thinking you're sleeping in someone else's sweat that sets my hair on end. At this point, I was too tired to give it much thought; I simply placed my sleeping bag between me and the sheets to and fell fast asleep.

It must have been six in the morning when I woke to the screeching sound of. (I could hardly believe my luck was going so bad) the wench! She, in all her vain glorious way, was acting like the queen bee. Years older than most of us, she bragged on her travels and seemed to be trying to make everyone feel inferior. Instead of dealing with the trials of losing a loved one with understanding and acceptance, she chose to layer herself in armor of steel and dominance. Ignoring her, Nikki and I went downstairs to have a bit of breakfast. Afterwards we walked down to the local department store where I purchased some condoms, and a new satin robe. I was going to make this a time to remember. "I can't believe I'm doing this," I told her as we picked out what she told me was the sexiest lavender satin robe in the store.

We walked down to the bus coach station to inquire about her trip back to Wales. I decided to go to McNamaras to see if Ciaran were there, telling Nikki I would meet up with her later. After stopping to check the ferry schedules for my necessary return to France, I walked to the pub. I would only be able to stay in Ireland five nights, since my last two days would be on the Continent, traveling to Frankfort to meet the plane.

There were only Michael and two other gentleman sitting at the bar when I walked in. My disappointment was evident, but I stayed to visit while drinking real apple juice (the non-alcoholic kind) which I had picked up in a shop along the way. I got involved in a conversation with one of the men whose name was Donel. He was in his sixties and told me he was a good friend of Ciaran. "Does he have a girlfriend?" I asked.

"Oh no, nothing steady. He's like any man and takes

it when he can, but no one special is in his life, oh no, don't you worry yourself about that," he told me.

"I wouldn't want to be causing any problems for him," I said. "Do you know where he lives, I understand it's somewhere near here?"

"No dear, for as well as I know him, as good of friends as we are, I have never been to his place of residence. I wish I could help but if you wait here I'm sure he'll be in. He usually stops by around noon."

It was almost eleven o'clock, so I decided to wait until noon to see if he came. I continued to tell myself it wasn't too late to turn and leave; "What in the world am I doing?" But, I knew exactly what I was doing. This Ciaran intrigued me and if all he wanted was something physical, then I was there to fill his needs as well as my own. I would enter into this with my head square on my shoulders. I rationalized all the time that my needing to be with Ciaran was a result of the "unfaithfulness" of my husband's lack of affection. After all, unfaithfulness can come in many forms.

Michael and Donel began speaking in Gaelic. I loved the sound of it but felt very much left out of their conversation.   So, with a sense of acting the slighted American, I said, "Now, if you keep going on like that, I'll have to leave. Must be talking about me," I laughed.

"Yes, we were talking about you," Michael replied. "On what a beautiful colleen you are and how lucky a man that Ciaran is for you to come back."

Well, that sure shut me up. Bless his wonderful Irish heart!

Half-three (3:30) rolled around with Donel cosily leaning back in the hardwood chair near the fireplace sleeping peacefully. I decided to return to the hostel to see if they would hold a reservation for the evening. The clerk kindly placed my suitcase in the office area for me after he told me there were no rooms available. I explained I was hoping to run into my friends and may not need a room tonight anyway. He told me that if no room came available, and I was unable to find my friends, I was welcome to spread my sleeping bag out in the lobby, "It's not much more than a place to lay your head," he said. I gratefully accepted his kindness and sat in the lobby watching television.

Nikki came in the front door and told me she had been successful in purchasing her coach ticket. I asked her if she wanted to join me later that evening to go to McNamaras; she eagerly took me up on it. After a quick bite to eat, we headed to McNamaras.

It was past seven o'clock now and there was a wee bit of a nip in the air. Nikki could talk faster than a New York minute and more than anyone I had ever met in my life, including me. As we entered the pub, I saw Tom sitting at one of the benches with several other people. He invited my friend and me to join them, which we did. I asked him if he thought Ciaran would be coming in that evening and he said he was sure he would. Between Tom and me sat his friend, Rose. She seemed friendly and we engaged in light conversation. She had heard me asking Tom about Ciaran and began to ask me questions about him when he appeared coming in the front door. Rose took special notice of how I followed Ciaran with my eyes as he walked towards the bar. Grabbing my attention with a touch of her hand on my arm and in anticipation of her inquiry, I turned and said, "I'm rather sweet on him you know."

She replied, "Yes, I can see that, and he's sweet on you too."

I asked her how she could know that. She told me he had told her about me the other night. She said he was very upset that I had left. "Where are you staying this evening?" She asked.

"I'm not sure if I'll still have a bed there or not when I get back, but I stayed last night at the youth hostel down the road."

"No, you'll stay with me tonight," she insisted. "But I'm afraid I have no room for your friend."

"Oh, I'm sure that'll be fine with Nikki," I said. "She's just someone I met up with on the ferry ride back from France. It's very kind of you to offer."

"Just as well, she'd be most like to keep us all night with that talkin' anyway," she joked.

Ciaran still had not seen me sitting near the support beam. I watched him standing at the bar exchanging greetings with everyone as they came near. He turned to inspect who else was in the pub when his eyes met mine. He had the most endearing puppy dog look of inquisitiveness on his face and smiled the most incredible smile I had ever seen. He continued to stand at the bar and I prodded Tom to tell him to come sit down. Instead of getting up to discreetly tell him, Tom yelled, "Come here Ciaran and sit with us. Colleen's here."

My head dropped with embarrassment, "Yes, yes, a minute, a minute," Ciaran replied over his shoulder as he continued his conversation with Michael.

Getting tired of the wait and feeling bold from the pints I had been downing on and off all day, I got up and walked over to where Ciaran was standing and whispered in his ear, "I came back to be with you, do you mind?"

"Of course not," he said with a happy sparkle in his eye. "Go, sit down, I'll be there in a minute."

I felt like a teenager and didn't care. I was not going to waste time in being shy and reserved. I felt the direct approach would be the best and he didn't seem to mind it at all. In fact, I'm sure he rather enjoyed it.

Moments later he came over to the table and sat directly across from me. With all the conversation around us it still seemed as if we two were alone. I would catch him glancing in my direction from time to time, always tilting his head with a puzzled look on his face. But he was obviously happy at my being there. When Tom, who had been sitting in between us got up for a moment, Ciaran jumped quickly into his seat to get closer to me. Now, with only a support pillar between us, I leaned over to him and asked, "Are you happy that I came back?"

"I say so. Where is your friend George?"

I explained briefly my return from France and how I had left George chasing after a pretty Spanish girl, and my new temporary traveling companion sitting at the end of the table was from New Zealand. Nikki was now showing them all the styles of her New Zealand money, which I must admit, embarrassed me a bit. I knew she meant nothing by it but, these were poor people, mostly out of work and living off the system. The thought of flashing foreign cash in front of them didn't sit well with me and I could see they weren't appreciating it either.

"Colleen is staying at my place tonight, Ciaran," Rose announced changing the subject. "Look at her, she's exhausted and needs a nice bath and a good night's rest."

Nikki hit it off with a couple that I hadn't met before and they left together to call on one of the other local night spots. I told her my plans for staying at Rose's place. She wished me luck and gave me a smiling wink with a side glance gesture towards Ciaran.

It was strange sitting there, knowing I was about to break every rule in my book and the belief system I had held on to so strongly. But I could not resist his charms and was not about to back away now. When the pub was closing, Rose and Tom purchased several cans of beer and cider before grabbing me up by both arms for the walk to her flat.

It was a small room, simply decorated, with an extra-small, convenient-sized kitchen area built in. Tom evidently lived upstairs in this apartment building. I felt as if I were going to fall asleep on my feet as the night before had brought little rest and the walking around town had just about knocked me out. There were several people in Rose's small flat: Tom, Larry (who Ciaran worked for), Rose's grown children, Keith and Alice, and one or two others who lived in the building including a fellow named Ed who looked exactly like my ex-husband. I was convinced it was some Irish relation of his.

It was one big happy family as we enjoyed drinking night-caps of beer at half-one in the morning. Rose noticed my drooping eyes and asked me if I wanted to take a shower. I gratefully accepted. She loaned me an oversized bathrobe before walking me up the stairs to the community bathroom.

The water was hot and felt wonderful cascading down my sore neck and back muscles. I stood under the shower head thinking about what was about to take place. "Not tonight," I thought. "Rose's place is just one room with one bed and I will share that with her. I can still escape in the morning, never to see him again." The continuing battle in my mind was quickly being won...but by which side?

I put on the satin night shirt I had tucked away in my backpack and folded myself into the warm flannel robe. After rejoining the party downstairs, Rose turned to me and said, "You look terribly tired dear, would you mind staying upstairs at Tom's tonight."

"Oh no, I wouldn't want to put you out, Tom," I told him trying to figure out this new development.

"It's no problem Colleen, no problem at all. I'll be staying at Ed's tonight," he said. "You and Ciaran can stay at my place. I've already made up the bed for you."

Rose leaned close to Ciaran and said, "And you must let her get some rest Ciaran, look at the poor thing, she's falling asleep on her feet. Go to bed now and we'll visit more in the morning. Go on now Ciaran, take her upstairs so she can get some rest."

Tom, Ciaran and I walked up the stairs to Tom's flat. A carbon copy of Rose's downstairs room, it was neat and clean. Tom had placed clean sheets and blankets over the fouton, evidently while I was in the shower. He turned on the television for us then left. "I'll see you both in the morning," he said with a grin on his face as he closed the door behind him.

This was it. Alone now for the first time all evening, Ciaran and I sat on the edge of the fouton talking. "Do you think me too forward for chasing after you this way," I asked.

"No, not at all. I'm glad you came back," he said. "I didn't expect to ever see you again."

I found myself feeling the need to explain why I came back to him. My rigid belief system couldn't bear the idea of him thinking me easy. "I've never done anything like this before," I told him. "As soon as I got on the ferry to France I knew I had to come back to be with you. I knew I couldn't come back without giving myself fully to you. I can't completely explain it, Ciaran, but you have touched me in a way I haven't been touched in many years. I want you to understand that my marriage has been over for a very long time. I needed the time traveling to France and back to be able to sort things out. Can you understand any of this rambling of mine?"

He sat staring at the television as I laid out my heart to him. He didn't say a word for several minutes and I felt the silence so thick and staggering, it would be cut with a knife through my heart. I was thinking that he would bolt from the room then and there. "Who is this woman?" he must have been thinking to himself. "I'm just here for the craic and here she is laying herself open to me when all I'm looking for is just to get laid."

If this were going to be a one night stand, then so be it. I wanted and needed him. I was not going to keep beating myself up or confessing my thought processes. "For once in your life, follow your heart...relax...just enjoy yourself, Colleen...give in to your desires."

Can't Help Myself

I love you and can't help myself,
no matter what I do.
I try to be cold-hearted,
to shield myself from you.

But immersed in waves of love,
I cannot bring my heart to die.
I'm hopeful for your waiting arms,
for to you with wings I'll fly.

Even though a fool for love,
I'll weather hurt if it arrives.
Why live these days in wondering,
in the end I will survive.

It's true I've never felt this way,
I can't explain it and won't try.
First true love felt far from home,
yet forced to say goodbye.

But I'll follow my passionate feelings,
and pray you feel the same.
That I am your true love found,
and not a lover's game.

Chapter 5
Ciaran

I tried to fight off the past memories filled with how I had been used by men most of my life. Acts of former betrayals whirled in my mind, making me feel, as we sat side by side in silence, the urge to bolt for the door. An overwhelming shroud of panic was draped over me. I tried to quiet the inner voices by telling myself that if he left, well, then that is how is was meant to be and I would just have to accept that.

He turned, stroking my hair with his long fingers, and said, "Your hair is the color of burnished gold...I knew it the minute I saw you." He continued to stroke my hair gently with one hand while the other wrapped itself around my shoulder, tenderly running a path down the curve of my neck to my shoulder. As he looked into my eyes, I felt as if I were falling into a long tunnel and he was the light at the end. He placed his lips on mine and slowly lowered me back onto the bed.

I was exhausted - his body felt comfortingly warm next to mine. He ran his hand gently down the inside edge of my robe, catching the sash to slowly open it, exposing my sheer night shirt. His hand mapped its way back up to my breasts and neck as he ran his long, wet kisses along my throat and shoulders, slowly making his way downward once again. As he started on my buttons, I asked him if he had brought protection with him. He jumped from the fouton with a panicked look on his face while checking his pockets and repeating, "Oh shit, I didn't expect you tonight, where..."

I interrupted his pacing, telling him I picked up condoms earlier in the day: "I knew if I came to you I would give myself to you completely." I pulled the package from my backpack and heard his sigh of relief as he sat back down next to me. "Are you really the biggest gangster in all Cork?"

"No, 'twas just blackhardin' ya. You've nothing to fear in me."

I undid the buttons on my shirt and took his hand in mine, placing it on my breast. He bent his head down to it and methodically caressed my nipple with his tongue. Lowering me back again on the bed, we lay on our sides, his hands now opening both my robe and night shirt to fully reveal my willing body to him. I very slowly unbuttoned his shirt while caressing his chest with soft kisses. I soon felt the warmth of his skin next to mine. He moved me further up onto the bed and lowered his entire weight on me while moving his body up and down against mine, continuing to place kisses along every sensitive curve of my neck, breasts and waist.

He took his weight off of me, angling his body to my side, never stopping his torrid affections. He ran his hand along my breasts to my waist, then down to my knee, only to return by a new route up my inner thigh. His foreplay was exciting, gentle and fulfilling. I found myself pulling ever closer to him, wanting to feel his weight on top of me and in me.

He penetrated me with a great thrust and I felt ecstasy welling up as he gave me an orgasm I never knew possible. I was used to the "wham, bam, thank you ma'am" type of love-making; his style was wild and new and seemed to last forever. And it did last forever. The force of him was now in me and my mind whirled in delight as I ran my hands up his back to his shoulders and back down to his buttocks to pull him even deeper inside.

He slowly pulled himself from me, laying back on the bed with an ecstatic smile on his face, saying, "Five minutes, give me just five minutes." After a short pause he asked, "Did you enjoy yourself?"

"Why is it that a man's main concern is if the woman enjoyed it or not?" I asked back, kidding him. "You ask me if I enjoyed it, then tell me I'll have to wait a full five minutes for more...as long as that?"

With this he pulled me to his chest and again began the rise of passion's flame. We must have come together at least four times that night and he was more than willing and able to continue, but I had to call an end to it. I put my head on his shoulder, snuggling up close to him, and fell instantly and deeply into the best sleep I had in years.

Destiny

How do people unearth so far away,
love's sweet sight known in a day?
When first their eyes gaze on the face,
they decree content desired place.

They smile and laugh as lovers do,
contentment in their sweetheart's woo.
They disregard their hearts' strong fort,
and frolic in the songbird's court.

With eagle's wings they make their flight,
their talons tangled in the night.
They accept as fact their destiny,
as I with you and you with me.

Morning came all too quickly, yet I awoke refreshed and, surprisingly enough, with no conscious sense of trepidation nor remorse. I thought I would wake to wanting to slit my wrists for what I had done and feel riddled with guilt. But instead I felt like a new woman. Ciaran rolled over and gave me a kiss on the cheek. We were about to fall into each other once again only to be disturbed by a knock at the door. It was Tom, wanting to see if we were up yet. I pulled the covers up over me to preserve some sense of modesty.

Ciaran got up, put on his clothes and let Tom in. He shyly smiled at me and turned his head away at the sight of the situation.

Ciaran ambled down to Rose's flat, giving me an opportunity to freshen up and put on some clothes. I joined him, Tom and Rose in her flat where we sat around talking for some time. "I need to go get my suitcase from the storage at the hostel. They won't hold it for much longer," I mentioned.

"I'll get it for you," Ciaran said. "You stay and relax, I'll be back in a few moments. It's just down the road." Without another word, he left to walk down the hill to where the hostile was. He returned a short time later with my baggage in hand, telling us how he enjoyed everyone watching the paddy walking around with the suitcase. He thought the police would stop him for sure to find out what he was doing with it. "I walked right by the guarda station and no one said a word," he boasted. We continued to visit with the myriad of callers that seemed to pour in and out of Rose's flat.

Ciaran called me out to the hallway, "I feel it only right to take Tom out for the use of his flat...I won't be too long." He then called Tom and they disappeared out the front door a few minutes later.

Hours passed while Rose and I visited. Several people continued to converge on her flat to seek out a beer or just to say hello. We talked in between the distractions. At one point she told me how she was married but left him on her wedding day. She said she didn't know why she married Kevin but knew it was a mistake right after the vows were said. With this, I let it slip that I knew my marriage was a mistake too. She asked me about divorce since it was illegal in Ireland and I told her of my first divorce, explaining I had been married twice. "And what about this one," she inquired with a look of concern on her face.

"Well, we haven't finalized anything yet."

Changing the subject she asked, "Is Keating his name then?"

"No, I've always kept my maiden name."

"I'll have to come visit you and Ciaran in America sometime. You can find me a rich cowboy."

"I'd be happy to find you a cowboy, but, what makes you think that Ciaran is coming to America?" I asked.

"Oh, he's planning on it. That's all he talked about the other night after you left. He planned on going to find you and now that you're back... Believe me, he thinks he's going to America to be with you!"

"That would be impossible and he knows that, Rose," I explained. "And as much as I would enjoy your coming for a visit, that would not work out either. My husband and I are still living together and I could not explain you to him for fear he would find out about Ciaran."

"You're still living with him!"

"Yes, but it's been over for a very long time. I have children to be concerned for," I said as I felt the tears coming on. "That's why I remain."

"And now you're feeling guilty."

"I wasn't. I thought I could handle this, but I guess I am...a little."

"You're going to kill him. Ciaran is my friend and you're going to break his heart with this."

"I've been completely open and honest with him about everything," I insisted. "I care for Ciaran a great deal or I wouldn't have come all the way back to be with him. I don't want to do anything to hurt him. If anyone's heart will be broken, rest assured, it will be mine."

"You don't understand, Ciaran hasn't been himself since his son died. He tried to kill himself back then and now you'll be the one breaking his heart. It'll be just the same as it was when David died."

"I don't want to hurt him, Rose. Do you think it

would be better for me to leave now before he comes back...?" We were again interrupted by one of her friends from upstairs.

"Hello, Rose, here's the cabbage for tonight," he told her as he handed her the bundle. "I'll bring down some extra potatoes later. Hello," he directed his attention to me to introduce himself. He was a man of small stature, in his early forties. He had the flat next to Tom's upstairs and was insistent I come up to see his record collection. I declined for the moment, telling him I would try to stop up later in my stay.

We visited for several more minutes until Ciaran and Tom returned from their outing.

"I'm going to cook a lovely dinner for you, Ciaran," Rose said. "You don't eat the way you should. Look at you, you're all skin and bones. Colleen, I'm sure you'll enjoy some beef and cabbage for dinner, now won't you?"

"That would be wonderful," I told her.

"Are you going to Black Rock today, Ciaran?" Tom asked.

"Oh, yes," he responded, taking my hand in his and lifting me from the chair. "Come along Colleen, we'll go for a lovely walk."

I welcomed the opportunity to get out of the flat and away from Rose and all the people coming and going. It felt good to be attached to Ciaran's arm and walking down toward the bus depot. "Where is it we're going?"

He stopped us for a moment, kissed me and said, "Have you seen Black Rock yet?"

"Do you mean the castle I saw from the boat ride I took to Cobh? Is that where we're going?"

"There's also a town near there where I used to have a place. I need to stop by the cemetery to tend to my son's grave, do you mind?"

"Of course I don't mind. But, are you sure you want

me coming along, Ciaran? It must be a very private thing for you."

"Of course...come along we'll have a day together. It's a lovely day out and we'll stop by the castle too."

He told me he tried to get out to the cemetery on Sundays. He also told me he needed to check on his cousin's place nearby as she was out of the country and had asked him to take care of a window that had been reportedly broken. He guided me to the back of the bus where a couple of boys around the age of twelve were sitting. He lit up a cigarette when one of the boys turned to him and said, "Give us a fag."

"Ah, and why would I be wantin' to give you a fag?" Ciaran said with sweet banter.

"Come on now, give us a fag," they insisted. Ciaran gave in to their persistence, after making them work for it, and handed them the cigarette.

"She's pretty, yer missus," the other boy shyly said.

"She is a pretty one to be sure, ya have a good eye," Ciaran responded.

He was a natural around kids and thoroughly enjoyed giving the boys a hard time. He asked them a series of questions, including who they were and about where they lived. I'm sure his white lies telling them that he knew their parents was to have them worry some about his giving them the cigarette. They didn't look too intimidated, however, and bade us a good afternoon, smiling and laughing as they stepped from the bus.

We got off the bus at the Black Rock stop and walked across the street to the cemetery. It was small and immaculately maintained. It's stone and cement headstones were neatly laid out in straight rows with large hedges and trees completely surrounding the area. The scent of freshly mowed grass hung in the air as the people tended to the grave sites of their loved ones. Ciaran took me by the hand and led me down one of the small dirt pathways. "Over here, I t'ink," he said. "There's a new stone...I'm not used to seeing it that way."

We walked over to the newly cut stone engraved with angels and flowers. It was the most beautiful monument I had ever seen. An angel was sculptured into the center of the stone with the usual information engraved above it: "David Short, born February 1, 1981, died June 2, 1985." "Ciaran," I asked, "why is his last name different?"

"His mother and I were not married at the time when he was born," he said. He told me the stone had just been placed, as he searched for something under the leaves. "I'm sure I left it here. It's a brush to clean his stone with, where could it be?" He continued to seek out the brush as I inquired of him, "Ciaran, it was almost ten years ago that he died."

He seemed taken back by what I had just said. He stopped his search to read the words on the stone, "Ten years, it doesn't seem like that long ago... "

"He was only four when you lost him. I'm sorry for your loss Ciaran, it must have been terrible for you. You must have been a child yourself when it happened."

"Sixteen when he was born," he answered. "It was a very hard time. But enough of this. Come along, we'll go check on my cousin's house now. I'll have to get a new brush for next time."

He took me by the hand again as we walked to the edge of the cemetery where he backed me up to one of the tall bushes to hug and kiss me long and hard. "Terrible way to be treating you," he said, "take you to a cemetery and not even kissed you once in all this long way."

"I didn't mind at all, Ciaran. I'm honored you would include me in such a private part of your life. I can see it is still very painful for you. Ciaran, it does not bother you that I am older than you?"

"No difference to me at 'tall," he said. "Why, it's a problem for you?"

"No, no problem."

He took my hand once again and briskly started walking, more like running, up the road to his cousin's place. I could not help but think that he was running away from his pain as it was clear, except for short moments, he didn't want to talk about it. Every once in a while he would stop us long enough to plant a quick or long kiss on me and we would continue on. I stood only five foot three next to his six foot stature and had to repeatedly slow down his long legs in order for me to keep up. He enjoyed making fun of my inability of being able to keep up with him, but kindly slowed down his gait for me.

We stopped by the house where his cousin lived. Sure enough, there was a broken window upstairs where it appeared someone had thrown a rock through it. He asked the next door neighbor who was outside at the time if they had a key so he could get upstairs to repair it, but they said they didn't. He told me it was too bad he couldn't have gotten a key or knew I was coming and needing a place, as we could have stayed there. So, with little we could do about the broken window, we started walking again towards the castle.

The winding road was trimmed with stone walls and a mature growth of ivy laced along its sides. Immense mansions dominated the landscape. Ciaran would tell me how we should live in a house like one of them someday. I told him it would be much too large for me to keep clean, so we would have to hire a maid to go along with it. We enjoyed the day-dream fantasy as we continued our stroll.

We ran into a gentleman who seemed well acquainted with Ciaran and stood visiting with us for several minutes. "Not with the Missus anymore?" He asked with a glance towards me.

"No, haven't been for almost four years now," Ciaran updated him then turned the talk to a different topic. He was good at that, turning a subject around before it got too serious or prodding.

   We continued along our way on the high road
overlooking the River Lee to Black Rock Castle. The castle
was small compared to many other castles; it had been
remodeled to serve as a tourist attraction and local high-class
social spot.   As we entered the main gate, I immediately
noticed the rich wool carpeting and fine oak trim.   The high
quality restaurant complete with oak bar and brass fittings
held a breath-taking view of the River from the windows.
Ciaran told me how they held many wedding receptions there
and perhaps we would be lucky and stumble on one inside so
we could mingle with the guests and have a free pint or two.
We, in our jeans and looking as he put it, "scruffy", hardly
like anyone's wedding guests were not likely to pull such a
caper off. Yet no one said a word as we made our way into
the restaurant, but it was as cold as January due to the stare of
the patrons and waiters. Ciaran acted as if he were the master
of the castle and took me by the hand, walking me around the
dinning room looking out the windows with a "lovely" and
"we should hold our reception here" thrown in for the sake of
showing up these stuck-up upper clansmen. We then walked
up the stone spiral stairway to the exclusive bar upstairs. It
was devoid of human presence. We looked at the view from
this high point enjoying our fun at being poor white trash.
After stealing a kiss, Ciaran turned to ask me if it was
Bailey's Irish Cream that I liked, gesturing towards the
deserted bar, showing how he could easily tuck a bottle under
his jacket for me.

   "You may be the biggest gangster in all Cork, but not
when you're with me, my love. Thanks for the offer, but I
don't want to be spending the night in the local jail." He
looked almost disappointed at this. He reluctantly agreed to
leave things as they were and we left the castle like a couple
of American tourists out for a Sunday walk.

   We laughed and got to know each other as we

descended back down the winding road towards the park that ran parallel to the River. The park was trim and had a long paved walkway extending the length of it. We stopped for short rests along the way, sitting on the stone wall that held back the waters of the river. At one stopping point Ciaran lowered me back onto the grass and gently caressed my neck with his lips in his own special way, teasing me while trying to slip his hand under my sweater out in this public area. I kiddingly slapped his hand and told him to behave himself.

On the more serious side, when the timing seemed right, I asked him about the son he had lost. He at first said he didn't want to talk about it. I explained that I was not trying to pry, but was trying to understand him by understanding his life. What Rose told me about him trying to kill himself back then was very much on my mind, but I was not going to bring that up to him.

"A victim of the troubles," he started. "He slipped out from our hands and then the bombing, it was all very fast. Paralyzed from the neck down, he was. Not quite two and a half at the time." I didn't say a word, just sat there feeling the pain this dear man had experienced. "I visited him all the time at the hospital. The nurses would never let him out of his bed." He began to change his sad tone to one of self satisfaction when he added, "But I'd outsmart them by sneaking him out every now and then. I'd put him in a wheelchair and take him for rides in the park. We'd spin 'round about and he'd want to see just how fast we could go." I watched him smile at this memory as he pointed to the children's hospital just above us in the distance. "'T'was just up the hill there...where he was," he said as I watched his smile again disappear at the sight of the hospital and the memories it left him.

"The priest said 'twas better that he died and I felt like hitting him, God forgive me. But, perhaps he was right, would not have been much a life for him like that. But enough of this now, we'll have to walk around the barricade...there's no other way."

I didn't bring up the subject again. He asked me some questions about myself, saying he wanted to get to know more about me. We were similar in that neither of us wanted to spend our time talking about sad or bad times. We kept our conversation as light and simple as possible.

As he again started kissing me, I commented that he needed a shave. "Yes, I must be getting a bit scruffy to be kissing your lovely face."

"It's just that it reminds me of bad memories from my childhood...the feel of your scratchy new beard. You see, there was a man who hurt me when I was young and he was always feeling like that," I told him as I ran the back of my hand along his face. I didn't volunteer any additional information and he didn't ask. He seemed to instantly understand what I was referring to and I appreciated his kindness not asking any questions. He held a special ability not to probe into areas that he instinctually knew were beyond our set boundaries of conversation. He simply took me by the hand and changing the subject, said, "How far do you think we've walked today?"

I was starting to feel the effects of the miles in my legs. We were approaching Rose's now, it was dark and just starting to rain. "A hundred, at least," I told him.

"More like seven," he said slapping me gently on my behind.

Even before we entered the flat, we could smell the aroma of fresh cooked corned beef and cabbage. The long walk had given us both quite an appetite and the traditional Irish meal would fill our empty stomachs.

Rose ushered us in and served us heaping portions of beef, cabbage, and mashed potatoes, which she called poppies. As I thanked her and commented on how good the meal was, Rose said, "I always feel you should cut the meat before you boil it, it's easier and more tender that way," The mounds of mashed potatoes reminded me of the movie, <u>Close Encounters of the Third Kind</u>, in the scene when Richard Dryfass was obsessed with sculpturing his haunting nightmare of Devils' Tower in Wyoming before his tryst with alients.

I told Rose I had to make my mound much lighter and started scrapping off most of the potatoes back into the pot. "She eats like a bird, Ciaran, look at that, like a bird." Then, turning her attention back to me, "You'll stay here tonight, Colleen. I insist."

****

Now settled onto our stools at McNamaras, Rose asked when I would be leaving. I explained that I would have to leave on Thursday in order to catch my flight from Frankfort on Saturday. It was now Sunday evening and I felt time slipping away from me. McNamaras was full and we stayed for only a short time before heading down the road to the Horse's Head Pub, leaving Tom and Ed behind. Rose had been joined by Pat, a stout and boisterous Irishman who seemed well under her feminine spell.

While at the Horse's Head, I saw Rose scoping out another man at the other end of the bar. She was singing and laughing, obviously doing this for the purpose of catching this other man's attention. "He's the husband, Kevin," she told me when she noticed my inquisitive looks. I overheard her asking Ciaran to go talk to him but I couldn't make out what about. By fawning over Pat, she was trying to make Kevin jealous. I thought perhaps there was more to their marriage story than I was led to believe. Perhaps it wasn't she who left him at the wedding reception, but he who had left her. When I asked Ciaran what was going on he explained that Kevin owed her some money and she was merely trying to get it from him the only way she knew how.

While I did not understand all that was transpiring, it was not long before Pat was out of the picture and we were joined by Kevin. Rose had been getting quite drunk and I caught from the gist of her flirtations with him that she was indeed after money. Whether it was an owed type of thing or not, I could not tell and felt it none of my business anyway. At one point she asked me to join her in the ladies room. In her drunken stuper she started cutting into me about my being no good for Ciaran. "He believes you're taking him back to America," she scolded, "but you're just going to break his spirit and go back to your husband and rich life." She successfully changed my mood from elation to depression. Ciaran asked me numerous times, after I returned to the bar, what was bothering me but I couldn't tell him.

"Who is this woman", I thought to myself, "to judge me so harshly." I convinced myself it was that she and Ciaran were such good friends and she was only looking out for his well being, as well as being drunk loosened her tongue.

After returning to the men, Rose soon informed us we could not stay at her place as she was hooking up with her husband for the night. She quickly added to both Ciaran and me how it wouldn't be right for me to intrude on Tom again. Knowing that neither of us had any money for a bed and breakfast, she told us that we would need to find another place for the night.

"Had a place for us the other night when you were here, but not now," Ciaran informed me. "Problems with the landlord, nothing more. Don't pay any attention to Rose when she's like this, we'll stay at Tom's again tonight." I told him that I hated to put Tom out again and perhaps it would be best if I just went back to the hostel as it would be easier for him to find a place to crash without me. "I'll have none of that. Don't worry...don't listen to Rose...she's like that when she's drinking...she doesn't mean anything by it. Tom won't mind at all."

With the exception of Rose and Kevin, who had gone off on their own, the rest of us found ourselves meeting back at the apartment building at the same time. Ciaran had pulled Tom to the side and arranged for us to stay the night. Tom didn't seem to mind the prospect at all - he made me feel welcome and comfortable.

We returned to the flat, where I stood staring out the window. Feelings of making the biggest mistake of my life were burning in my mind thanks to Rose's lecture. Ciaran asked me to come to bed but I could not and would not join him in an evening of love making while I was feeling more confused than ever. I told him that I needed some time to think and insisted he go to sleep. In a few short minutes, he curled himself under the blankets and was peacefully in dreamland. I stood there for what seemed like hours watching him sleep. He was like an innocent child, and even in his sleep, beckoned me to him. I stripped off my clothes and snuggled underneath the blankets with him. He stirred and drew me close to him and our love making reached a crescendo once more.

"Don't worry about Rose," he reassured me, "she's like that when she's been drinking. It means nothing."

"You know you can't come to America with me...as much as I'd like you to."

"I know that."

"I can tell Rose cares a great deal about you, Ciaran. She's concerned I'm going to hurt you and I'm growing concerned as well. I wish things were different for me, that you could come visit me in Montana. But, I told you that even though my marriage is nothing more than a piece of paper...I can't have my children think bad of me for being with you."

"Why, I'd walk right up to your husband and shake his hand like an old friend," he joked.

"Oh, a grand moment for me that would be!" I kidded him back.

When morning came he wanted me to join him downstairs at Rose's. I refused, explaining I couldn't go to Rose's flat after the way she treated me. He went ahead downstairs and several minutes later Rose came into the room to talk to me. She did not back down from her feelings of my being no good for Ciaran, but did seem apologetic for treating me the way she had. Having come to an agreement that we wouldn't bring up the subject of my relationship with Ciaran again, I followed her downstairs. Ciaran was standing in the kitchen and tugged me to him when I entered. He kissed my cheek and told me how he needed to be running some errands and that I should wait at Rose's flat until his return.

After he left, more of the locals descended into Rose's flat, including Keith and Alice, her children by a previous marriage. She was easily able to end that marriage in divorce as she was in England at the time where divorce was legal. All her children were adults and living on their own with the exception of one daughter who remained with the father in England. Kevin was still there, along with a few other new faces. I was amazed at how many people this tiny room would hold.

Thoughts continued to whirl around my mind and I grew increasingly uncomfortable. Several hours had passed and I, in all my great insecurity, decided I did not want to put Tom out of his place another night and that Ciaran would probably appreciate my not being there when he returned, especially after my emotional outburst the night before. I was imagining, by his long absence, that he wouldn't be back anyway. I also didn't want to be responsible for leading Ciaran into a relationship that could never work out and, in the process, would hurt him. It would be better for me to leave giving him an easy way out. After making a few phone calls to some of the local bed and breakfasts, I found one just down the hill that was only sixteen pounds for the night. More than my near empty pockets could handle but, it was Monday now and I could get to the bank to get some cash from my credit card. Only a few more nights left and I would be sleeping on the ferry and train on my way to Frankfort. I wouldn't need much cash then. I would have to budget myself carefully or else spend the next year paying for this trip.

I asked Keith for his help getting my suitcase down the disintegrating front steps. I asked Rose to tell Ciaran that I would be staying at the King's Inn. "If he wants to see me then tell him he'll need to fetch me there," I told her, thinking that I'll not be chasing after him this time. He'll need to come for me. "You will tell him where I'll be, Rose?"

"Of course Colleen, I'll tell him," she promised.

As I walked down the hill with suitcase in tow, I couldn't help wonder if she would tell him at all. She seemed bent on destroying our relationship. It would be easy for her to let me just disappear from his sight. I made it clear I would not be at McNamaras unless he called for me and she, or he, might take the opportunity to never see me again. "So be it," I said to myself. "It may be better for both of us if he doesn't come, anyway." But deep in my heart, I knew I wanted to see and be with him again.

I checked into my room at one in the afternoon. The bartender said he would turn on the hot water for me so I could wash up. While it was heating, I made a run to the bank and reaffirmed my ferry ride for Thursday. When I returned the water still wasn't warm, so I laid back on the bed to watch the news on the television and fell asleep.

Around four-thirty the phone rang. It was the woman who owned the establishment telling me there was a man to see me by the name of Patrick. I could barely hold back my elation and laughter at his calling himself Patrick. I asked if she would send him up, but she said she wouldn't do that. I asked her to tell him to have a seat and I would be down in a few minutes. The bed and breakfasts in Ireland have a strict rule about allowing men up into the rooms of single women. In the States he would have been directed to the room number and left to his own devises in finding it. But, here that was not allowed. I entered the bar and saw him standing near the end of it looking sweetly out of place. This was a more upper crust styled pub than the ones he frequented and, since it was right next door to the guarda station. I knew it made him very uncomfortable.

Wanting to thwart off any preconceptions by the owner, I walked up to Ciaran, or should I say, "Patrick", and asked solicitously, "And how is your dear mother?"

He caught on immediately and retorted, "Oh, it's her heart you know, she seems much better, but has far to go."

The woman ate up our conversation as we ordered a couple of glasses of apple juice from her, then retreated to a table at the other end of the bar. We sat talking for some time when he asked me to go somewhere else. I told him I still hadn't been able to take my shower yet and was feeling pretty scruffy, then asked if he would wait for me. He was uncomfortable with the idea of waiting in the bar, "I thought you said you were kidding about being a gangster?" I said.

"Still, doesn't mean I like being around the gardai!"

I walked over to the owner and said, "If you wouldn't mind, the water wasn't hot yet for my shower when my friend got here. Would you be so kind as to let my friend up for a while to wait for me while I get ready." She nodded her head somewhat reluctantly, but seemed to accept the idea well enough.

We retreated to my room on the third floor and immediately fell into the single bed. After we completed our love making, he again asked if I enjoyed myself. I told him, "No, actually I faked the whole thing...what do you think? And you...did you enjoy it?"

"Of course." He said smiling and offering to make it even more enjoyable while starting his dear advances once again.

I pulled away excusing myself to enter the shower, that by this time I had expected to be warm, ready and waiting for me. But, I couldn't get anything warmer than ice cubes out of it. I could wait no longer so went ahead, one foot in the tub and one foot out, drenching myself in the frigid waters.

I returned to the room to find a more-than-willing Ciaran waiting to help warm me up from my Titanic-like experience. He laughed and blackharded me about it. I told him he should try it himself if he thought it would be so grand; he took me up on the offer!

He returned to the room about twenty minutes later looking refreshed and...warm! "I think you must not have adjusted the controls properly," he laughed. "I had a lovely shower, quite hot and lovely."

"Well, I'm glad you enjoyed yourself," I said as I teasingly slapped his arm. "You'll need to show me how to adjust it so I don't freeze my ass off next time."

He laughed more and told me, "Must keep that police woman's ass of yours nice and warm."

"Do you think you're capable of that task?"

With this he grabbed me and pulled me tight to his chest on top of the bed and told me again, "I knew it the minute I saw you."

We spent the evening at McNamaras where we ran into Rose and Tom. They teased us both, exclaiming many times during the evening, "tear into her" or "tear into him." They seemed to enjoy that we both were happy. I was glad that Rose didn't appear to hold any further animosity towards me. Still, I decided it best to stay clear of her since she was drinking. I did not want a repeat of our last time out together.

One of the older gentlemen patrons at the pub came up to Ciaran and me every now and then and said, "A lovely colleen, she's lovely, Ciaran." To which Ciaran would glance over at me and reply, "I say so."

"I say so" was a catch phrase in that when one said it, the whole pub joined in a chorus of, "I say so, I say so." On and on they would go like one big happy family playing a game of telephone down and around the bar. I had never felt happier or more gentle of spirit than I did right now. He had come for me when I had feared he wouldn't and now, here we were, passionate lovers. He leaned over and whispered to me every now and then either "I knew it the minute I saw you," or "I love you."

While at the pub I told him how I still had a coupon for a free rental car and had earlier reserved one for next morning. He was quite pleased with this and solicited some ideas from Michael on where we should go. When I mentioned that I was anxious to drive on the left side of the road, I thought both Michael and Ciaran were going to have cardiacs. "Fuck, no, I'll do the driving," Ciaran asserted.

Michael backed him up with genuine concern and said, "Better to let Ciaran drive as he drives the lorries and we're always hearing of Americans getting themselves killed from driving on the wrong side of the road."

The pub was closing, so we retreated to sneak Ciaran up to my room. It was after one-thirty now and the pub downstairs should be closed. I held the key for the large wooden outer door of the pub with the second dangling beneath it for the room.

I quietly turned the key and we both stepped inside. Not wanting to raise an alert, I held onto the latch handle, easing it off slowly so as not to make any noise as I closed the large main door.

When we got to my room, Ciaran said, "I do believe you are the true gangster between us two...sneaking us up so quietly."

After several rounds of passion, Ciaran and I quietly

made plans for the next day. He enjoyed the idea of getting away together for the day, but when I reminded him that I had my international driver's license with me, said, "No, I'll be doing the driving." I teased him at length about wanting to drive and he said that he might 'let' me on one of the straightaways... if I behaved myself.

The night passed quickly by, finding us wrapped in each other's arms. We rose early in order to slide back out of the building without anyone seeing him. We then headed out to the airport to pick up the car.

I felt myself falling endlessly and hopelessly in love with him. "Well, Colleen," I mused, "you really did it to yourself now." I talked myself into enjoying the moment and to quit beating myself up mentally about how I would never see him again and how I was committing the act of adultery. We were honest with each other on this point and he understood that our ecstasy would last no longer than Thursday morning when I left on the bus for Rosslare Harbor. Today was Tuesday and I was wrapped up in our intrigue.

I mentioned that I would need to find a place to park the car that night and sleep in it, as I had only enough for one more night at the bed and breakfast.

We picked up the car with no specific destination in mind. I left all the driving and the decisions on where to go up to him. We drove through the farm roads which were winding and tall with hedgerows on either side of the road. Along the way, we saw gypsy wagons and farmer's carts. He told me how, when he was younger, he used to race horses. When I asked him why he quit, he told me he grew into a much-too-tall Irishman. This was the true Ireland. Serene, away from city traffic and noise, I teased him about pulling the car off into one of the fields where we could re-consummate our love.

As we drove to Waterford, skies turned from gray to blue. After stopping in a pub his relatives used to own, we started back towards Cork. He even gave in to my need to drive a short way. I found I was not able to get the car into fifth gear since the shift was on the left side. He helped me and enjoyed teasing me about my clumsiness. When he saw my frustration getting to me, he explained he understood how difficult it must be for everything on the car to be backwards for me and took over driving. It was raining now and I teased him once more saying, "Don't you Irish ever have a place where you pull off the road and make passionate love in the back seat? I'd love to make love to you where I didn't have to hold back my cries of ecstasy." A few minutes later he pulled off onto the back roads, stopped the car and kissed me. After brushing his new growth of a beard across my cheek and noticing the scratchy feeling, he said, "Too scruffy, I'll have to take care of that. Have you any soap?"

I went to the back of the car to my suitcase and pulled out some soap. I watched in awe as he pulled a razor from his pocket and shaved himself with rainwater. "I'll not have you thinking of anything but me by being scruffy," he said. He stole my breath away at that moment. Here was this man, who rather than reminding me of any memories from my childhood, after having only given him a small hint of what that was, shaved for me with rainwater!

He sat on the front passenger seat and I straddled his lap. He unbuttoned my blouse and worked his tender, wet kisses over my breasts, as he undid my front-hook bra. Then he moved his hands under my buttocks and stroked my inner thighs with both hands. We helped each other pull down each other's slacks. I lowered myself onto him, slowly impaling myself onto his full erection. We blended our motion with the now pouring rain. The rocking back and forth, up and down motion sent us both into multiple orgasms and I bit my lower lip holding myself back. He picked up on my lip biting right away and said, "You can scream out here all you want...make all the noise you want. No one will hear you out here. I love you."

The passion inside me overflowed. My heart felt as if it was going to explode. How long had it been since anyone had treated me with such consideration and affection?...it didn't matter. Here I was wrapped tightly in his embrace, looking deeply into his eyes, eyes that held nothing but love for me. I was feeling in love, truly in love, for the first time in my life.

****

"Have you ever seen our rabbits here in Ireland?" He asked as we continued on the winding back country roads heading back to Cork.

"No, I haven't. Why, are they the extent of your wildlife?" I joked.

"There look, in the field, see the rabbits..." When I looked into the distant fields I saw finely groomed thoroughbred horses running free in the fields. "You see, they're as big as horses." He said completely enjoying blackharding me. "Ah, but you should see the size of our deer some time."

I happened to see two of the sweetest bunnies standing just off the side of the road. They were huddled together and looked like something from a Currier and Ives lithograph. "And those there," I said trying to maintain a serious tone, "must be the Irish mice." He was completely taken back with my analogy and laughed heartedly...so heartedly that he almost caused us to wreck. "Perhaps would be best if I drove," I kidded.

"Fuck...just keep your eyes on the mice...I'll watch the roads." He told me.

Irish Mice

We sped along the back roads
viewing countryside and sea.
You pointed out the Irish rabbits,
looked like thoroughbreds to me.

Then drove around the next curve,
beheld the gypsy wagons there.
Viewed fields where farmers toiled.
We were happy and had no care.

Then sharp to the left and to the right,
furry sentries peeked out at us two.
My eyes grew wide in wonderment.
I smiled and spoke these words to you.

"If the horses are truly Irish rabbits,
then no doubt these beasts I see,
sweet gentle creatures of your land,
not bunnies...but Irish mice must be."

We stopped in Fermoy for a quick Guinness and then, safely back in Cork, stopped by McNamaras. We were greeted by Michael (and the rest of the gang) who asked how our day went. I told them Ciaran had let me drive a short way and had survived the experience with great bravery. Michael was still very concerned about Ciaran's letting me drive, so Ciaran jested with him about my driving and his near having a heart attack from the experience.

Ciaran especially enjoyed telling them about how impressed I was at the size of the Irish rabbits which I caught on was a common joke among them in calling their horses rabbits. He went on to tell them that I stated that the Irish mice were the size of American rabbits. The patrons, including Michael, thoroughly enjoyed my comparison and I knew at that moment that I would always have friends to return to here.

Since Ciaran had several pints at the pub, I drove us to the park bordering the river where we had walked from Black Rock the day before. He sounded a bit nervous about the possibility of my driving right over the rock walls, that had no barriers, into the river. I added to his tension by lightly turning the wheels from left to right as we proceeded down the grass. Safely parked and completely alone we quickly fell into another round of auto-rocking, this time in the back seat. There's nothing in the world like trying to make love in the back seat of a compact car, but we accomplished the act very nicely, with only minor cramps. We lay in each other's arms and started to drift off.

Only a few minutes had passed by when we saw headlights approaching, pointed in our direction. Another vehicle of lovers and not gardai, we hoped. Lovers it seemed, as they pulled off near to us. While I could see nothing in the darkness, Ciaran, who had the eyes of a cat, told me what was taking place. Evidently there was a lovers' quarrel going on or...an unwilling girlfriend. The two had gotten out of their car, arguing with each other; then there was silence, then back in the car. They sped off down the grass to the exit. "Must have had a headache," I said.

"Just one of the five fs," he said. "You know about the five fs?"

"No."

"Find her, feel her, fillet her, fuck her, and forget her," he told me. "It's especially easy with married women." I knew he meant it as a joke, but I couldn't help feeling crushed at what he said. Could it be that he was trying to tell me that it would soon be over and that would be no problem for him? In one way, I was glad of it but still my heart pounded at the thought this was about over. Earlier that day I had felt confident in our affections...now once again the insecurities flowed back over me like a dark veil.

After spending a very uncomfortable evening scrunched up in the back seat, we packed up our goods and went on our way. Ciaran mentioned he would need to work that day and we parted, he to his work and me to the bed and breakfast, after dropping off the car at the airport. He told me he would be by to 'fetch' me at nine that evening.

Nine o'clock came and went with no sign of him. I had decided to wait in the bar downstairs rather than have him call up for me. I ordered a bottle of Buhlmer's cider, borrowed the local newspaper and sat at one of the tables waiting. At ten, I was growing very anxious, yet made up my mind that I would not seek him out. "He must have come to his senses," I told myself, "and chose not to see me tonight."

The other owner of the bar, a well-dressed and groomed man in his fifties (obviously the husband of the lady I had talked into allowing Ciaran to my room just two days before) came over to me and asked, "Is everything alright?"

He seemed sincere in his concern for me and I told him I was fine and had been waiting for a friend, "A cousin really." I don't know what had made me say that I was waiting for a cousin...perhaps it was just my way of making this nice man not feel sorry for me at being stood up.

"Oh, so you have relatives here in Cork," he happily asked me.

"Some...very distant ones," I told him. I was enjoying the story telling at this point which came easier than the truth that I was being jilted. I added that my cousin's mother was ill and he must have gotten hung up with her, adding to the validity of the story Ciaran and I had earlier told his wife. He was very kind and was glad that nothing was wrong.

At ten-thirty, I told myself that I should at least go to McNamaras and say goodbye to Michael and the gang before the pub closed. If Ciaran were there I would simply by-pass him, stay a few minutes and return to my bed...alone.

During my walk to McNamaras, I continued to tell myself it would be better if we didn't see each other again, anyway. After all, I was headed back to the States the next morning and where could this relationship possibly go? I would never see him again. I convinced myself I was nothing more than a good lay (all of the 5fs) to him and he must have found someone else to keep him warm this night. I passed the train station and with McNamaras less than a block away, I noticed the figure of a man walking towards me. It was late and I was somewhat frightened; I had heard that just the day before, an American tourist had been knifed down by the docks. My eyes focused and the man's gait appeared to be like Ciaran's in the dark shadows and I could feel my heart skip a beat wishing it were indeed him and not some mugger. To my delight, it was him.

"Where are you going?" he asked.

"Well, a handsome tour guide named Patrick was to meet me over an hour ago but stood me up, so I thought I'd go for a walk."

"I'm sorry I was late, I only now got back into town. I stopped at McNamaras hoping you'd be there and when you weren't, started straight away to you," he told me as he backed me up against the stone wall. "Remember Fermoy, where we drove through yesterday?"

"Yes."

"Wound up working there all day and couldn't get away any sooner."

I kissed him slowly and gently and told him that I loved him. "Are you sure you were headed to see me and not off to Rose or Toms?"

"To see you, of course. Look at my clothes," he convincingly replied, pointing to his dirty pants. "Do you want to go to McNamaras or somewhere else? You like McNamaras?"

"Must be McNamaras," I told him. "I need to say goodbye to Michael and the others." I continued to tease him that he wasn't headed to see me at all when we ran into each other and he continued to try to convince me that he was. But I acted stubborn and jilted to his constant cries of innocence.

It was near closing time when we walked into McNamaras and ordered our ciders. Michael was busying himself clearing cans and glasses from tables. "Here now, I'll prove it to you," Ciaran said. "Come over here a minute Michael." Michael quickly came over to where we were sitting. "Tell Colleen where it was I was going when I left here a few minutes ago."

"Oh he was off to get you," Michael insisted. "He stopped in for a moment, didn't even get himself a Guinness, when he asked where you were. When he learned you weren't here, said he needed to go get his American lady."

Ciaran was very self-satisfied to have been pardoned. With a slight tone of fun-spirited-cockiness told me, "See, told you I was off to get you." As closing time approached, Ciaran asked if I would mind us walking Ed home. He explained that he was concerned about Ed because he had some drunken words with some fellows in the pub and Ciaran worried they may try to harm him if he walked home alone. Ed was small in stature and inoffensive most of the time. But, when the pints ran freely, which was the usual case for him, he sometimes forgot his nature and tangled with the wrong sort.

We stopped at the street in front of Ed's flat where he drunkenly slurred, "I'll be cryin' in the morning when you're gone Colleen, cryin'. And Ciaran will be cryin' too."

Ciaran took him once again by the scruff of the collar in order to keep him from falling flat on his face. I waited on the sidewalk as they ascended the concrete stairs leading up to Ed's flat. I do believe that thanks to Ciaran's strong arm, Ed was kept from an inevitable fall. "He'd most like to kill himself falling down cracking open his head, even if the other fellows didn't do it for him." Ciaran said.

Back in my room and finally deliciously alone, we made love as if there were no tomorrow...after all, there wouldn't be. I wrapped my arms around his neck as we stood just inside the door of the room where I told him that I loved him. We stepped backwards towards the bed. He stripped the buttons from my shirt slowly and with a rhythm that could only be described as "andante'". I took off his jacket and shirt, dropping them to the floor behind him and started gently kissing his chest, working my way down to his belt. Unstraping it, I continued to kiss him exposing his already firm penis. He jerked me up to him, "I knew it the minute I saw you," he whispered. He removed my bra and drew my arms behind me then quickly plummeted with me to the bed. Undoing the zipper to my jeans he slipped his hand down inside and slowly positioned his hand to fondle my innermost region. Easily finding one of my erogenous zones, he stroked it...back and forth...up and down...spiraling me into a fantasy state of climactic ecstasy. We tumbled and rolled on the bed, flinging our remaining clothes to the floor. He gently spread my thighs, positioning me perfectly to receive him. We were lost in a passion I never would have believed existed. I found myself crying inside knowing it would soon be over and I would never see him again.

I lay there for some time with my head on his chest, as he spoke Gaelic phrases, telling me what each one meant in English. He had a sense of serious longing in his eyes and I began to stroke his neck and locks of hair with my fingers. "I wish I didn't have to go, Ciaran," I whispered. "If you can ever get away, Layla, my friend, has a place in Pennsylvania. I know she'll understand and let us use it should you ever come to the States."

He drew me fully on top of him and told me he loved me. "How do you like it best?" I shyly inquired.

"Anyway with you is lovely," he answered. "And you, what do you like best?"

"It doesn't matter to me, Ciaran. I love you and every way you touch me. I just want to please you." By the look on his face I could tell he had never had anyone who said they wanted nothing more than to fill his needs. I was sure he felt the same hurt and betrayal that I understood so well from my own personal past. He knew my words went beyond wanting to fulfill not only his sexual fantasies, but his spiritual ones as well.

Intense desire grew in him as he pulled me even tighter to the soft hair of his chest. I straddled him and felt the fullness of him inside me again where he seemed to so naturally belong. In the heat of passion, my face safely hidden in the curve of his neck, I whispered in his ear, "tell me that you love me, even if it's not true."

After a short pause, he held my face in his hands, stared straight into my eyes, and said, "I do love you, Colleen."

We passed the night making love repeatedly. I had lost all sense of shyness with him. We eventually fell asleep feeling an overwhelming sense of both contentment and exhaustion.

In the morning, Ciaran told me to take a nice long shower and enjoy my breakfast, as he had to run up to Ed's to make sure he got up for work. He said he'd meet me at the bus depot where I would catch my bus to Rosslare Harbor. He left before anyone at the bed and breakfast would be aware he had spent the night. I am sure he did this to preserve my modesty and spare us the embarrassment of being caught in my room.

Forever trapped within my lack of security, I found myself at the bus depot thinking he would never come. "Find her, feel her, fillet her, fuck her and forget her," he had said. His words were ringing in my ears even as I tried to shut them out.

He showed up ten minutes sooner than he had said he would. I saw he looked anxious and had a somewhat frightened aspect to his eyes as he first entered the station. When he saw me and sat down, he completely relaxed. We both passed light conversation with nothing of any real importance being said until my bus pulled up to the depot. I told him that I would write, care of McNamaras as he had asked, and send off the photographs we had taken as soon as they were developed.

He walked me outside, and while I stood in line waiting to board, kissed me and said, "I love you, goodbye." Without my having a chance to say a word, he turned and walked down the street. I wanted to run after him but knew his was probably the best way. I watched until he disappeared into the crowds and out of my sight.

The bus took me directly to Irish Ferries' docks where I boarded for the long trek back to France. Once again, I was not in a socializing mood. I spent most of the trip sitting in the lobby, politely avoiding the conversational advances of several other
passengers.

I decided to sleep in the ship's lobby that night and placed my sleeping bag near to the stairway. I passed the night miserably. I was exhausted from lack of sleep and the toll of passion from the night before. I was unable to catch even a nap in the lobby. We finally docked at Cherborg, France. I made my way to the train station and readied myself for the long trip to Paris, then on to the Frankfort airport.

I couldn't stop thinking about Ciaran. Now that I was well away from Rose's imposed guilt, I didn't experience even an inkling of remorse at what Ciaran and I had for those five nights. It would have to remain my lifelong secret. If I risked sharing my experience with anyone, it may easily slip out and I couldn't take the chance my children might hear of it, I wouldn't have them think their mother a whore...and I wasn't one!   I hadn't planned on falling in love, it just happened and now it was over.

Adieu

*In the light of day
or the dark of night,
how can I sense remorse
when you feel so right.*

*My heart runs like a river
up the stone walk to your door.
Knowing it's improbable
yet wanting you all the more.*

*The stars they hold no challenge
to the sparkle in your eyes,
for they see this tug of heartstrings,
say adieu and not goodbye.*

Chapter 6
Back in the USA

Kent and the kids met me at the airport. Angel ran over to give me a big hug, wrapping her arms around my waist. She wasted no time asking what presents lay hidden in my baggage. Jimmy was equally excited to have me back after my long absence. He reveled in telling me immediately how he had picked up the mail, cut the grass, and cleaned the house prior to my return. Kent stood off to the side saying his usual nothing.

At first, I thought I would break down into deluging confessions of my sin. However, when I saw Kent in his consistent state of apathy, I felt absolutely no sense of remorse. I found I could look him straight in the eye and not feel any urge to cleanse myself by breaking down in tears because I had betrayed our marriage vows. After all, I figured he had been doing so himself.

Kent and Angel were leaving the next morning for the national volleyball championships in Lake Tahoe. This was Kent's one area of interest where he found total elation. His annual excursion to Lake Tahoe was his idea of a vacation and our daughter didn't need to badger him to let her go with him this trip. While he failed miserably as a husband, he tried to be a good father. Angel found it easy to get her dad to give into her even if she missed a week of school for it. It would give them some time alone together and, with Jimmy usually off with his friends or working at the nearby convenience store, I would have no problem getting some needed space to myself. There were still many tangled thoughts I needed to sort out.

It was after midnight when we pulled up to the house. I unpacked my bags and handed out gifts I had purchased during my travels, then collapsed on my bed. The warm waving water of the bed felt good against my aching muscles. It was Memorial Day weekend - I had a day or two to recuperate before having to return to work.

The house was quiet when I woke up, Kent and Angel had already left, and Jimmy was off to work until later that night.

I decided to call George to see if he had gotten back alright. It was good to hear his voice, "Hey, kiddo. How did things work out for you? Are you all right?"

I told him I had a wonderful time and was feeling happier than I had ever before. He told me that he had become very ill on his way to Spain. He had lost sight of his newest love interest in Barcelona when he stepped off the train, she was lost in the crowds. He didn't seem to mind though; he was gearing up to meet his Oregonian lady friend in just another month. He told me how he had a terrible time connecting with any Army flights back to the States. He wound up spending a couple of days in Idaho where he finally telephoned his father to come pick him up.

"I gave Ciaran and Tom your address so they can write me," I told him. "I hope you don't mind, but I didn't want to take any chances that Kent or Jimmy might pick up the mail. Besides, I doubt I'll be hearing from them anyway."

"I'm sure you will. No problem kiddo, glad to help out," he said.

We set a time to get together after our journey's pictures were developed.

I dropped off the eight rolls of film at K-Mart and told myself that I would mail Ciaran the copies and that would be the end of it.

On Tuesday, my first day back at work, I found my overall attitude had improved. I felt rested and fulfilled. I knew in my heart I wanted to get back to Ireland as soon as possible but didn't know how I would come up with the money or time off to achieve that feat. And, really, what sense would there be to my hasty return if I wouldn't see Ciaran again?

My coworkers commented on how well and content I looked. I heard a lot of, "You look great," and "You're glowing you look so happy."

When I picked up the pictures a week later, I immediately placed my set in an album and sent many off to Ciaran. It was early June. I wrote a letter to send along with the pictures and told Ciaran that I thought about him the entire way back...how I wanted so much to be with him again. I wrote, "I don't understand why you left so quickly from the bus station the day I left. All I can think...even if it's wrong...is that perhaps I was just one of the 'five fs' you told me about. All I ask is for your honesty as I will not hold you to this impossible situation." As I typed out the words, I knew I could waste no flowery speech on him and that life was too short not to tell him how I felt. If I were playing the fool, so be it. I could only hope he would write the letter that I so yearned for.

I had sent some photos off to Layla the same day. She called me when she got the pictures a few days later. We talked at length about my trip, VE Day, Scotland, Wales, and of course, Ireland. I found it difficult to tell her anything but the basics I experienced. As much as I loved her, I thought it best not to reveal the whole story. Better to keep that secret to myself. Not that I couldn't trust her, but I didn't know how to even begin telling her of my total joy.

I should have known better, after so many years of friendship, I hardly had to bring it up. It was as if she read my mind. She knew how miserable I was in my marriage, but also knew my beliefs about marital fidelity. How all that had changed; I had changed; I was a new woman feeling sensuous and whole again.

She inquired about the people in the pictures I had sent and we easily fell into a discussion about the good-looking tour guide she immediately took note of.

"Oh, he was very kind. He would drive me anywhere

I wanted to go and was very protective of me," I said. Then I tried to change the subject to some of the other people in the photos but, she consistently brought the conversation back to him. I eventually found myself confessing my sins to her and should not have been surprised at the fact she was not even shocked.

"Good for you, Colleen," she said. "And don't you go beating yourself up over this either. God, don't get some hair up your butt about telling Kent!" I assured her I wouldn't be telling anyone but George who already knew due to the circumstances. When she voiced her concerns over his knowing, I explained he had been very supportive of my decision to return to Ciaran in the first place. I told her George had encouraged me to act and I wasn't concerned about his telling anyone. Content with my reassurance, she asked if I would be seeing Ciaran again and I told her that I wanted that more than anything, but didn't feel confident our being together meant as much to him as it did to me. "He said he loved you, didn't he?" She asked.

"Yes, and I can't explain it Layla, but, I really think I've fallen in love for the first time."

"Oh, he loves you, I'm sure of it!"

"I hope you're right. I can't explain these feelings of mine. I returned to him from France thinking we could simply pass the time satisfying animal desires, but I really do believe I love him. I know it's wrong, and an impossible situation, but all I can do is think about him. Every song on the radio reminds me of him and I can't sleep at night for wanting to be curled up next to him. When I close my eyes, I see his smile and hear him telling me 'knew it the minute he saw me'.

"What did he say?"

"He told me on many occasions that he knew it the minute he laid eyes on me."

"Knew what?"

"I'm not exactly sure. He never did explain it, but, I believe he meant that he had fallen in love with me. I know this all sounds insane, and maybe I have lost my mind. But I believed him."

"Does he know about Kent?"

"Yes, I was very open and honest with him. That's why I don't think I'll ever hear from him again. It bothered him that I was married, yet he seemed to accept that we would have just a short time together and enjoyed it for what it was. And so did I," I reaffirmed.

"Enjoy it for whatever it turns out to be, day by day, Colleen, day by day. And, if you start thinking about telling Kent, you call me first so I can talk you out of it. I know you, Colleen, and I don't want that Victorian-styled mind of yours kicking in and you spilling your heart out."

Now reassuring her I said, "Don't worry Babe, I really do feel okay with all this, besides, Kent and I have been through for years. I'm too busy thinking loving thoughts about Ciaran to think about anything else. Besides, I told him if he ever made it to America, you'd be willing to put us up at your house in Pennsylvania."

"You know I would! And, I'm sure you'll hear from him. Quit worrying so much, Colleen. If it's meant to be, it will happen for you both." She declared just before saying good-bye, "It's about time...you deserve some happiness in your life."

After hanging up the phone my thoughts again turned to Eire. As I reminisced on our times together, I was reminded of Ciaran's love for his dead child. I didn't write poetry often and shared it only on a 'need to know' type basis...mostly with Layla's 'need to know' basis.

I found the words flowing naturally and didn't feel the need to change a single word at it's completion. "Would he ever get to see this?" I wondered to myself.

On Wheels of Thunder Run

Old beyond your youthful years,
man of laughter, man of tears.
You try your sadness on the side,
and with majestic stallions ride.

A son long ago was lost to you,
happy thoughts were turned to blue.
David was the dear lad's name,
you rode his wheels in joyful game.

And clean his stone on Sunday's best.
You give your love and pass the test.
Don't feel you guilt, your heart is loyal,
he's with the Lord, crown jeweled royal.

He loves you still, I have no doubt,
he knows it now and gives a shout.
So don't give up but live your life,
no dismal shadows nor dwell in strife.

I do not know the reason why,
young children suffer or have to die.
But this I know, the Lord is near,
and holds sweet David close and dear.

Past are many years, now live anew,
love, be happy, sup raindrops dew.
Again in Heaven he runs and plays,
'tis no ones fault those dreadful days.

And loved again someday you'll find,
God give you solace and peace of mind.
For on that day, you'll with your son,
again on wheels of thunder run.

The next night I went to a movie. I first heard about the show, <u>Bridges of Madison County</u>, while home ill earlier in the week when the author appeared on the Oprah show. It sounded wonderfully romantic and starred Clint Eastwood and Meryl Streep. The story is about a man and married woman who had an affair. "'Affair', what a vulgar word for two people falling in love," I thought, "and how inaccurate. It makes it sound like some type of casual business arrangement. And there is nothing casual about how I feel for Ciaran."

Now, suddenly, the movie I hadn't heard a word about until just a few days ago, was showing at one of the local theaters.

I sat in awe as every aspect of the movie seemed to speak personally to me. Here was a woman whose husband and two sons had gone off to the State Fair for a week, leaving her home by herself. She welcomed the peace and quiet, soon intruded upon by a very handsome stranger she immediately felt attracted to. Whether it was being fed up with the routine of farm life or being taken for granted after years of marriage, she found herself falling totally in love with the man. The feelings and emotions were welling up inside me as I thought of Ciaran and me. I related our experience to this movie that took adultery to a more acceptable realm in the minds of the viewers. It wasn't the first time an extramarital relationship was digested by audiences. My mind was also drawn to Camelot and Guenevere's love for Lancelot. Neither of them wanted to hurt King Arthur, but were drawn together by a force much stronger than their human wills.

The days went by with quiet, yet painful acceptance, that I would never hear from Ciaran again. I had been checking in daily with George to see if any letter had arrived, but the weeks were dragging by without any word.

To my great joy, just three weeks after I had sent off the pictures and letter, George called me from work to tell me he had a letter for me from Ireland! He hadn't been able to read the return address hand writing and wasn't sure who the letter was from. I began to think it was more likely from Tom. My heart was pounding and even George remarked how I looked like a teenager with her first crush. George handed me the letter, taped shut to the point I could barely open it. But, when I looked at the return, I knew it was from Ciaran. "I'd better read this before I go back to the office," I told him. "I may need your shoulder to cry on, you never know." I opened the envelope just enough to reveal the closing words where Ciaran wrote, "I love you, xxx, Ciaran."

Dear Sweet Presence

Your letters have touched this fragile heart,
sweetly swirl my mind from end to start.
I remember your every dear sweet line,
and tenderly kiss the name you sign.

I envision me resting in your dear arms,
bewitched by all your magic charms.
The hole that once was called my heart,
Is newly filled and maps your chart.

Mind trapped agonies that filled my years,
yet you have wiped away my tears.
You have placed in me delightful elation,
never before known in my creation.

Ere if forsaken from your protective glove,
no matter our outcome, I'll remember with love.
For know this my darling within my essence,
will always abide your dear sweet presence.

I was in heaven! Whirling, twirling revelations of hope and joy filled me instantly with thoughts of seeing him again. I was no longer thirty-nine but sixteen, sweet and virgin and in love for the first time. George was beyond happy for me - he was ecstatic. I told him some of the bits from this one-page letter of love, then returned to work with a smile that could not be erased.

In response to my letter he wrote, "To answer some queries you have raised. No! You are not one of the five fs. I left the bus station in such a hurry because I could not stand to see you go out of my life. But now, on reflection, this may not be forever. As I think of it, do you have any sinks on your cars in 'Montana' as one has to shave daily. I could dearly do with your police woman's ass over here, but no doubt that will take some time. I am blighted by your absence and await your next letter with delight. I love you, xxx, Ciaran."

I could have hoped for no more than that. His writing was simple, to the point and raised the one memory that held my thoughts more than any other...that he shaved in rainwater out of consideration for my feelings. I had placed my trust in him completely.

I wasted no time, writing him back that same day. I told him that I rode on wings of angels to pick up the letter from George, and how delighted I was to hear from him. I went on to tell him that I was walking around work with a foolish grin and was sure everyone would wonder what was up. I mentioned his picture on my wall at work and how I found myself looking at it constantly. I mentioned I had told my coworkers and friends it was the picture of a very kind "paddy" who acted the "tour guide" for me while I was away. How they commented on what a good looking "tour guide" he was. I thanked him for telling me how he felt when we parted at the bus depot and that I too watched him disappear from my sight, wondering if I would ever see him again. I went on to say that we didn't have sinks on the cars in Montana, but would gladly provide one special for him and thanked him again for being so considerate of my feelings.

I found myself writing him about the <u>Bridges of Madison County</u>, giving him an overview of the movie, then stating that the two had only four days together, while we had five. That the woman decided to stay with her husband and children I could understand. What I couldn't understand was how they never saw each other again. I told him how after thirty years she received a letter from his attorney after his death including the photographs he had taken of her so many years before. I explained how amazed I was at the similarities of her feelings to mine but, the one thing I could not imagine was how they could not go on being together as best they could and how I needed to go on being with him as best we could..if he wanted.

I went on to say that I was working hard at both my full-time and part-time jobs to put enough money together in order to get my "police woman's ass" back to him as quickly as possible and I might even bring the 'cuffs' with me; I hoped it would be as soon as October. I explained that Layla said he would be welcome at her Pennsylvania home anytime he wanted and we could meet there someday if he chose.

"Ciaran, I hope you don't mind my taking the liberty to write a tribute to your love for your son, but I am so moved by your affection for him that I was inspired and am enclosing it for you." I enclosed the <u>Wheels of Thunder</u> poem and sent it all off to him the next morning. I hoped I hadn't overdone my letter. But I reminded myself all we had for now were our letters, and I would hold nothing back from him. Better a fool for love's sake, than protect the increasingly stone-cold heart I had developed before.

Weeks went by with no word. "I must have frightened him off," I told Layla during our weekly bull session. "I was too forward with my last letter and now I've scared him away."

"No, you haven't," she assured me. "You know how most men are, they hate to write, I'm sure he loved your poem and letter. Relax and give it some time. I'm sure you'll hear from him again."

"Do you think I should write him again?" I asked although I already knew that I would.

"Yes. He probably just needs a bit of a poke to get him going."

The next day I picked up an aeromail envelope from the post office and hand wrote a brief letter to him. Having received a letter from Tom a few weeks earlier, I referenced this and wrote, "Tom said you were all turning into brown Irishmen from the heat wave you've been having. It has been a bit warm here as well but not as humid as Ireland, so not as miserable I'm sure. My friend, Layla in New York, said it has been over one-hundred-two degrees there and terribly humid, causing many deaths and problems in the area." I went on, "It has been some time since I heard from you and grow concerned you are either angry with me for being so long-winded in my last letter, or perhaps I have frightened you off with all my talk of bringing the 'cuffs' with me. My boss has approved my time off and I hope you want me to come...you'll need to let me know as I need to make reservations soon before he changes his mind. All my love...I await your reply with great anticipation!"

Hardly two weeks had passed when I received his response. "Colleen, loose your angel wings...as for your grin, keep it on your beautiful face. Your tour guide misses you very much. My waking thoughts are with you always; however, as with the Bridges of Madison County, I am a lazy letter writer. But have no worry, if I'm not in every way with you, it's my fault. I look forward to seeing you in October with longing. Say thanks to the 'boss' for me. You can 'cuff' me anytime you wish. You haven't frightened me off...to the contrary...Colleen, your poem words have changed... and loved again someday I've found solace and peace of mind...'cor tu solas I mo speir'...Gaelic, meaning, you put the light in my sky."

Cor Tu Solas I Mo Speir

Caress my neck with your dear sigh...
Until morning comes I'll draw you nigh.
And stroke you gently with my hair,
I'll give my warmth with great a care.

Your fervor burns within my heart,
the heat of you sets each new start.
Set your sword to my waiting vault,
my crimson tide feels sweet assault.

I will hold you deep inside of me,
and give you my best of ecstasy.
With passions flame I'll set afire,
your deepest fancy and great desire.

You whisper to me your inmost thought,
how in your heart 'twas me you sought.
Cor tu solace I mo speir,
you place in me a childish fare.

It was August - I was walking two feet above the ground.

Kent approached me one evening and asked if I wanted to go to a show with him. It had been years since he asked me to go to a show. I replied, "Thanks but no thanks." When I told Layla of this during our next talk she said, "Oh, sure, you don't want to go to a movie with your husband for fear of cheating on your boyfriend." We laughed till we cried over her banter. She knew well that things between Kent and I hadn't improved at all.

"I know I've heard that sometimes a relationship

outside of a marriage will better your marriage connection, but that's not so in my case," I told her. "Kent continues to make me feel powerless where the kids are concerned. He tells me things after the fact and was even telling Jimmy how he could go ahead and get a place of his own if he wanted. God, Layla, he's only sixteen and way too young to venture out on his own. How would he support himself and finish school?"

"What the hell is wrong with him," she said. "A little common sense would sure go a long way. Doesn't he realize he's losing you because of the way he's been treating you all these years?"

"Lost, Layla, already lost. He wouldn't understand if I tried to explain it to him, how mentally abused I feel." I said in addition to telling her I didn't want to get into a Kent bashing session. Down deep I tried to convince myself he was a good man doing the best he could. But I found myself completely, if ever I was in the first place, out of love with him. He had belittled me too many times for us to return to any semblance of a friendship. I knew I was settling in an easy relationship when we married and was partly to blame for my heart growing cold towards him. He was, however, constantly negative about me and it had worn my spirit down and out.

The next day I wrote Ciaran back with a passion I hadn't felt I could ever express in a letter.

"As you have already guessed, I am a 'hopeful' romantic. I can see you are a lazy letter writer, but not in comparison to Bridges...as he took over thirty years to write his love again and this she did not receive until after he was dead (lot of good that did)! So there is hope for you yet...though I hope you will not take too long to write me again as your letters touch my heart and the grin on this face of mine cannot be wiped away as I think about you and reflect on them. Remember the coupon for the free rental car," I wrote, "George was not permitted to use the other two since they were in my name. While I felt terrible about this at the time, he has returned them to me and I hope we will put them to good use when I arrive. If you would have the tour guide, Patrick, I think his name was, meet me at Shannon Airport, perhaps we could pick up a car and visit the Aran Islands and the Cliffs of Moher." I assured him, "Don't worry, my love, I'll not do the driving and we'll stop and have a Guinness or two along the way...and there will be no spending my first night with you in a car...we'll find a lovely bed and breakfast and sleep (do you think?)" I asked him to write back to me at my home address since George was planning to pick up his children in California and if a job presented itself, might not return for quite some time.

"I couldn't resist sending you this poem also, my love. I only wish it held some sweet Gaelic phrase to give you in return for yours, but, you are my teacher in this regard and I'll have to rely on you for my education. Eight more weeks!!!" Taking my inspiration from his letter to me, I wrote flowingly, inspired by a love I had waited for all my life.

Pronounce Our Love

Among the willows make love to me,
on castle clouds and emerald sea.
From noon to night and dusk to dawn,
encircling wildlflowers and new spring fawn.

In your strong arms you hold me tight,
and love me gently with all your might.
I will lay me back and breath you in,
immersed in pure delirium.

And in the morning rise we may,
for there's no tomorrow nor today.
We can frolic in sunshine's heat,
pronounce our love, quiet and sweet.

I heard nothing for the next month but felt content in my knowledge that he did indeed love me and his absent letter was merely a laziness on his part, not a lack of caring. I wrote him again telling him I would be arriving on October ninth at ten-thirty in the morning and asked if he would like me to bring anything for him from America. I wrote, "Time has been dragging by terribly, but I am content in knowing that I will soon be looking into your eyes and wrapped in your arms. I know how I've frightened you with all my talk of the 'cuffs' so I am enclosing them in this letter and hope you don't find them too intimidating." The cuffs I enclosed were a small keychain variety that I picked up in one of the local novelty shops. I didn't tell him I would be bringing a full size pair with me. I closed my brief letter giving him all my love and telling him I would be eagerly waiting for reply.

All the stresses in my life, and there were always multiple stresses, didn't seem stressful at all as I lowered myself into warm bubble baths. I placed a photo of Ciaran and me, where I could gaze on it from the tub, illuminated by the flickering light of the scented candle sitting near by. The music on my cassette player was a rhapsody of love songs that reminded me of Ireland...and him. I sipped on a glass of Irish Cream and lost myself in my memories. When I closed my eyes, I could almost feel his embrace and large, gentle hands caressing my body and his lips on mine. Here I could find peace in my tub and close out the world...well, almost. Even this escape into near-Utopia was constantly interrupted by Angel needing me to help her find socks, a phone call from Jimmy wanting to stay out just one more hour," Dispatch needing me to come in to work, or the squeal of my pager urging me to respond to an emergency scene. After a series of interruptions, I finally told everyone that when I was in the bath, they would have to wait until I was through to ask me any questions or take any phone calls. This was my 'time out' and I needed to be left alone. The kids were naturally cooperative once it was explained to them and really seemed to enjoy protecting me in my sanctuary from the outside world. As Kent was almost never home, he posed no problem. When he did happen to show up, I would give him and everyone else in the house an opportunity to use the bathroom before I took over. This occasional hour of refuge helped me make it through the long days until I would be with Ciaran again. Angel was especially understanding as she mimicked her mother in taking long bubble baths from time to time.

October ninth was rapidly approaching. I hadn't received any word from Ciaran. I told myself that if he didn't meet me at the airport I would either go to Cork or figure something had gone wrong or he had changed his mind, and plan on going to Wales. I was going to travel blindly, trying to keep my heart intact, not knowing exactly what I would do upon my arrival.

I couldn't help but feel apprehensive after so much time going by and not hearing anything from him. He had told me, the night we slept in the car, that he could have been a murderer and could have killed me at any moment; how I could be equally dangerous...how we had opened ourselves to danger without thinking about it. I had told him I saw it in his eyes and his heart that there was nothing he could ever do to hurt me. But I was unclear if he saw me this same way. Perhaps he did change his mind. It had been two months since his last letter and I had made up my mind not to write him again.

Five days before my flight, I received a post card from him stating he would not be able to meet me at the airport due to an appointment with his attorney on a pending court case but looked forward to seeing me on Wednesday night at McNamaras.

"Wednesday night!" I exclaimed to Layla. "I arrive

on Monday. And what's all this about a pending court case. Maybe he really is a gangster. What could he need with an attorney?" I had feared the worst and Layla tried to calm me as best she could.

"Colleen, what an imagination you have...you think too much. Quit worrying. Everything will work out," she said. "What else did he write?"

"That he wanted nothing from the USA but my lovely self," I told her. "I don't even know if he has a place for us to stay and I've heard nothing more from Tom, who had promised me a place." The anxiety attack I had never before experienced was now finally in control. "I can always stay at Tripp's in Wales, I suppose."

"Well, there you have it then. Take it as it goes and if worse comes to worse you can stay with Tripp." She added, "Colleen, I've never heard you this way before and you're starting to worry me; so quit it! You're a strong woman and can handle anything that comes along."

She was right, my internal insecurities always seemed to get the best of me and I was a worrier. I knew she was aware that my strong exterior was merely a facade to cover-up the abused, gentler heart within.

I resolved to be spontaneous on my arrival, while still hoping Ciaran would find a way to meet me at the airport. My instincts told me this was unlikely, yet I reminded myself that he did write that he loved me -- I would take him at his word. After all, what other choice did I have? I had placed all my hope and trust in this wonderful man so far from my reach. The mystery of him mixed with my insecurities and this great distance between us. Perhaps it was that I felt I was doomed never to be this happy in my life. Yet, he made me happy and I needed him. I could only hope that I made him equally happy and that he needed and wanted me.

Kent never questioned my lone vacations. He was indifferent on this subject -- only a dry-drunk silence emanated from behind his newspaper. His complacency might have derived from the fact that several years earlier we had agreed to put aside our income tax refund of one-thousand dollars towards the rental of a travel home. We planned to take the kids that summer to Washington State for a couple of weeks. When the time drew near, I asked him about what he was able to find out about renting the mobile home. He had waited until then to inform me he had spent the money, 'on bills': Kent tried to make me feel guilty because he believed it was my fault he carried more of the financial burdens of our household than I. He never gave me credit for paying for child care, groceries, water, phone, and cable television. He didn't want to accept the fact that more money came out of my paychecks to cover our taxes because of his self-employment and the fact he refused to pay quarterlies. He forgot, or didn't want to acknowledge, that the first five years we were together, I covered the majority of our expenses. We used to have annual arguments, always near tax-time, mostly due to financial differences. I finally gave up trying to point out my personal participation in paying our bills to him. There was just no talking to him. It was one of the areas in which he tried to make me feel inferior. Perhaps he didn't question me now, because he spent most of the time ignoring me. When I tried to speak with him, he would hold the newspaper between us, even after I asked him to put it down. I didn't want to believe that he meant to intentionally wear down my self-esteem but, when he belittled my responsibilities, activities in emergency services, or as a mother, my confidence hit an all time low. I had always beaten myself up enough mentally without his adding to my torments. At times, he could be supportive and I was always openly grateful for it. At other times, he could be a real shit, and I grew to detest him for it.

When Angel was five years old, I started my own business. I had no problem allowing Kent to take over more of our personal bills in order to get my business off the ground; therefore, I never offered to pay more than the necessary. I continued to cover additional taxes, Christmas presents, household items such as furniture, and some needed home improvements.

Our problems went well beyond finances. He had once told me, in front of the kids, he thought I was an alcoholic. This because once a week or so, I indulged in a glass of wine or Irish cream. I felt the children start to show a lack of respect for me and I'm sure his absurd observations didn't help. He had been an absent father most of our marriage; I found myself always having to discipline the kids when they misbehaved... which he would disagree with and put me down for it.

He stopped showing any sign of affection for me years ago. A woman gets tired of playing the aggressive role in love-making. Our problems were numerous. He would blame me and I him. I knew, and I believe he did too, that it was over long ago.

I knew he didn't appreciate my capabilities as a wife -- or as much else. He told me what a 'demanding' bitch I was, even though I never asked much of him. When he'd stay out up to four nights a week until after four in the morning, I never questioned him or started an argument over it. He stayed out all hours and did not call to tell me if he was safe or when he would be home. He was never considerate about my feelings. More than once, I explained to him how I had been sexually abused as a child and how his unshaved face brought brutal memories back to me, but he didn't care. He consistently approached me sexually with his scratchy face. After so many years together, I started reflecting some of his characteristics like not communicating or showing affection.

For a long time now, I had no longer wanted to talk to him, be touched by him, or show consideration of <u>his</u> feelings. I felt he was unfaithful to me in many ways, including adulterating our marriage with his move to the living room sofa over four years ago, leaving me feeling repulsive and inadequate.

Because of him, I had come to believe "love" was just another four letter word for fuck. It was because of Kent's mentally brutish behavior and the other abuse I had experienced over my lifetime that I was so insecure where Ciaran was concerned. I wanted to believe true love really existed...and hoped it did with Ciaran. I prayed this romance would not prove to be a game of sexual gratification or worse, power. Sex seemed to be the only thing that made some men at least temporarily happy and I thought perhaps that's why some women also use it as a weapon of power as well.

Yes, it would be good to get away again. Ciaran made me feel beautiful both physically and spiritually and gave me the strength and permission to think well of myself again. He filled me with a joy I never knew possible with any man. I wouldn't allow myself to lose this new-found sensation of loving and being loved.

I boarded the plane with the great anticipation of soon being in his fond embrace. Yet, I could not shake the mixed feelings of self-doubt that I was making the second biggest mistake of a lifetime by returning to Ireland. I could have left well enough alone and not written him that second letter urging him to write me. I might never have heard from him again which may have proved the best for both of us in the long run. But I couldn't help myself as the heartfelt compulsion to be with him was stronger than my mind set against it. If it was wrong the first time, then perhaps I was making it even more wrong by returning to him. God forgive me -- my love for him makes me refuse to feel ashamed.

I don't remember any other time when I felt so inspired to write poetry. But my memory of him made the simple flow of words set to paper sound musical and rhythmic. During the long flight I pulled out some of the poems and read them again.

I could set my heart to rest whenever I reminisced about the things he said to me. I tried to convince myself I couldn't have been so blind to have played the fool, nor could he be such a good con as to reel me on a phoney line.

At the time I wrote, 'Replete New Start', I was still waiting for a reply to my second letter. I hadn't received his letter yet, but, I woke with a vision clear in my heart that he was indeed setting pen to paper.

Replete New Start

Oh blessed love, my soul refreshed,
your letter read in heart is meshed.
I've waited so long for small a word,
dreamt brought to me on wings of bird.

It appeared like sad eternity,
with no pale utterance sent for me.
Yet in my dream with charge well said,
you sent your thoughts to me instead.

I heard your voice so sweet and clear,
spiritual sight took away my fear.
That I could never be forgot by you,
as Cupid's arrow struck sure and true.

A peace crept over this foolish heart,
I felt content and replete new start.
All trepidation and doubt is gone,
My love eternal, I breathe new dawn.

The day after I wrote 'Replete New Start' I received his letter telling me that I was the 'light in his sky' and how he had been 'blighted' by my absence. My premonition had been a vision after all, a wonderful anxiety releasing blessing from my feelings of self-doubt that I had held up to that point having not heard from him. Now I could write with even more confidence after reading his romantic yearnings.

Tranquil Theft

Your love proclaimed, sweet delight.
Your words declared my dearth a blight.
So you were sad when there I left,
your heart I stole, oh tranquil theft.

Think I could walk out of your life,
and continue mine with no due strife?
For dear you are to me my love,
I'll back to you on wings of dove.

Though dismal days where now I stand,
beautiful thoughts on your sweet land.
Until afresh again your arms I fold,
my world's thoughts will have no hold.

When Autumn comes I again will see,
your splendid smile look down on me.
And all my worries, toils and snares,
will flee me all these worldly cares.

I deplaned knowing I would not see him at the airport, yet found myself looking for him all the same. It was still uncertain to me what had been going on with him and I wasn't sure what I should do. "Perhaps the legal concern was hanging him up," I told myself. I went to the travel agent located within the airport who told me she didn't think the ferries were running to Wales that day. That helped me make up my mind to bus straight to Cork instead of visiting Tripp right away...which was what I really wanted to do anyway.

I purchased two three day bus passes to assure me that I would be able to return to Shannon to meet my return flight even if I wound up broke by the end of my trip.

I left my things at the King's Inn not knowing if I would be needing a place to stay. The bartender, Aiden, told me he would keep them in the kitchen until I was able to finalize my plans. He recognized me from my first trip and was especially accommodating. He was a handsome man in his mid to late thirties with light brown hair and pleasant, friendly manners. Muscular in build, I couldn't help watch his biceps bulge as he carried the luggage to the back.

Since I was traveling on a very tight budget (having returned so soon). I prayed Ciaran had managed to arrange some lodging for us. "Surely he must have a place by now," I told myself.

I walked up the hill past one of the many cathedral-styled churches to Rose's apartment building. Her's was the first floor flat at the front of the building with a large picture window near the outside stairs. When I approached the building, I noticed the curtains missing from her window and, when peered inside, saw that remodeling was taking place. The flat was completely empty from any furniture or signs of life. I rang several of the doorbells hoping to find Tom, Ed, or Rose, but no one answered.

I decided to continue to McNamaras, hoping to run into someone I knew. They had all seemed to drop off the face of the earth. "Maybe my entire experience here was a trip through the Twilight Zone," I teased myself. "How could so much change in so short a time?"

It was just after three in the afternoon when I walked into McNamaras. I was fondly greeted by Michael and Donel, who were at the bar in the same positions I had left them in so long before. "At least some things haven't changed," I thought with a sigh of relief.

Michael said, "Oh, you only just missed him, Colleen. He was here not five minutes ago.   He's off with Ed somewhere. Payday you know." Before the words were out of his mouth, he gave me a great, welcoming, gentlemanly hug. I was glad to hear that at least Ciaran was not off in some jail or out of town until Wednesday. However, I grew even more puzzled why he didn't meet me at the airport.

"I'm sure he's just down at Jackies," Michael said. "Go on now, he'll be glad to see you. If he's not there...come back...he'll be here sooner or later."

I followed his advice and walked down to Jackie's Pub, hoping against hope that I could locate him. Ciaran was the first one I saw as I opened the door. His back was to me and he hadn't heard me come in. Ed was sitting with him at the bar and immediately started to say hello. I gestured to him with finger against closed lips to remain silent, thus allowing me to hold an element of surprise.

I quietly walked over to Ed and shook his hand then turned my attention to Ciaran saying, "Hello." He didn't say a word, just sat there staring at me. I immediately felt that perhaps I shouldn't have come. Overcoming these thoughts, I took his hand, shook it, and told him hello again. Ed quickly retreated into the men's room leaving Ciaran and me alone at the bar. "Aren't you glad I came?"

"Of course," he replied. "I didn't expect you until Wednesday."

"I wrote you that I would be here on the ninth Ciaran, a Monday...today." He still wasn't offering me a kiss, hug or any conversation and I was feeling increasingly uncomfortable not understanding what his strange behavior meant.

"Ciaran, I'll be plain with you. I'm very short on funds having come back so soon. Is there a place for us to stay or would you rather I make other arrangements?"

"We'll work it out, don't you worry yourself about that," he told me.

"Tom promised me a place in his letter but I haven't heard anything from him since. My suitcase is down at the King's Inn and I promised I would let them know if I needed a room or not."

He told me the place he was living was not a good place to take me since all bachelors were living there and that he would come up with something more appropriate. "I received your post card. It wasn't a very good idea to write so openly where everyone at the post office could read it," I told him.

"Didn't say anything that should have caused you any trouble," He said.

"Not really. But you did say not to bring you anything but my lovely self. Perhaps they'll just think it to be some sweet Irish phrase. But, it could have proved a problem...it's a small town."

"Sorry, I mustn't been t'inkin' when I wrote it." He concluded.

We walked to the King's Inn and enjoyed a drink. Aiden looked somewhat dejected when I told him I wouldn't be needing a room after all. We then walked up to McNamaras where Michael let me put my luggage in his store room. Ciaran seemed to be warming up to me some, but I still felt a great distance between us. As I watched him trying to secure a place for us from several different friends, I knew why he had been so silent...he was ashamed of not having a flat for me to stay in.

When Larry came into McNamaras, Ciaran took flight from me to go speak with him. When they returned from their conversation, Larry greeted me like a wonderful old friend. Ciaran had arranged with him for us to stay in his trailer, which was parked with the lorries in a deserted area of town. Larry ordered us a cab as he said he never took one of his cars with him when he was out drinking, due to the stringent DUI laws. There was no power to the trailer nor running water, but I didn't mind as long as Ciaran and I would have this time to ourselves. Immediately after getting Larry's help in securing the door from it's broken latch, Ciaran grabbed me and pulling me close said, "I missed you." This was the Ciaran I had waited all day to see and feel! He started running his hands up and down my back, then down inside the back of my elastic banded stirrup pants. The passion I felt was intense and I found myself wanting to lie down right there in the middle of the floor when the door opened. It was Larry who had forgotten to tell us something. With a look of obvious embarrassment on his face, he quickly said he would be back in the morning for us, then retreated to the waiting taxi.

A bit shyer after the sudden visitor, Ciaran and I retreated into the bedroom where I readied myself to be with him. I pulled out the box of condoms from my suitcase and the lavender satin robe I had purchased during my last trip. It was not long before I found myself placing the condom on his familiar bulge. We made love all night long and it felt as if we had never parted. We talked little except to tell each other how much we had missed each other with an occasional 'I love you' spoken passionately in the midst of our desires.

He was apologetic about our surroundings and said he would find a better place for us the next day. He hoped to get us a cottage he knew of down near the river. I told him I didn't care if we slept out in the cold October rain as I was content to be with him anywhere.

"You didn't seem very happy to see me earlier," I said.

"What are you talking about? Of course, I'm happy to see you."

"Then why didn't you kiss or hug me when you first saw me this afternoon?"

"It's a public place and wouldn't be right. But, don't

t'ink I'm not glad to have you back with me." He reassured me. "Besides, you surprised me, didn't t'ink you'd be here until Wednesday."

"Funny, you didn't seem to have any problem when I was last here, molesting me in the pub." I returned in jest.

"Well, t'was different. 'Twas McNamaras, not Jackies. Everyone knew we were together," he replied as he pinned down my arms to the side. "I love you, I missed you, now be quiet woman and behave yourself."

We fell into the most delightful rumble and tumble, naked on the bed. He quenched my hunger for him with his long wet kisses as he ran his hands up and down the length and width of my body. First he would position me under him, familiarly and tenderly opening my thighs to welcome him home. Just as my climax was about to reach an all time peak, he would toss me, like a rag doll, on top of him. I pulled him deep inside me. He was poised and acted like a man who hadn't made love since last I saw him and I relished that thought. His seduction well established, he turned me over yet again to culminate the splendor with a great, climactic drive of ecstasy.

Larry arrived early in the morning to take us to his mother's home. He needed Ciaran to work with him that day and left me at his parent's house. I enjoyed a bath, talked with Mr. and Mrs. O'Hara, took a nap and waited for my love to return. Ciaran said they should be back by four, but Mrs. O'Hara told me Larry had mentioned they would not be back until late. She made corned beef, cabbage and poppies for dinner.

When seven o'clock rolled around, Ciaran and Larry came in. They walked into the kitchen and sat down. Larry's mother served them heaping helpings of the Irish mix. When she returned to the living room where I was sitting, she prodded me to go in and talk with them but I declined, telling her that I would leave them to their meal. After what I felt an appropriate time span, I joined them at the table. Ciaran looked apprehensive and I could not help but think something was wrong. I could tell he had no place for us to stay and when Larry left the room for a moment Ciaran said, "We can stay at the trailer again tonight."

He told me not to worry about it and that he hoped to have a better place for us. It had turned cold and with no water, lights or heat, neither of us were enthusiastic about the proposition of staying in the trailer. I had moved from my chair to stand behind him rubbing the back of his neck. "Don't worry about it Ciaran. It's not important where we stay...as long as we're together." He whirled me around placing me into his lap. Captured in his strong arms, he kissed me passionately and said, "I love you...right?"

"Right, I know that. But I never get tired of hearing it." I said.

Larry seemed to have a habit of walking in on us at the worst of times. As he entered the kitchen, I started to bolt out of Ciaran's lap, but Ciaran seemed pleased to show off our affections by pulling me back down, and kissing me long and hard. Larry didn't seem to mind and said, "Ah, you two will be married in no time. Bless yer Irish hearts."

We soon made our way to McNamaras. After some discussion with Rose's estranged husband, Kevin, Ciaran announced that we'd be staying there, but not to let on to Rose as she was upset about the idea. Evidently she had a brother who she wanted to stay at Kevin's place but Kevin had declined. She would be upset that he would let us stay there instead.

Kevin had recently rented a building a few doors away from McNamaras. Rose's daughter, Christine, was staying in one of the four bedrooms. She was a pleasant girl of about nineteen and had agreed not to let it slip her mother we were staying there. She soon retreated out the front door to party with her friends at the local 'Colosseum', a hot spot for the young people to bowl, play video games, dance and have a good time. This was Rose's other daughter I hadn't met on my earlier trip as she was then living with her father in England. She recently returned to stay at Kevin's since he had the room and Rose didn't. She and Kevin got along well; I instantly liked her.

Kevin's house was in need of repairs. The wallpaper was stained and peeling off in several areas. The carpets smelled of mildew and the only shower was broken. Kevin had been living there for only three months. He had moved in hoping that Rose would return to him, but this idea didn't even cross Rose's mind. She merely wanted his financial support. Kevin worked for the city as a maintenance man and I couldn't understand why she thought he was well off. He planned to fix up the house in hopes of purchasing it at a reasonable price and so, took responsibility for making the many repairs. He was sick for several weeks with a stomach ailment and had an appointment for the next week to have some tests run at the local hospital. His sickness didn't allow him to start working on the house and Ciaran offered to fix at least the broken toilet, which he did right away.

Kevin showed us to the room we'd be staying in. The blinds were black with filth, but the double sized bed was newly made with clean sheets. He and Ciaran pulled in a wardrobe from another room, then Kevin retreated downstairs, leaving us to ourselves.

"Ciaran, there are so many things we need to talk about," I said as he looked at me inquisitively. "I decided to go on birth control pills before I came back here but I must tell you that due to my work as a medical technician, I'm considered in the high risk group for contracting AIDS. I have been checked and I am clean but it is something you should be aware of. In truth, I don't know what your sleeping arrangements have been while I was away and I'm equally concerned about that. I do love you Ciaran, and will do without the condoms if you'd like, but we must be clear on the dangers."

He explained he used protection with other women and was glad that we wouldn't have to use the condoms. He told me, "Rubbers are for sluts, not for the one you love!" With this we fell back on the bed bathing in affection and basking in each other's touch. Disrobed and well on our way to a new round of ecstasy, I said, "I want to feel you in me, Ciaran. I want to feel your warmth and be one with you with no barriers between us." He rolled me onto my stomach gently caressing my breasts which now lay imbedded in the mattress. Coming from behind, he placed himself inside me. He slid me along the mattress slowly at first, then increasing in speed, rubbed me from both behind with his body and against the mattress to the front creating a double orgasm I wouldn't have thought possible. I had never experienced anything like this before and never believed it possible to enjoy this position, declining his offer of it when I was here last. But now I felt him fully in me and I knew we were joined forever. He reached his hand down to my most secret place and gently stroked my formerly forbidden sector as he continued his onslaught of propulsion deep inside me. He had not just my body but, my heart, completely and totally. I felt beautiful for the first time in my life and would never let him go.

He gently dismounted and lay next to me stroking my long hair and telling me he loved me. I believed it entirely now. He, although in poor circumstance, had secured us a place to stay, was joyous at my being there and gave me the affection I had been so starved of.

"Why do you love me?" I asked.

"I can't explain it," he answered at first giving me a look that it was a bit of a silly question, "I just do. Why do you love me?"

"It's not fair you should give me such a short answer

then expect me to tell you my innermost feelings," I teased. He looked at me with his blue-gray eyes playfully acting as if I wounded him and beckoning for my answer. I made him wait several moments for my earnest reply, "I love you because you are kind and treat me with affection and consideration. I love you because I have looked deep within you and find a man who is well beyond his years in wisdom from a pain-filled life. And, I love you because of the way you love me and make me feel." With this he rolled me to my side and placed his hand along the curve of my neck. He kissed me sweetly and repeated how much he loved me. "Ciaran, there is something else I must tell you..."

"What is it?" He inquired with genuine concern.

"When I was with you last, in the heat of my passion, I said for you to tell me that you loved me even if it were a lie. I knew it was a mistake at the time and didn't really mean it and I still don't understand why I even said it. But, it has been the hardest memory for me to deal with these four months. So, I will say to you now, my love, tell me that you love me only if you truly do. These are words of great meaning and should not be spoken light heartedly...I never believed in falling in love so quickly was possible. I've settled for things all my life and I want you to know that I have never loved, truly loved...anyone but you."

"I'd marry you tomorrow if things were different, I'd marry you tomorrow, Colleen," he told me as he caressed my neck and hair to start our love making once again. As he ran his hand down the curves of my breasts, waists and inner thigh he whispered, "I love you because you are beautiful, you have a gentleness and kindness in you that I love."

Making love to him came easy. The way he brought all my senses alive sent me into a euphoric state. Dizzy and filled with him, I was soaking in every moment as a sponge soaks up the water. I was immersed in his love and already knew that I never wanted to leave him again. His bringing up marriage had startled me, however, and I asked, "Then what? As much as I love you we would grow apart because you would think me a bitch after a time. I wouldn't want you in the pubs every night but with me; your love for me would fade. But the primary reason I can't be with you, Ciaran, is my children. I wouldn't have them think me a whore, which is exactly what their father would have them think if I were to leave him now. In truth, I would stay with you forever if it were not for my kids. My marriage has been over for years as I told you. I know you can understand this as you have children of your own."

We passed the evening enveloped in each other's essence, neither wanting to let go of the other. I felt his power, he my gentle side; we were held in a magical spell, bound together even if only for this brief time.

The next few days passed by quickly, too quickly. I felt our time together slipping out of my hands. I had made a commitment to visit with Tripp in Wales by Monday, forcing me to leave Sunday in order to make the late ferry docked at one in the morning. I felt this would give Ciaran an opportunity to get a few days work. He had been spending all his day time with me going for long walks around Cork.

How unfair our circumstance. I was older than he but he, had no problem with that and while I was uncomfortable with this aspect early on, it dissipated in the light of his maturity. He was knowledgeable beyond his years from all his life experiences. Then there was our long-distance relationship. We lived thousands of miles away from each other and could snatch only brief periods of time together. He told me he could live with this, as it was our only choice, I concurred. I was Protestant and he a Catholic. I had believed this would be a big problem based on the "Troubles" in Ireland but he had no problem with it. I had attended more Catholic functions than Protestant over the years and was more than content with the difference. I however, couldn't help but think that it could create a problem for him somewhere down the line. Then of course there was the difference in life-style. He was dirt poor and while I was far from financial independence, I didn't want to imagine going backwards in time to a single room apartment, struggling to make ends meet and going hungry much of the time as I had when I first moved to Montana. Yet, I knew that to be with him I would more than willing to start over again.

It didn't seem to make sense to me he wasn't working, since I knew about all the hard jobs he had held and told me about. I figured it was a lack of work availability, not laziness. He voluntarily explained to me his legal concerns that he had written of in his last postcard. He had been injured in a car accident a few years prior, hurting his lower back and unable to perform work-related responsibilities on any regular basis. He was concerned even working what little he did for Larry that, if he were spotted by a fraud investigator, he would have placed himself in a compromising position. This was why he needed to see an attorney. I was relieved when he told me. I kidded him when he told me about the pending claim saying, "Just call me to the witness stand and I'll say how you were unable to perform any manly duties, leaving me to do all the work. I'll tell them that I always have to be on top because of your bad back."

Finally, what stood between us more than age, distance, religion, and lifestyle was my marriage and our children. He had confessed to me he never actually married Jane, the woman he lived with for over nine years. They shared three children together: David, dead at age four, and the two remaining: a girl now eleven and a son four. He separated from Jane near the birth of their newest son and he said he didn't love her anymore. He confessed openly she was the only other love he ever knew. I was struck by his honesty in telling me these things. He had been so much more elusive when we first had met. Lying to me about his real name, telling me he was a gangster, and that he was married when he was not.

I explained to him that due to the age of my children it would be some time before my daughter would be old enough to deal with the fact that her father and I must part ways. This was the reason why I still lived under the same roof with him. Angel was her father's child and most certainly daddy's little girl. However, this was the time in her life, at age twelve, where she would be needing me the most. I couldn't part from my children even though I could from my husband. Ciaran sincerely understood my plight and I could see the love he held for his own children whenever he spoke of them.

With all this working against us, how could we possibly hope to continue with any sense of permanence? We placed no demands on each other and decided we would simply enjoy the time we had.

One evening we walked to McNamaras. Rose and Tom were sitting at the bench near the pillar where Ciaran and I had united months before. I stopped off to visit with them for a while. Another woman, Mary, was also there. I had seen her on my last trip one evening out at McNamaras where she had been ranting at me -- something about Ciaran being no good. I had paid no attention to her as she had an obvious drinking problem and I could understand only half of what she was saying.

I learned Rose had been informed Ciaran and I were staying at Kevin's, but didn't bring up the subject up, for which I was thankful. I didn't want to get in the middle of estranged marital discussions. I visited for a while then returned to the bar.

Ciaran and I sat just above where Mary, Rose and the others were sitting...we on our high stools at the bar. Michael and several of the other patrons were sitting at the corner table playing cards while Maggie tended bar. The pub was full with blackharding and banter which were well established for the night. We exchanged in light conversation with Larry, who had joined us.

Mary, who evidently had been patronizing the pubs for some time that day, started talking in a very loud voice, "Michael, didn't know you let whores and prostitutes in your pub." I knew immediately she was referring to me as she repeated her accusatory statement several times. Unlike when I first met her last May and couldn't make out a word she uttered, now, suddenly, she was speaking clear English and obviously wanted me to hear and understand every syllable. Ciaran as well shook off her vulgarity and Michael, busy with his cards, seemed not to notice at all. I felt the anger building inside me and thought I would become volcanic at any moment. But I contained myself, exhibiting exceptional self-control, for Ciaran's sake. I didn't want to waste my time on this loud and obnoxious drunkard.

Alice, Rose's oldest daughter who I had become acquainted with during my last visit, was sitting with them. When I noticed her at the end of the bar waiting for a beer, I decided to ask her what Mary's problem was. "Why is she treating me this way?"

Alice explained that Mary had a crush on Ciaran, that they all felt sorry for her and had seen her in tears because of it on many occasions. I told Alice that I could empathize with that. I also told her if we were in America and someone was speaking that way about me in my favorite pub, a dozen friends would run her way out.

Again, Mary voiced loudly that prostitutes and whores shouldn't be allowed in the pub. She repeatedly got up to play a song on the juke box about swearing about promises being made, then broken, yet love would always remain the same. She played the song at least ten times back to back. I could see the anger welling up in Ciaran's eyes yet he tried to make light of it. Hardly able to contain my own anger, I commented loudly on what a lovely song it was. Upon hearing me say this, Maggie looked at me and alluding to Mary's off pitched singing along to the tune and said, "Well, it used to be."

When another song came on the juke box, I sang it sweetly to Ciaran's ear. It was about being far apart, and going crazy...but that, no matter the heart break, we would always remain faithful.. I had already felt it was our song and my singing it was easily overheard by the 'wench', as I was now referring to her. It seemed to put her in her place and quieted her somewhat.. I wondered, as the song stated, how Ciaran and I could survive this distance. But, as the lyrics touted, I knew that if someday we could be together we were more than willing to take the risk.

Ciaran and I handled the situation primarily through ignoring her crudeness. He commented to me that he couldn't understand why Michael wasn't telling her to leave. I explained that I didn't think Michael heard her from his far position at the other end of the bar or he most certainly would have. The bar was closing now and Mary had finally, completely quieted down. She looked about to pass out and this was probably her saving grace as Ciaran and I left.

In our room, Ciaran continued to tease me about my 'friend'. I told him it was lucky for her that I did not mop up the pub with her. Further, that had we been in my stomping grounds, she would not have faired so well. He enjoyed winding me up yet seemed pleased with my self control. As he began his evening's advances, I told him I wouldn't sleep with him until he explained to me the whole situation of his involvement with her. He eventually gave in saying, "I wouldn't be with the likes of that now. It was a long time ago, I was her first, she was just seventeen and me twenty. It was just one time but, she's been after me ever since."

"So you were with her while already involved with your Jane?"

"Yes," he replied without any further explanation.

"I would hope you'd have better taste than that!"

"I'd never be with her again. If ever there was a slut...you should see the men she's with. Catch something for sure from that one."

I was content enough with his explanation and refused to dwell on the fact he had been with her when already involved with someone else. When I figured out the time span, I knew it must have happened not long after David died which had added stresses on his marriage. I imagined Ciaran, in a drunken state, must have just been lonely from the loss and she happened to be available and willing. I lightened the serious mood saying, "Well, I can see how much of a heart-breaker you are and absolutely amazing under the sheets...no wonder she still wants you!"

"You're a wicked woman," he said laughing as he pulled me to him to prove to me again just how amazing he was.

The next morning, we took the bus to the airport to pick up our free rental car with one of the coupons I got back from George. Ciaran drove us to the Ring of Kerry, a place I had heard of and had mentioned wanting to see with him. We drove along highway seventy-one to Bandon, then Glandore and Skibereen. We'd stop occasionally along the way but the weather had turned to intermittent heavy rain that kept us mainly in the confines of the car. Still we enjoyed the ride and scenes along the way. The winding roads to Kenmare were full with animated visual effects on the mountains from the clouds that hovered around the peaked crowns. The place was rich and alive with color. We continued to Killarney where we found, with some difficulty, a bed and breakfast to spend the night. After settling in and dropping off our bags, we walked downtown to a traditional Irish pub. The music flowed freely and so did the people in and out of the double oak and Tiffany glass doors. We sat at one of the long benches with several other patrons, enjoying the revelry and tunes from the band, such as 'O <u>Danny Boy</u>' and '<u>My Wild Irish Rose</u>.'

We sat for sometime -- Ciaran speaking with the man to his left and me the American tourist on my right. The American was from Long Island and was here visiting her sister and brother-in-law who lived in the area; they sat to the other side of her. Ciaran and I played the lovers we were and it seemed he wasn't having any problem with public displays of affection now. The woman next to me asked if I lived in Ireland. "No, but I plan on it someday. I'd love to spend the rest of my life here."

Ciaran picked up on our little talk, joining in, saying, "I'll get her to stay!"

I introduced Ciaran to her as my fiancé; I thought I caught a look of surprise from him at the announcement. But he quickly caught on, showing off my "engagement" ring of garnet and sapphires I had brought with me.

"I thought you two were already married," she added. "At least, newlyweds. I hope you've thought things out, you know it will be a hard life for you, my dear. It is so poor here."

She didn't seem to be enjoying her trip very much and obviously wished for the warmth and conveniences of her mansion in New York. Her sister and brother-in-law appreciated the announcement of our upcoming nuptials and told me, quite contrary to their sister's ideal, how splendid everything had worked out for them and they had been married for over twenty-five years. I was touched by the way they still looked at each other after all those years and yearned to have what they did.

Later when alone in our room, I asked Ciaran, "Ciaran, when I was here last time you continually told me how you knew it the minute you put eyes on me. What exactly did you know?"

He sat silent for several minutes with a slight twinkle of a grin on his face, when I decided to interrupt his happy little train of thought and, in giggling laughter said, "You knew you wanted to get laid, was that it?" He grabbed me and admitted his thoughts of sexual prowl were what first drew him to me. He added however, that he fell completely in love with me. We passed the night with only one roll of love making, a most unusual feat for us. We were spent after the long day and quickly fell into the quiet of the room; sleep came almost instantly. The next morning found us back to Cork.

It was Saturday: I would leave the next day for Wales. We spent that entire evening madly and passionately in each other's arms. Again I felt the power of him in me...he truly was amazing!

I did have some family research I wanted to do, but would have gladly put it off if it were not for my promise to Tripp I would be by to visit.

Ciaran walked me to the bus depot the next morning, but not before we visited with Kevin telling him of our trip to Killarney. Kevin mentioned how he wished he knew where we had gone as he would have come with us. Ciaran and I had quite the laugh at the thought during our walk to the bus depot. I told him he shouldn't mind sharing our time together with Kevin as he had been so kind in letting us stay at his home.

"What a grand time we would've had what with Kevin in the bed right next to us in Killarney!" he laughed.

"But then again, you two could have slept in the large bed together and I in the smaller one," I added.

"Oh, right, that would've been even lovelier," he said playing along with the scene I had painted.

I told him I would rush back to him Tuesday morning and copied down the return bus schedule for him. He promised he would try to meet me at the eleven o'clock return and if I weren't on that bus, would come back each time a bus was due from Rosslare, until I arrived.

****

My head was spinning his taste on my lips as I stepped inside the bus. As the bus approached Wexford, I started to look forward to seeing Tripp and seeking out my ancestor's tomb in Carmarthan; this would, I kept telling myself, be better for Ciaran, so he could catch a bit of work while I was away.

The ride to Rosslare Harbor was familiar to me now and I found myself napping and waking to the sound of the midday rain spattering echoing against the windows of the bus. I was deep in my dreams of Ciaran and wanted nothing to disturb my sweet thoughts. There was going to be a several hour wait for the ferry to Pembroke, but it would be only a four hour boat ride to its docks.

The boat landed near one in the morning. Tripp met me with a big hug, like a wonderful old friend. We had been corresponding regularly for many months. It's wonderful how much you can get to know someone by their letters. He was a graduate of Cambridge University, an English major, who spent his time teaching children on an individual basis. He'd pick them up in the bus in the morning, teach them during the day and drop them all off home after classes. In addition, he was a part-time bartender at The Watermans, and was fond of and involved in the local theater and choir. He had converted to Catholicism many years before and was active in his church. He loved to travel and I had sent him many brochures about Montana where he said he would trek sometime. He had just returned the week before from a three week trip to India where he met a couple of friends and traveled to all their exotic and not so exotic places.

His house was very cozy. A single story framed home

with attached garage where he lived with his father. His mother had died over ten years earlier, leaving his father and him to "bach" it together. His dad now had a girlfriend who enjoyed traveling with him and they were currently off in Scotland together. Tripp showed me to the guest room, complete with double bed that had an endless amount of covers on it. The shower, which I had yearned for so much after sponge bathing the past week at Kevin's place, was very inviting, but I was much too exhausted to even imagine being able to jump in it that evening.

Tripp and I sat in the living room, sipping on home-made wine and getting to know each other. It was getting quite late and we both needed to get to sleep. He had school and theater rehearsals the next day and I wanted to get an early start for Carmarthan.

I barely heard him when he left in the morning, but he did stop by my door with a knock to wake me in order to catch my train.

I could have slept all day, but forced myself from the warm and comfortable surroundings to the shower to which I begrudgingly had to call an eventual end. Walking down the steep hill to the train station, I reveled in the beautiful Welsh landscape. At the train station, I visited with another passenger who gave me directions to St. Peter's Church, where my ancestor was rumored to be entombed. The Welsh are as helpful and friendly as the Irish, and I found no one here that wasn't willing to go out of their way to help me. I had even read once that if you asked an Irishman for directions, he would jump in your car to show you the way and I had no doubt that was equally true of the Welsh.

The gentleman's directions were splendid and I had no problem making my way up the winding, hilly road to the church. It was awe inspiring. The church was Gothic style with a large stain-glass window at the head of the alter. A solid brass angel made up the base of the pulpit. The tomb was to the right of the choir box. I thought it wonderful that churches here still left their doors unlocked. In America, with all the vandalism and burglaries, the churches had closed their doors...locking out the bad-guys along with the homeless who might otherwise sleep huddled under the pillars.

I took several photographs of the church and tomb where Sir Rhys and his lady, Janet, lay. Gazing at my ancestor's tomb made all my research come alive for me. It wasn't just a character in a book anymore, it was Grandfather, fourteen generations removed. A gentleman stepped in through the front doors, inquiring if I needed any assistance. I asked where the local library was and to my good fortune, and his enjoyment, he showed me the very place just across the street from the main doors.

After spending several hours photocopying books about Sir Rhys, I rushed to the train depot to catch the return to Pembroke Dock.

Tripp arrived home shortly after I did and heated up a marvelous speciality of his father's for dinner. His father, knowing that I was coming, made it for me before he left on his trip to Scotland. Lasagna -- one of my favorites. We put the heated bounty on trays and sat in the living room, visiting briefly over our meals. Tripp's theater rehearsal was in less than an hour and he had invited me along. They were performing a play which involved characters from the mountains of Tennessee. Tripp was elated to find out that my father's family was from this very same area and hoped I would be able to help with the accent.

It was fun to sit in the theater, sipping on wine, watching these Welsh men and woman putting their best try at a southern American accent.

In one of our earlier letters, Tripp had told me that if he were to have choir practice when I visited, he would ask me to sing along as I had told him of my singing talent and past experience with theater and choir in high school.

So, at the end of the theatrical rehearsal, I sang for him (and the remaining troop) my signature song version of <u>Amazing Grace</u>. I was humbled by their kindness and how much they openly enjoyed the song.

We enjoyed the brief ride down the stone lined roads back to Tripp's house. My ferry back to Ireland would leave at three in the morning.

We watched Tripp's video from his trip to India. The movie was incredible. His videotaping talents were obvious. There was little hunting and pecking with the lens and he had tape of not only the incredible architectural skills of the Indians, but also an obviously poor family baking him bread in their meager surroundings. "They love to be photographed," he told me as he narrated the film. "They're a wonderful people." He was a thoughtful, educated, and gracious man and I totally enjoyed this chance to get to know him. He held a deep interest in weather and I had been sending him various newspaper articles from America, which he put in his catalog of albums.

As he dropped me off at the docks, we both exclaimed how we wished we would have had more time together. I was anxious to return to Ciaran however, and had promised him I wouldn't tarry in Wales any longer than necessary. Ciaran would be expecting me at the bus depot the next day and I couldn't wait to feel his arms around me again. Tripp, of course, was unaware of my reasons for returning so expeditiously and did not question my desires. I told him that if things worked out for me someday, I might even find myself living in close proximity to Wales. He said it would be several years before he made another trip to America, but would be certain to come see me if I were still there at that time. He had friends in California and went to see them every few years, but his immediate plans were to other places of the world, including a trip to China.

That night the waters were choppy on the ferry ride

back to Ireland. I was unconcerned as I had never had any problems with sea sickness and was excited about the return. I had washed some clothes at Tripp's the night before and had put them out on his line to dry but it had rained while we were at rehearsal and they were still wet when I left. I sought out a place on the ferry to hang them to dry. I found myself in the television room where only two or three persons lounged around the fifty or so chairs.

As I put my clothes on the backs of several chairs, a woman who was either on drugs or booze, came over and while scanning the contents of my suitcase, sat down with her back on a pair of my wet jeans. I had seen her earlier as we were boarding and she was acting very suspicious at that time, as well. There were more than enough places for her to have sat which raised my suspicions even more at her sitting near me. I removed the jeans from the chair she sat at and said, "Oh, let me get these out of your way." She started throwing a fit of sorts, telling me that I better not get in her way. After her tirade and a look from me that clearly stated my position of not messing with me, she retreated. I would rather cling to the gentle side of my nature that Ciaran was able to bring out in me. I had lost this side of myself long ago thanks to women like this and a series of betrayals in my life. But, I found it better in the area of self-preservation to act the bitch at times.

Thinking it more prudent to take my things to the front of the room, I moved everything to the empty chairs near the television. A young man in his twenties was sitting in the front row. We talked as I laid out my clothing on the large red recliners and I told him of my experience with the woman in the back. "Dodgy, that one," he said. "Be careful of her, she's dodgy for sure. I saw her when we docked and there's no trusting that one." He offered to watch my things while I went up on deck to find a ladies room and grab some crackers. My stomach was not cooperating at this point and every roll of the sea went the opposite direction of it.

The young man's name was Stewart and he had just finished college in Wales. He was returning to his home in Galway for the first time in over a year. The excitement of returning home was evident in his voice. He was friendly and placed himself in the chair next to me for easier conversation.

He asked where I was headed and if I needed a ride. I told him I'd be riding the bus as I was going the other direction.

After a short while, the tossing motion of the boat became too much for me and I found my head stuffed into one of the stand up ash trays, emptying the contents of my belly into it's opening. Stewart was very understanding and after several repeat performances, we both fell asleep in our chairs.

We woke as the boat was about to dock. Even with my earlier demonstration of unfeminine ash-tray hugging, he asked me to join him in Galway. I declined graciously as we bid each other a fond good-bye.

The bus back to Cork was only a few minutes from leaving. I waited visiting with the driver until the rest of the passengers were ready to load. I had the same driver on my trip to Rosslare and, recognizing him immediately, commented on this to him. He asked me where in America I was from and told me of his relatives there. "Oh, all of us have some relatives in the States," he said. "After all, there are only four million Irish in all of Ireland and over forty million in America." I told him how I wish I could stay in Ireland forever to which he flirtatiously offered that I could come live with him. He continued to banter with me for the next several minutes and never bothered to check my ticket as I boarded the bus.

A man approached the bus who was, by his leather cowboy boots and feathered hat, obviously an American. He seemed confused and unsure of how to get to his destination of Sneem. He explained to the driver how be was here to visit his mother and wanted to know if this were the right bus. He was sitting behind me when I pulled from my bag one of the complimentary maps I had picked up at the airport. As I handed it to him I told him I knew he had a long trip ahead of him. "Sneem is over by Kerry, the other side of Ireland. It'll probably take you all day."

"Thanks, this'll help a lot," he said. He introduced himself as Jay Roberts. He had just left London where he had conducted some business and was now on his way to his mother who he hadn't seen in several years.

At the next stop, after a stretch and a cigarette, he sat next to me. He began telling me of his life in Pennsylvania. His mother had lived in Ireland for many years. He was a successful businessman who at one time worked for the Federal government. He owned several apartment buildings in Pennsylvania and enjoyed telling me he was financially well off. He was an attractive, large framed man, mostly muscle, with handsome chiseled facial features and a brilliant smile. His conversation was open and he seemed to thoroughly delight in talking about himself!

He wanted me to continue to Kerry with him, but I explained I had a special friend in Cork that I planned on joining. He picked up on the fact that this "special friend" was a lover, but continued to entertain me and still wanted me to meet him in Kerry later in my stay. He started pestering me to exchange mailing addresses and insisted on giving me his mother's address in case I changed my mind.

As we pulled into the Cork City Depot, I expressed my good luck to him and said goodbye. Ciaran was no where in sight to meet me. I therefore started walking up the road to Kevin's. He had given me my own key and I expected that Ciaran must be off working and that was why he hadn't made it to the bus depot. I took the small piece of paper with Jay's mother's address and, without hesitation, tossed it into the River Lee.

I was feeling rather full of myself by now, three men had made advances at me in less than a day. "Perhaps the twenty-five pounds I lost this summer made more of a difference than I would admit before," I told myself. I had been getting pretty chunky and had been experiencing some health problems. This, coupled with my desire to be more desirable for Ciaran, helped motivate me to lose. Ciaran had not mentioned a word of it when I first arrived, but Larry had commented on the difference right away. Jokingly, I told him that Ciaran hadn't even noticed it. "Of course, I did," Ciaran said, "but I liked you just as well the way you were, makes no difference to me. You're beautiful either way." He had such a wonderful habit of saying just the right thing, God, I love this man.

When I arrived at Kevins, I found Ciaran in the kitchen washing up. He told me he was just about to leave to meet me. "Then, you'd be a little late, don't you think?" I kidded him.

He told me he needed to meet with Larry in half an hour "up the hill" and expected Larry needed him to work awhile.

"And how did you expect to be meeting me at the bus depot and meet Larry at the same time?" I asked. It seemed I had caught him up in my question as he avoided volunteering much of answer, but said, "I would've met you both." He promised to be back by six that evening so we could go spend some time together and quickly kissed me goodbye.

Six o'clock came and went, so did seven and eight. "Perhaps I'd have been better off staying in Wales if he were only going to now take me for granted or perhaps he was upset feeling that I had deserted him these last few days." I felt it was me doing all the chasing and he simply relaxed enjoying the attention I fawned over him. "Jesus Christ, Colleen, are all men really the same."

I am not much of a drinker and a small glass of any type of alcohol in more than capable of altering my state of consciousness. Although it wasn't my way of dealing with problems, I found the fresh bottle of Cream I had just purchased; it went down easily and quickly. The anger of being taken for granted turned to feelings of hurt and rejection.

The bottle over half empty, I continued to 'sip' on the Cream and was now joined in the living room by Christine. She was a darling girl and we talked for some time she picked up on the fact that something was bothering me. Between the effects of the Cream and the emotional state it was bringing out in me, I let on that I was upset due to Ciaran's not being back by now. "Now" being after ten. She tried to comfort me by telling me how excited Ciaran had been when he talked of my returning. This helped me somewhat, but the Cream was winning the battle between mind and heart.

Christine offered to go to McNamaras to see if he was there. She was gone just ten minutes and told me that Michael said she had just missed Ciaran. That he had left only a few minutes before she arrived. "Maybe he's just getting even with me for going to Wales. Maybe he did mind my going after all," I thought to myself.

But going to McNamaras and not checking in for me was inexcusable. And still he wasn't back. Christine decided to head to bed; I told her I would take care of the wet pants she had put on the back of a chair near the fire to dry.

Still no sign of Ciaran. I went upstairs, packed my things and had my mind made up to leave first thing in the morning. Returning to the living room, I wrote a note for him, telling him I was sorry if I had been a burden to him and I felt it best to leave, adding that perhaps Mary was right in her assessment of me being some kind of whore since that was how he was treating me. The tears streamed down my cheeks as I wrote the note. It was a byproduct of the Cream and my mood which was set to the side of doubt, rejection, and mounting anger.

There was nowhere for me to go now as it was past one in the morning. I was sitting in the living room with the lights out, watching the fire. It was half-one when he walked in the front door with a smile on his face and two cans of Buhlmer's in each hand. He walked into the living room and turned on the light. I turned my face from him and asked he put the light out but he didn't. "A bit cranky are you?" he joked as he tried to present me with a can of apple juice. I declined his offer as I got out of the chair and flipped the switch, turning out the light.

He was not apologetic and I thought to myself again how all men are the same, after all. They meet their needs and nothing more. That love, even true love, was not enough unless each party thought more for the other than themselves...it's called consideration!

We began to bicker about his being late. He told me at one point during the discussion, and I don't even remember what I said to bring it on, that he wouldn't even take what I was saying from his wife.

I replied, "Then it's a damn good thing we're not married! You have time enough to be at McNamaras tonight, but no time to come see me. And after me rushing to be back with you! I could easily have stayed in Wales!"

"I wasn't at McNamaras tonight! I've been working. Why do you think I brought you the apple juice." He said.

"Then why would Michael tell Christine that you had just left there when she stopped in earlier?" I demanded.

"He must have been confused with my being there the other night," he said. "Enough! I'm going to bed."

He retreated to the bedroom. I wasn't satisfied with the answers he had given and so, less than a half hour later, went to join him only to find him fast asleep. "How nice," I thought to myself, "that nothing seems to bother him." I decided to remove my suitcase to the living room for a speedy morning exit and woke him in the effort.

"And where would you be going?" He asked with a smile.

He lay me down next to him and I found myself apologizing for my attitude. "I'm not much of a drinker. It's why I don't like to drink much," I explained. "I drank the better part of a full bottle of cream. I'm sorry Ciaran. I just don't understand why you never came to get me and why you were so late getting here."

"I was working, I swear," he told me. "There's no phone here and I had no way of telling you. We were out of town all day -- look at me, I'm a mess." It was true, he was covered with grime from the day's labor. "But, I should've found some way to get word to you before we left. When I met Larry I didn't know where we were going or how long I would be or would've stopped off then to let you know." He wrapped his arms around me, adding, "Will you forgive me?"

"Will you, me?" I gently asked as I stretched up my face to meet his lips with mine. I never enjoyed the smell of a man's sweat before, but his was like sweet perfume after our brief battle. "You need a bath," I told him.

"True, I can barely stand the smell of myself."

"Wait here my love, don't move a muscle."

I went down to the kitchen and grabbed a large bowl from the cabinet, filled it with hot water and brought it up to him. I was glad he hadn't fallen asleep again in my absence. He watched me as I removed a wash cloth and soap from my suitcase, placing the items next to bed on the table. "What are you up to?" He asked.

"A special treat for you, mo muirneach. Relax, you don't need to do a thing. I'll do all the work." I rolled the wash cloth in my hands through the hot water, squeezing out the moisture before I ran it over his face. He sighed deeply enjoying my attention and feeling the refreshing cloth across his eyes and forehead. "A sponge bath for you. Ever had someone give you a sponge bath before?"

"No...can't say that I have," he said with exhaustion in his voice.

"Tonight I'm your slave and will please you beyond your wildest desires," I told him as I rubbed the soap against the wash cloth, creating a light lather, then proceeded to clean his neck, working my way around to his arms, chest, and waist. After rinsing the suds from his skin and re-soaping the cloth, I started to massage his genitals softly and slowly in a swirling motion against his tired body. His arousal was almost immediate and he moaned gratefully as I continued to bathe the workday sweat from him. He started to pull me up to meet him for a kiss, but I dutifully returned to my work. "I'm not through yet," I said.

I rinsed the cloth once more to delicately remove the soapy film from his eagerly waiting body. I followed each stroke of the cloth with my lips sweetly kissing the same route around his full erection. I gently pulled down his foreskin and placed my pursed lips around him. Slowly, then quickly, then slowly again, circling him with my tongue with varying rotations. He would moan softly, tell me he loved me, and moan again. I never felt so uninhibited. I wanted to spoil him for any other woman and felt I was well on the way of achieving my goal. I ran my hand up his inner thigh, never letting go of his area of primary interest, and playfully kneaded his most private jewels. He was in a state of euphoria and I was going to make it last for him forever. I positioned myself between his legs, while never leaving the post I held dear between my lips. Slowly, I moved my body up his, rubbing my well-endowed breasts along his thighs, then into position surrounding his most private place. I positioned my breasts moving my chest in an upward and downward motion against him which created an even more delightful groan from deep within his being, "You're going to make me arrive right now," he managed to say.

With a deep and penetrating passion exuding from him, he suddenly pulled me up even with his body. With a new found energy he tossed me on my back. He teased me only momentarily by rubbing himself around the lips of my inner regions. Then, in one great sweeping motion, thrust himself into me. I could feel the warm sticky fluid coming from him even before he entered. Unlike the few I had known before, this was no deterrent for him as, for well over an hour, he continued to move around inside me creating a climax for the two of us that finally threw him back in exhaustion and both of us into new heights of delirium.

"Did you enjoy it?" I asked, mimicking his own words to me after earlier rounds together.

"Yes, of course." He said smiling.

"I've been reading a book...could you tell," I teased.

"Must be some book!" He said as he gestured for me to place my head on his chest.

After a short pause of quiet, I added, "Let's not waste any more time arguing. I love you and only want to make you happy."

"But it's so lovely making up." He jested then with the deepest sincerity said, "No one else has ever made me happier, Colleen. I love you as I have loved no one else."

"What would you have done if you woke in the morning not to find me here?" I asked.

"Why I'd go after you!"

"And where would you look?"

"Near Shannon of course," he said with a bit of a smirk and we both knew he was right as that would have been exactly where I would have headed.

The next morning he greeted me with a tender smile and kiss. He had the most incredible smile, capable of melting even the Devil's heart. As we started into the living room, he noticed the almost empty bottle of Cream sitting on the floor near Kevin's favorite chair. "Did you do all that on your own?" He asked.

"Yes...although Christine did have one small drop, but I did most of the damage. This is why you don't see me drink much, Ciaran, I don't like what it does to me. I think strange thoughts and turn either into the life of the party or the worst bitch in the world."

He laughed and lightly wrestled with me telling me that he loved me and that he wouldn't be late again without trying to somehow let me know. I didn't doubt him at all. "Michael must have made a mistake telling Christine that Ciaran had just left. He was so used to having Ciaran in there...yes, it must have been a mistake on Michael's part," I convinced myself.

Ciaran announced he would be making dinner for us that night. Then, taking me by the hand declared we would being going for a walk around Cork.

"Don't you have to work today?"

"Not today. Today I spend only with you." He said.

He walked me to Barracks Street, which he said was the toughest part of town and where he once lived. We toured around for miles and was passing by a beautiful Gothic style cathedral, St. Finbarrs, when I asked him to go in. He agreed somewhat reluctantly, and I told him that although it probably wasn't a Catholic church, I didn't think the walls would fall down around him.

We went in and it reminded me of my last trip here when he and I had stopped by St. Coleman's Cathedral in Cobh, on our way to Waterford. He jokingly had sprinkled me with Holy Water as we left and I explained to him that the church we were in now obviously wasn't Catholic.

"How can you tell?"

"No Holy Water for you to sprinkle me with...and no statutes of Mary or the saints." He looked around the enormous Anglican church, while I explained my observations.

I reminded him that I was Protestant and he replied that Catholic or Protestant didn't make any difference to him.

We continued our walk to Fitzgerald's park and took a brief rest there.

"I love you, Ciaran," I told him as I laid my head on his shoulder.

He smiled and put his arm around me and said, "I love you too, right!"

We sat and enjoyed the pond which lay before us and watched a man sleeping on one of the benches across the way.

We found ourselves at the top of a hill looking down over the entire city. I asked him to stop for a minute so I could take some pictures and he relished acting the 'tour guide' once again. He explained what the different buildings were in the distance, including pointing out Saint Finbarrs, the church we had just left. It seemed so far away now as the late day fog rolled in and around it's spires. He more than made up for his lateness the night before, showering affection over me at every opportunity.

We had walked for miles, not as far as our May sojourn to Black Rock, but according to the gang at McNamaras when we arrived, at least four or five miles. Ciaran enjoyed telling them of our trips and getting their impressions on distance and direction. He especially enjoyed asking Michael, who would go into a ten minute dissertation for each left and each right turn that we traveled.

We returned to Kevin's house where Ciaran cooked a wonderful dinner of blood sausage, which he called pudding, bacon, and of course the ever popular poppies. He insisted on washing all the dishes and chased me from the kitchen, out of his way when I offered to assist.

Kevin and I sat together in the living room watching television while Ciaran served us then he swamped up. When Ciaran returned to the living room I commented, "You're going to make someone a grand wife someday!"

"Damned lucky she'll be too," he quipped. "Cooking the dinner, washing the dishes, and mopping the floor!"

We spent the evening with Kevin quietly watching television. Ciaran, more exhausted than ever, retreated to the bedroom to catch a nap. I don't know where he got his energy -- when I went upstairs to check on him, he woke up, snatched me into his arms and made passionate love to me.

When we were done, an hour or so later, I told him he needed to get some rest. I went back to the living room to rejoin Kevin who had turned on a soft porn type show. There had been much controversy about this new channel that appeared on cable in Ireland. I had read several articles in the newspapers about people wanting it banned. The articles stated that most people preferred to get the Disney channel instead but it was unavailable. This pornography, however, was available and being taped by teenagers, who sold copies of the explicit programs to their friends. I never did enjoy those shows. I had even been shy about reading books about the art of love-making, until recently. It took less than a New York minute for me to feel embarrassed and to return to Ciaran's side to turn in for an early night of sleep.

The next few days passed quickly and without any unusual event. Ciaran would work when he could, always being sure to be home when he said he would. I cooked dinner for all of us a few nights and Christine made us a wonderful shepherd's pie one evening. She promised Kevin she would cook dinner for us one night and prepared the same dish for a group of French visitors to her school earlier that same day. Shepherd's pie is similar to a meat pot pie, but is covered with mashed potatoes in place of a crust. She cooked it to perfection, we all enjoyed the feast.

My heart grew heavy as I knew my time in Ireland was nearing an end. I asked Ciaran if he thought he could get away my last two days so we could use up the last free rental coupon. I would splurge and charge an extra day of rental to my credit card. He was apprehensive, not about taking the time off, but if he would be able to put a few pounds together in order to go.

He picked up a day's work with Larry, who told him he would be able to pay him before we planned to leave.

However, when that evening rolled around and Larry hadn't been paid for the job yet, (in addition to not expecting to receive the cash until the following week) Ciaran grew concerned about our going. "I won't have you paying for everything," he said.

I reminded him that I would be taking care of the car and our rooms, but fell short on money for spending along the way and that was all he would need.

His mood all evening had been one of anxiety and he was still obviously upset. I knew more than the money concern was bothering him but he didn't say anything.

When we walked over to Kevins, I inquired what it was that so deeply troubled him. He was hesitant at first, but explained to me that he was having problems with Jane, his ex-wife.

"She informed me she's selling the house and moving to London," he hung his head as he spoke the words. "She's taking the kids away with her." His anger grew as he said, "She has no right to be selling the house, it was the money we got from the death of our son that bought it and I'll not let her get away with selling it out from under me."

I asked him if the house was in his name and he told me, "No." He said that he had gone into a deep, drunken depression after his son's death and hadn't paid attention to what else was going on back then. She had purchased the house in her name only without him knowing or caring about it at the time. I told him since they hadn't ever married and with the house in her name there would probably be little he could do about her selling it now.

He said that he had gone to the house to take some pictures of his children with the disposable camera I had given him and that Jane was snotty and wouldn't let him take them to the park. According to Ciaran, she snarled saying "and what would you be wanting pictures of them for! I'll not be dressing them up for you. Where have you been for the past two weeks?"

They evidently had quite the discussion. He left without seeing his children and was now deeply depressed by the experience.

"To hell with her," I told him. "Let her have the house. When you come into your settlement you won't have to feel obligated to share any part of it with her."

"I would never do that to my children," he answered. I felt ashamed that he thought I meant to abandon his children in any way so I explained that I didn't mean that he shouldn't provide for his kids but that if she were taking his share from the sale of the house that he would probably be best off placing some cash into trust funds for the children so she wouldn't be able to get to it.

I did what I could to comfort him. I knew it would be hard on him to have his children taken so far away and I felt this was more at the bottom of his anger than the house was.

"I'll not let her get away with it," he repeated. I knelt at his side as he sat in the hardwood chair, quietly listening to him vent his pent up anger.

Seeing him slip deeper into despair, I changed the subject saying, "We'll have a lovely drive together, Ciaran."

He apologized for telling his problems to me, especially since I was nearing my last few days there. I, in return, told him that I was glad he told me what had happened, as it made me feel closer to him and helped me understand what he went through while I was so far away in the States.

His frustration was released in the love we made. His anger had turned into an energy that was fully directed towards me as we fell into our rabbit roles that evening. I must admit I enjoyed it, as always, and it lasted well into the early morning hours. We were devoted to each other in our desires and I enjoyed not having to be the aggressor. We took our turns at navigation in our tumbles during the night. He always smiled, allowing me to see part of his inner self through his wonderful, blue-gray eyes that sparkled in the candle light. He was as much wanting to please me as I him. That night he would pull me tighter to his chest than ever before, all the while professing his love and fondness for me.

He found some spot work the next day with another of his friends. I told him not to worry about money for his return from our trip as I had an extra day on my bus pass for him to use to get back from Shannon Airport.

He didn't mention any more about his problems with Jane and I didn't bring it up. I could see in him a hard working man who, if an alcoholic at all, was most likely a functional alcoholic. He had a lived a hard life his few years and was devoted to his children. I prayed he was not still in love with his ex and that I had stolen, fully, his affections.

The next evening, the gang at the pub wanted to throw me a farewell party. Ciaran had to work and I waited for his return. But now it was half-nine and he had not showed up. I decided not to disappoint my friends and walked down to McNamaras knowing Ciaran would be joining me as soon as he was able.

I was sitting with Rose, Christine and their relatives who were in visiting from out of town. Rose presented me with a gift of two purple bud vases for which I graciously thanked her, telling her that purple was my favorite color and that it was kind of her to think of me. Christine had earlier given me a lovely scented lamp. These were people struggling to survive, and the kindness and generosity shone me cleansed me of any possible negative feelings.

I sat visiting with them and was joined occasionally by Tom or one of the others who would give me a hug and bid me make a speedy return.

Ciaran was in the best mood I had seen him. He entered the pub, and told me he earned enough to have a few quid in his pocket for the trip. He kissed me fondly and deeply, and in front of all his friends! I was totally content after these past two weeks that his love for me was true. For the first time in my life I wanted nothing more than to please a man. I wanted to run away with him and forget all my past life. But, reality always set into my thoughts and I knew that all that held me back was my abiding love for my children.

Patience

If I could run away tomorrow,
into your waiting arms so strong.
The world would never hold it's power,
knowing full well where I belong.

My life holds many obligations,
though greatly tempted I may be.
To hurt the little ones I share,
would abate love you for me.

So with patience and understanding,
our love must be placed on hold.
Until such time as change does come,
to break away this gloomy mold.

Michael presented me with a bottle of Paddy's Irish Whiskey and the walking stick which Ciaran stored in his kitchen for me to take. "How very kind these folks were to me," I kept repeating to myself. Larry came over, apologizing for not having a gift especially after I had given him a box of tobacco when I first arrived. I explained to him I didn't give gifts with the intent of receiving any in return and kissed him, old friend he had become, on the cheek. I could tell he felt terrible about not having the money to give Ciaran, but told him not to be too concerned since Ciaran was able to work that day for someone else and we were leaving in the morning as planned.

All was well with the world: Ciaran and I would leave in the morning, my new friends showed their affection towards me and I them, and, of course, we all enjoyed the banter and fun of that night.

Ciaran wouldn't stop sweetly pestering me until I sang a round of <u>Amazing Grace</u> for the crowd, which fell silent listening to every word. I do not think he believed me when I said I sang well and I watched him never take his eyes from me as I sang. "Again, another verse, again," he and several of the others prodded. Michael had been trying to usher the crowd out as it was well beyond closing time; however, gave me special permission to sing <u>O' Danny Boy</u>, just once. Never had I found a place that felt like home as much as this. Never in my life would I be content to settle for less than true love.

I turned to say a final farewell to Rose and whispered to her, "take care of Ciaran for me!"

"Oh, there's no worry about him and other women, if that's your concern," she answered.

I told her that was nice of her to say when she interrupted with, "It's the drinking I worry about."

I believed Rose meant well but I hated being left with this final thought on my mind. It had been a concern to me that Ciaran drank too much. Yet, on this trip, he drank moderately, and at times, not at all. I knew he had entered into drunken states when depressed, as when his son died. I couldn't help but think she was alluding to the possibility I would break his heart and send him into the despair he had experienced so many years before. My instincts told me not to trust her. I was forgiving but not forgetting. I could not help but hold these concerns of mine. I reminded myself of what I had told her last May: "I'm sure it will be my heart to be broken, not his."

We drove to a flat owned by a girl named Susan. I had met her on my last trip to Cork when she was over eight months pregnant. I gave Tom gifts for her and the baby when I first came back, since I hadn't had a chance to see her. Ciaran had seen her a few days earlier; she gave him her address and phone number, asking us to call. Unfortunately, she wasn't home so we continued along our way. "She said we would have been welcome to stay with her and that she had told Tom to tell us." Ciaran was upset that Tom withheld that information these last two weeks. Evidently she and Tom had some falling out and even though he knew, and had promised in his letter to me that a place was available, he didn't tell us about her invitation.

"All that time, and he didn't say a word about it." Ciaran couldn't understand how Tom couldn't keep his own promise then neglect to tell us there was a place we could stay that first night I arrived since he knew Ciaran was frantically trying to locate one.

I was concerned, as Ciaran was such a giving person, that his friends tended to take advantage of him. He refused to admit they were capable of that, yet I was reminded of one evening in McNamaras, when Ed, who was fond of sucking on my knuckles and singing his version of New York, New York to me, had in his possession a photograph I had sent Ciaran of Layla and me. I didn't understand what he was doing with it. I had grabbed it and approached Ciaran, who was livid. Ciaran told me the only way Ed could have the picture was if he were the one who broke into his last residence. Ciaran had several items missing and upon seeing the picture, would have nothing to do with Ed, convinced of his involvement in the crime.

It was good having Ciaran to myself again. I popped in a cassette that I had brought with me for just this occasion and hummed along to the tunes of Bryan Adams, Elton John, Michael Bolton, Reba McIntire, and Ciaran's favorite, Garth Brooks.

We drove along the main road to Limerick, then on to Galway. We took the long winding coast road which ran along the Conamarra Mountains to Kikieran and Clifden, known as the Capital City of the Conamarras. We spent some time walking along the roads of Clifden but, with dark rapidly approaching, returned to Galway by way of Ballynahinch, Maam Cross and Corrib. It was a beautiful drive, the rain barely holding itself back for us. But hold itself back it did as we traveled along enjoying the view of clouds hanging low over the mountain tops and ocean. "God and all His Angels are smiling on us," I told him.

I would run my fingers through his hair and along the outer edge of his left ear as we drove along and he would pretend to be an America tourist, changing his accent to one of a prep-school American. "Oh my," he would say in his best English, "look at all the lovely sheep." He enjoyed black harding me in this way and repeated his rhetoric many times as the day went on.

By the time we arrived in Galway, it was raining heavily.

After checking into a bed and breakfast and putting our bags away, we walked down the main avenue to find ourselves in a traditional pub named the Horse's Head. It was already crowded, but we managed to find two stools tucked neatly into the front corner. We sat listening to the music, keeping mostly to ourselves, when I spotted a pay phone next to me.

"I should try to call Layla," I told him. "I told her I would try and call while here, she would love to say hello to you." It was impossible to get a call out and Ciaran could see I was disappointed, "Don't worry," he said, "we can try tomorrow, it's too noisy in here anyway."

The bed we found ourselves in that night was the noisiest we had experienced. He always seemed somewhat embarrassed if a squeak sounded during our love making and I noticed him stuffing pillows behind the headboard trying to quiet it.

Caught up in the act and not the noise, I pulled his arms down away from the headboard he was trying to silence and said, "I don't care how much noise we make."

The next morning we were joined at breakfast by another couple who had spent the night there. Like us, she was an American and he Irish. They told us how they had come from Dublin and were headed on their way up north. We exchanged light conversation over our meal as they told us of their traveling plans.

As Ciaran and I loaded the car with our things, I commented on how I had heard one of them get up to use the bathroom as I had just closed our door the night before.

"You mean to say there we were making all that noise, with them in the next room awake!" He exclaimed. "Then, there we were sitting across from them at breakfast talkin' about our travels."

He was sweetly shy and truly enjoyed giving me a hard time about my passion with him the night before. "Do you really mind all that much?" I questioned him.

"Well, no, I don't suppose I do. I love you, right!" He answered.

"Is that a question, or a statement," I queried at his use of the word "right."

"You know what I'm sayin' to you," he said as I began to tug at his ear. He swatted at me as if it were a bee trying to sting him then kissed my hand, saying, "Now, don't be playing with me ears."

It was my last day with him -- our last night together too soon ahead. We grew quiet along the roads to the Aran Islands and Cliffs of Moher, stopping to walk along the rocky beaches. The clouds continued to hold back their moisture and even parted occasionally to reveal the blue skies hidden behind.

Along the way, he pulled the car off the side of the road. In the middle of nowhere was a pay phone. "Now you can call your friend," he told me. I was touched by his remembering I wanted to call Layla the night before and proceeded to dial New York, hoping I would catch her in. Her boyfriend refused the collect call which signaled me that she was not in at the time. "We'll try again later," I told Paul over the voice of the operator who was about to disconnect us.

We did phone again several hours later to find Layla home and excited about our calling. "I'll pay you for the call when I get back," I told her.

"Don't worry about that! I take it everything is going good for you. I got your postcards," she said with a happy sly, "I know what you're up to", tone in her voice.

"It's going better than I ever imagined," I said. "Would you like to say hello to Ciaran?"

She naturally replied, "Yes" and I was amazed at the clarity of his English as he exchanged greetings with her. "Tell her about the sheep," I told him.

"Oh, Layla, they have the most wonderful sheep here. You really must come and see them for yourself," he blackhardingly told her.

When they were through he handed the phone back to me. "He sounds wonderful!" she exclaimed. "What a lovely accent." I said. I told her I'd call in a few days from home.

"I'd like to be a fly on the wall for that talk between you two," Ciaran joked as I hung up the phone.

We continued along the coast road to Kilkee, then on to New-Market on Fergus. My flight left at ten the next morning and we needed to stay close so I wouldn't miss it, much as I wanted to.

We stayed in a very comfortable bed and breakfast which held the quietest bed we had been fortunate enough to find in the whole of my two weeks there. I pointed this out to Ciaran upon our arrival and he tossed us both on top of it just to be sure. We spent several hours talking as we rested, I on the bed and he in the chair near to it.

"Don't go tomorrow," he whispered.

"I don't want to go."

"Then stay," he said rising from the chair to sit down next to me.

"Then what? My children would hate me, then I would be deported in a short time to return to no one."

He wrapped his arm around me. We tried to talk of other things so not to grow sad at my impending departure. "Are you hungry?" I asked, changing the subject.

"Yes, I am a bit hungry." He answered. I could see he appreciated the change of subject as much as I. Neither of us wanted to think about tomorrow.

We walked down to a local cafe' and sat quietly alone as we ate fish and chips. When we finished our meal, we walked towards our room, checking out the local drinking establishments along the way. Finding one that suited us, we entered. The pub was small in size, similar to McNamaras, and was deserted except for the elderly woman who owned the place. Meg must have been at least eighty, dressed in a simple cotton print dress with the ever present drooping knee-hi nylons and orthopedic shoes. She was friendly and served us promptly. She told us the history of the area and her family's ownership of the pub for over four generations. She continued by telling us how it would pass on to her daughters someday. She and Ciaran exchanged information on where they were from, who they knew, and what was happening around the country. I remained silent, enjoying their conversation and found myself staring at him, not being able to hold back my thoughts of my future loneliness.

Meg disappeared into a back room then quickly reappeared with two small cone shaped cordial glasses in her hands, she placed them in front of us. The liquors inside had separated and formed the colors of Ireland. "An Irish flag," I told her. Which, as it turned out was exactly what they were called and were her specialty. She wouldn't part with the recipe, but it appeared to me to be made up of Creame d'Menth in the bottom, with a narrow layer of Cream, then topped off with either Irish whiskey or some unidentifiable orange mixture on top. Ciaran and I thanked her for her lovely farewell gift and drank them down. The taste of mint lingered on our tongues with the warmth of the whiskey giving a cozy after effect. We sat for sometime enjoying another pint, then bade her goodnight and returned to our room.

We were slow at first to embrace each other, each thinking about our imminent destinies. But, soon we lay snuggling. He laid his head on my shoulder, stroking my neck and face ever so gently. Without any words between us, he found his familiar way down my chest. Rolling me on top of him, he kissed me as if there were no tomorrow, and we both, in our silence, knew there was not.

"Oh Ciaran, I love you so much," I said breaking the silence. He continued to caress my back down to my buttocks, pulling me tightly against his loins. I cradled him between my thighs. Laying my chest to his, he rolled me onto my back, with his fullness well inside. He again changed our positions, putting me on my stomach while he rocked himself slowly into me. Placing his lips near my ear he whispered, "I love you Colleen and always will. I'd marry you tomorrow if you'd have me."

There was no sense in trying to respond. We both knew the impossibility of my staying. I fell asleep with my ear near his heart feeling secure in our love for each other. "I will be with you again come May," I reassured him.

Ever Yours

Ever in your arms I'll dwell,
and place upon you my magic spell.
I'll take my rest in your dear arms,
and fall beneath your mystic charms.

The days will melt into enchanted nights,
no longer starved by sweethearts blight.
The moon our heat and the stars our cover,
fantasy realized my own dear lover.

Endearing moments pass all too soon,
as cheerful songs turn to lonely tune.
For I'll leave again on morning flight,
depart too soon out of your sweet sight.

But ever yours know I'll always be,
I'll come again over heartless sea.
And pray these times we're so far away,
take not a toll from next dearer day.

Waking early the next morning, I freshened up leaving him tucked safely under the blankets. When I returned to the room, I curled up close to his back and reached my arm around his waist to begin gently stroking him. I had thought about bringing in a bowl of warm water to bath him but could find nothing that would serve. He didn't mind my advances and once aroused and awake, quickly turned and mounted me as a stallion mounts a mare in spring.

Our love-making completed, I commented, "A quickie. Never had one from you before."

"Thought that's what you wanted," he replied with a hurt look in his eyes.

"Not what I necessarily wanted, but I enjoyed it all the same."

"So, you enjoyed yourself then?" He teased.

"Oh, yes. With you, as you already know, I always enjoy it," I said as I kissed each of his eyes. "And, hope I've spoiled you for any other woman!"

"To be sure," he said. "To be sure." He was pleased with my response, kissed me again and retreated to take a shower before we had breakfast.

We were the only guests at the establishment and enjoyed having the dining nook to ourselves. I found him quietly looking at me constantly and myself doing the same to him. Our eyes would meet, the sad answers written in each.

We arrived at Shannon Airport only half an hour before departure. After dropping off the car and checking in, we sat in a quiet place readying our final words. I commented on how beautiful the walking stick was that he had handmade. "I'll place it near to my bed as a constant reminder of you...Ciaran, I'll place no demands on you. All I ask is that you to be careful. You have no idea how hard it is for me to say this at all..."

"You can say anything to me."

"...all I ask that if you find yourself with someone else before I come back that you use protection." The words came with difficulty and I hung my head not able to speak directly to his face. I didn't even want to think of him being with any one but me.

"I'll not need them," he assured me. "I'll wait for you."

I was ecstatic at his response of fidelity and in like manner reminded him I too would be with no one but him.

But, then again, he already knew that.

"Will you promise to write me more regularly this time." I asked. "I know how you hate to write, but it's hard for me with you being so far away. Not knowing if you are alright or thinking of me. You would not have to write too often, but once a month would be nice. Would you do this for me?"

"Of course...I'll try...I love you, right?"

His sincerity overwhelmed me. There was still so much I wanted to say, but couldn't find the words nor need try to shake off any prior insecurities. It felt as if they had all disappeared now. I was never more myself.

"Don't go." He asked raising me to a standing position while wrapping his arms around me.

"You know I'd love to stay, Ciaran. But, I can't." I told him. "Are you sure you can deal with this?"

"I have no choice," he said then fell silent once again. I knew he understood as we had been honest with each other about our circumstances.

"Delta Flight 209 boarding at gate five," rattled over the public address system. We both held horrified looks in our eyes, but gathered up my things. We walked discontentedly down the wide hall to where I had to board. We stood at the gate for several minutes, making plans for my return.

"I'll have a place of my own when you come back," he promised.

The PA squealed the final boarding announcement.

I felt a panic well up inside me. "If only things were different, I'd stay with you forever."

He took me into his arms and with the same abrupt parting as in May, looked deep into my eyes and said, "I love you, right! I'll see you soon."

"I love you, Ciaran," I cried as he quickly turned and walked away. I could now understand the Shakespearean quote, "parting is such sweet sorrow". Never before had I experienced this feeling of panic, mixed with sadness, even though now, certainly more so than in May, I felt secure in the knowledge that he really did love me and I would rejoin him soon.

Lost in my thoughts and with tear-filled eyes, I boarded the plane and gazed out the small portal, watching my Ireland, my Ciaran, fade out of my sight.

Abide

Our heart's passions set ablaze.
This hazy water-colored maze.
Our unkind world keeps us apart.
Random togethers set each new start.

Can't seem to halt these outside forces,
that set afar our different courses.
Our hearts breaking oh cruelest score,
yearning to be at distant shore.

If only my life could take a change,
and close this cold unfeeling range.
How long will I wait to feel embrace,
to touch content desired place.

Can you wait for me, dare I ask.
Long, arduous and lonesome task.
For to you I swear I will be true,
as my tears melt into morning dew.

So steal us moments as we can,
there draw our marks in golden sand.
To be swept away with afternoon tide,
we have no choice but to abide.

Chapter 8
Lonely Once Again

The loneliness crept over me, almost immediately, like a smothering blanket of thick, darkening fog. It took nineteen hours to fly back to Montana, I struggled to hold back the tears every minute.

"What are you doing to yourself Colleen, not to mention to him?" my inner voice interrogated me as the plane landed. "What illusion overrides your senses? How could this relationship ever be more than an occasional fling under the sheets? Sure, you've won his heart and lost yours, but will you ever be able to be with him the way you want?" The anxiety was overwhelming and I attempted to force myself to find contentment in the fact I was finally, completely loved and in love.

True love had always seemed an unattainable goal for me. I had never felt much loved as the middle child among my siblings. My grandparents, whom we had moved in with when I was just two years old, were openly attached to my younger sister who was only two months old at the time. My mother's favorite was obviously my older brother. She was constantly getting him out of trouble, therefore he took all her attention. I found myself standing on the sideline looking in on this family that I felt no part of. It was no illusion that I had always been left out of their affections...and I had made a conscious observation, when only eight years old, that I was unwanted and already on my own. Until that point, I was an extremely shy child...but I was fast becoming street-wise and stone-hearted. I was not going to fall into a "poor me" complex, but I was going to take on the world headfirst!

At six, until I was ten years old, I had been molested by a man who should have been protecting me from such atrocities. The experience left me knowing that affection, so-called 'love', lay only in how much a man could sexually gratify himself with a girl. I also fell victim to believing I could never trust anyone, along with all the other emotional lifelong baggage. My ideas changed slightly when my mother remarried. Josh was a good man who immediately took me under his wing...and his mother did the same. For the first time in my life, I felt parental style affection and had enthusiastically accepted every facet of it in my life. Josh and his mother treated me with dignity and respect and made me finally believe I was possibly special. Still, the ghosts of my early childhood never stopped haunting me.

It was the evil forced on me as a child that formed much of the person that I was to become. I had grown untrusting of relationships and unwilling to reveal too much of myself to any one person. Created in me was a never-ending difficulty accepting that love between a man and a woman could ever really exist. Even though I had come to realize that it had been a crime perpetrated on me and that I wasn't responsible for his actions, I felt confused about my feelings at times. My child's mind had somehow taken responsibility for what had happened and it took years before I found enough faith and fortitude to forgive myself for something that was not my fault. Eventually, I was even able to forgive him.

Now, I could no longer allow what happened to me as a child to interfere with the love that waited for me with this wonderful, gentle man who had delightfully ruined me for any other. Still, even with this rationalization in mind, I could not help but fight the battle raging inside me that I was somehow unworthy of such fondness.

Even when I had determined to lose my virginity with Don, it had been a conscious decision, well thought-out. I needed to know if I would be able to handle any intimate relationships; which was why I allowed myself to finally be seduced after so many before him had tried to no avail.

Kent picked me up from the airport with hardly a word passing between us; we located my suitcase, loaded it in his car, and drove home.

The children were still up waiting for my arrival and the new round of gifts they knew I would have for them. "I missed you mom," Angel said greeting me as Jimmy descended the stairs from his room to chime in with her.

Angel was a beautiful young girl nearing thirteen. Her hair had grown even longer over the last few months and gave her long, slender body the look of a model. She was stubborn and hardheaded, but I always saw within her a caring sensitivity. Kent was trying to push counseling on her due to problems at school. What I saw was a child trying to cope with frustration and a sense of powerlessness in dealing with a new principal who seemed not to like her. This, in addition to puberty, finding her hormones gone wild and a home life that was devoid of affection between her parents. No, I didn't think she needed private counseling, rather some incentive to learn and practice self-control. I offered to have her hair permed if she stayed out of trouble in school for the remainder of the year. She had been bugging me to perm her hair and I had always declined, thinking her too young. Thirteen was fast approaching and I thought no harm to giving in to her wish if it would help her achieve my goals for her. She was pleased with the idea but asked if she could change her reward to having her ears pierced instead. I agreed, but under the condition she get just studs so she wouldn't tear her ear at play; she gained the approval of our contract from her dad. She accepted my conditions without argument and I looked forward to watching her attain, what was now, both our ambition.

She enjoyed leaving me notes, scattered around the house, telling me daily that school went well and she had no trouble that day. She would always sign it, "I love you, Mom!"

Jimmy, nearing seventeen, was taller than me and loved to remind me of it at every opportunity. He had a good head on his shoulders and planned on joining the military after high school graduation in order to work toward a college education. He was independent, old fashioned and I loved that in him. His maturity had made it difficult in the past for him to make friends within his age group but now he was surrounded by what I deemed fair weather acquaintances that he didn't recognize as such.

Jimmy had run away two years earlier with another boy and two girls. One of the girls had told him that she was being sexually abused by her step-father and wanted to get to Virginia where she could safely live with her grandparents. So, Jimmy, soft touch that he was, felt he would help her get to Virginia with the other two in tow. He had withdrawn all two hundred dollars from his savings account and took off on foot with the three of them. Discovering the plan, albeit late, by one of the other parents, I called the local police and requested they designate him as a runaway. The night had passed by miserably for me. I was deep in tears and filled with guilt at every harsh word I may have spoken to him through the years. Not knowing his plan, I had even contacted his biological father in Washington thinking he was headed there. Matt was very supportive. He had quit drinking several years earlier and had asked me permission to contact Jimmy just a few months earlier. He said he would send him home immediately if he showed up on his doorstep. Falling asleep in my bedroom chair, I passed the night tossing and turning, praying for his safe return.

The next day I was surrounded by the parents of the other children and inundated with phone calls from other parents, friends, and finally the nearby county's sheriff's office. The children had been spotted about twenty miles from town near a forested area. It had been cold out the night before and this evening promised more of the same. I joined the other girl's parents in their car and drove out to where the kids reportedly were.

Dark came quickly that night. When we finally came

across the kids walking down the frontage road, they appeared to be in beginning stages of hypothermia. After hugging them with eyes drained of tears, we quickly placed them in our respective vehicles. Kent and Angel had joined me by then and we drove home. I asked Jimmy why he had run away and what the problem at home was. He said there was no problem and asked if he could wait to explain it to me until later.

Once home in his room, out of earshot of his sister, he explained to me about the abuse the girl had been experiencing and I had no choice but to look into the bright blue eyes of this fourteen year old and believe all that he said. Relieved at his reasoning and respecting his sense of chivalry, I told him while I respected his motives; however, if something like this happened again he would be grounded for life!

Angel was just ten at that time and devastated by her brother's absence. After our talk she joined us in his room where they hugged and she lectured him on how he better not ever do something like that again.

It was great to see them so closely entwined. He was the big brother and protective of her every move and she, the little sister, had no problem whacking him upside his head at times to bring him to his senses. They fought like cats and dogs at times, but God help the one who stepped between them as they would turn their joint attention to the intruder.

I hadn't experienced too many problems with Angel other than her somewhat devilish attitude at school and at home. She was impossible to deal with at times, yet could win you over in a heartbeat with her smile and charm...she truly was my angel.

Oh how I dreaded these teenage years. Their hormones out of control and feeling invincible, I now was experiencing all the pain and heartbreak that parents for generations had, even though my problems were mild by comparison to those of many of my friends whose children escalated to stealing cars and joining gangs. "Yes, I can count my blessings where my children are concerned," I relished telling myself.

I had been such a rebel growing up, continually cutting school to go off and party with my friends. I was not particularly close to my mom during my teen years. My perception was that she seemed to enjoy pointing out my pudginess and other imperfections.

By fourteen, I was already passing for legal age and frequented the bars with Layla. When I turned fifteen and she seventeen (with a driver's license) we would head over to New York City where the drinking age was only eighteen compared to New Jersey's twenty-one. It was easier to pass there and we took advantage of the opportunity.

I was truly a child of the 60s and was already smoking pot regularly and experimenting, with the exception of sticking a needle in my arm, with every drug I laid my hands on. It was my escape from the pain of reality.

My children were much easier on me than I had been on my parents, so it was difficult to feel sorry for myself. I was rather proud of their accomplishments -- I, we, must be doing something right.

Jimmy had run away again just after my first return from Europe. I had just co-signed a loan for his purchase of a new reliable car when, persuaded by two female acquaintances, he cashed in all his savings bonds and treated them all to a wonderful cruise to California. I refused to be the grieving mom this time and called juvenile probation in order to have a runaway status and unlawful use of a motor vehicle placed on him. This would, as I knew from my work as an emergency dispatcher, help give authority to the police in picking him up rather than simply lecturing him and letting him go. On his voluntary return, the fourth of July, he again told me it had nothing to do with any problems at home. I recognized his adventuresome spirit, yearning to be free.

How well I could relate to that! But, I laid down the law that he would need to contain his spirit else would lose his car for good and he was grounded from everything but work and school for the next month. I held the title in my name and refused to back away from what I felt a pretty light sentence for his spending all his college money and pulling the stunt.

Kent acted outraged that I would pass such sentence on Jimmy. The following week he announced that if Jimmy wanted to move out of the house he would back him on it. I told him then that Jimmy was only sixteen and it was ludicrous to think he could support himself on his own. I told Kent that just because his father had told him to get out at eighteen didn't justify Jimmy leaving at sixteen. It was episodes such as this that made me wonder if Kent ever really accepted Jimmy as a son.

I had already been working full time for some time and taking care of myself, so I had calmed down considerably by the age of eighteen. I couldn't wait to move out of my house and, with the help of Layla, found my own two-bedroom apartment. It was in old building with tall ceilings owned by her aunt and uncle. The building, only a few doors away from Layla's house, gave us many an opportunity to get together painting and searching out furniture items to brighten up the place. I loved the independence that came with living on my own which was why I understood so well Jimmy's desire to be independent...but if I had had to wait until I was eighteen...so would he. The world is even less kind these days and he would need the extra time at home to prepare for the vigors of life.

Jimmy did agree with my wish that he remain home until he was eighteen. He was quite the young man. I explained to him my marriage problems had nothing to do with him or his sister. I felt him old enough to understand and was impressed by his maturity. My talk had not come as any surprise to him and he even suggested Kent and I get counseling. I knew in my heart I wanted no counseling, just to get out, but this I did not let on to my son.

A multitude of other thoughts raced through my mind. I told myself it may be better just to fade out of Ciaran's life knowing it would be years before I could hold any hope of being with him on a permanent basis. How could I leave my daughter, even if Jimmy would be out of the house in another year or so? She was approaching the age when she would most need her mother. After all, how could Kent hope to relate to her changing body and needs. My first night back and already I was inundating myself with guilt.

The next day on my way to work I dropped off the pictures with an order for an extra set.

My absence must have further raised the awareness of my coworkers, who commented on how fine I looked and how much weight I had lost. Perhaps it was because I glowed after being with my love, or perhaps it was just proof of the old adage that "absence makes the heart grow fonder." I didn't care, nor dwell on it, but merely relished the compliments.

I found myself still obsessed by thoughts of Ciaran and as soon as the pictures were developed, did not hesitate to send him a set with a letter proclaiming my love for him. I told him how I thought of little but my next plan of escape back to his waiting arms. I was disappointed in myself for not being able to let him go, which I felt would be better for him. I had determined that he was a grown man and would have to deal with, as I did, whatever lay ahead for us and pray that our love was strong enough to see us both through together or separately.

Kent and I were even more oppressed by the silence between us. After having words with Angel over her behavioral attitude problems one evening, Kent poked his head in my bedroom doorway and with a look of evil in his eyes said, "Satan is in you!"

I pointed my finger at him and said, "If Satan is in me then you helped to put him there!"

****

This was the opening. There had been so little communication between us that I seized the opportunity and asked him to join me in the bathroom out of Angel's earshot. He immediately started cutting me down by pointing out my fault in yelling at the kids when they were younger. This was one of his favorite arguments against me and I felt it was because he knew that this, my fault, bothered me so much.

I turned to him and said that I wouldn't get suckered into an argument with him as it would just turn into the usual he's right, she's wrong discussion. I told him I had had enough and that things between us were over and had been for years. We had a similar argument earlier that year, prior to my going to Ireland for the first time, when he wouldn't back me in my discipline of Jimmy. I had walked away that time. He had asked if we could discuss it and I told him then I had taken on his same character traits, therefore I had given up talking to him years ago. I felt it a waste of time since it would just be 'his way or no way'. There were too many bridges burned to back away from laying it out clearly for him now. My concerns had been ignored for years. His lack of attention and communication led to my frustrated outbursts of anger and slamming doors. He would have meetings with teachers at school, waiting until the last minute to tell me about them, making it impossible for me to attend. He would consistently contradict me where the kids and discipline were concerned. But I was complacent now and my mind made up, it was over and there would be no going back. All our tomorrows would bring about too many yesterdays and all I wanted now was *out*!

The next morning we were scheduled for a meeting with my son's teachers. Kent showed up and sat quietly to my left. Another group of parents with their teenager sat waiting sitting to my right, Jimmy had not arrived yet.

After the other parents were ushered into the conference room, I turned to Kent and told him that we needed to talk, no accusations, just to put finality to our miserable existence. "I think we need to go to counseling," he started.

"It's beyond counseling," I explained. "Too much has transpired for counseling to be effective. Truth is I'm at a point I don't want to even try to make this work." He fortified himself with his usual silent treatment while I continued, "When Jimmy is eighteen and Angel out of eighth grade, we'll need to sell everything off, split it down the middle, and go our separate ways. I think it important that we maintain some resemblance of civility to one another for their sake and remain as we are until Angel gets into high school." The high school was in a different town and he understood my wanting not to tear her away from all the friends she had grown up with by splitting up now. I didn't like hurting him, but I knew for so many years, and felt he did too, that our only reason for being "husband and wife" was the children. They were getting older now and I couldn't see us staying together any longer as it was as harmful to them, living in our ever-growing disfunction, as it would be if we parted our ways once and for all. He sat listening without a word. I attempted to make it clear to him in a quiet yet determined voice that he should consider us "officially" over and we could talk about it more after the now rapidly approaching holidays. He decided to leave before our turn came to go into the conference. Jimmy showed up a few moments later. He and I entered the room together, met with the teachers, and he was lectured about raising his now falling grades or be placed back in the main school, which he hated.

Thanksgiving came and went without word from Ciaran and I could not hold back my old insecurities anymore.

He promised he would write. I rationalized his lack of communication by reminding myself he must be busy with the difficulties he had been experiencing before I left. In addition, he told me he hated writing.

Christmas was less than a month away and I decided to spur him along with another short letter asking him if he had forgotten me or what. I received a letter from Christine, but she didn't mention him. I got another from Tom who also didn't bring up Ciaran's name, leaving me an impression that something was wrong or Ciaran had found someone else. When I sent cards to them, I asked straight-out for word of Ciaran and hoped they would speedily reply with some small news of him.

Time continued to drag by without any word from Ciaran or anyone else in my Eire. I felt my heart and spirit breaking. Any joy I thought I had achieved was now overshadowed by the murky haze of despair. I tried to justify not receiving a Christmas greeting from him as the mail was moving slow due to snow storms on the East Coast. Even Layla's card to me took over ten days to arrive and she had told me she sent Ciaran a card also...how much longer then for word from Ireland?

It was nearing New Year's Day, over two months since I last saw him and I couldn't purge from my mind thoughts of him...why hadn't he written? Was he safe? Was it all a game to him?

Breaking Heart

Why do you wait to proclaim your love?
To send sweet word from heaven above.
My heart is breaking, do you care?
Gray-blue eyes and darkest hair.

Each passing day brings me new pain,
I wander aimlessly in drenching rain.
My suffering heart is torn in two,
as no sweet word has come from you.

You asked me how to prove your passion,
I said to write in sweet a fashion.
In the past you wrote with dear reply,
yet now I think you've said goodbye.

Please don't let it end this unknown way,
to touch sweet locks again I pray.
But if it's over before it's begun,
then I will not to your strong arms run.

Am I just being naive? Should I go to Ireland come May as I originally planned? Ah, now, that was the question.

To return to Ireland and find him in the arms of some other woman could prove the final straw to my increasingly fragile psyche. It would take great mental preparation to even approach him. If only I could somehow see him without his seeing me...but that would be impossible.

The wheels in my mind continued to churn when, (perhaps it was my reading one too many mystery novels) I came up with what I thought would be the ultimate plan. My memories turned to when I was eighteen and out with some friends for Halloween. I wasn't usually one for dressing in costume but we had all partaken of the festivities and the various costume parties going on at the bars that night. I had found a long black wig and covered my face with eye shadow, liner, rouge and the like. I didn't normally wear anything more than a bit of cover and blush so my appearance was certainly different. Different enough that I was not recognized at close range by several of my closest friends. Even an old boyfriend had not recognized me when I ran into him at one of the bars as he tried his same old lines on me in trying to win a conquest for the night. I never did let on to him who I was but enjoyed the satisfaction in rejecting his advances instead.

So went the general scheme of things that night. I started thinking that this may work for a return to Cork. I was proficient with accents and could easily dye my hair possibly fooling everyone after a six month absence. But how would Ciaran react to this act of deception if he found out?

No, I told myself, it would be better to not return at all even knowing that I had to have answers before I could ever again sleep at night. I could return to him as myself and point-blank ask him why he was rejecting me.

On New Year's Day, I came across Tom's phone number. I had completely forgotten he had given me his number on my last trip. I toyed with the idea of calling and thought it wouldn't be out of place to call and wish him a happy holiday.

With trembling hand, I dialed the number. "Hello, is Tom or Rose in?" I asked the female voice on the other end.

"Yes, this is Rose."

"Rose, this is Colleen. How are you?"

"Oh, Colleen, how very nice of you to call. Tom is down at the hospital. Janie, his friend, just had a baby."

"It's so good to talk to you Rose. How is everyone...Christine?"

"Oh, she's pregnant you know. She showed me your letter...it was very nice."

"Is it her Thomas' baby?"

"Yes. They're living together now."

"Ah, so he's made a commitment to her and the child then?"

"Yes, at least he's done that much."

"She's a sweet girl and I could easily scoop her up."

"And how are your children?"

"They're fine...simply beautiful and fine. Rose, I must ask," the words sticking in my throat, "how is Ciaran?"

"He's a miserable sight," she told me with a genuine sound of concern. "He's been doing nothing but drinking and won't talk to anyone. No one knows what's bothering him."

My heart broke at the news. "Oh, Rose. I hate to hear he's not well."

"Won't even tell Tom what's wrong. When are you coming home? Would be a help for him...not until May is it?"

"I'd like to come as soon as March. I've worked many extra hours at the police department and should be able to put the plane fare together sooner," I explained. "But I haven't heard a word from him since I was last there."

"Oh, you know how he is...hates to write. But, he loves you, rest assured, he loves you Colleen. All he's been doing is drinking and he's been losing even more weight since you left." She said.

"He had many items on his mind other than just us," I explained. "Tell him that I phoned to say hello and please give my regards to Tom, Christine and the gang. But don't tell him that you told me of his condition...he wouldn't like that."

"Come home, Colleen, he needs you. We'll see you soon."

Pulling out a fresh pad of paper, I began to write and rewrite and rewrite, a letter to Ciaran. I didn't sleep at all that night trying to put words together that would not be harsh sounding, yet would clearly let him know my concerns. So much had been on my mind. I knew that Rose said he needed me but how could I know that I was the root of his withdrawal and not one of the other concerns. He told me he drank heavily when his son died and perhaps now Jane was the one who left him so depressed. He hadn't drank much at all when

I was last with him and so knew that he used it as an escape from his aching mind. How could I blame him for that as I found myself increasingly locking myself in the bathroom to enjoy solitude with a glass of Cream and warm candle-lit bubble bath.

It took me a full two days of revising the letter. Having used up completely the writing tablet I started out with, I finally felt comfortable with the wording and mailed it. I told him in the perfumed letter that I had heard quite a bit with regard to Ireland lately...the new divorce law and President Clinton visiting Dublin in addition to hearing a new Irish group, The Corrs. I told him how I had talked with Rose and based on that conversation coupled with my heart of faith, had booked tickets to return to him in March. I continued by telling him, "I feel compelled to tell you that I am not what Mary would make me out to be...I am no whore! Not that I care what she thinks (truthfully, I feel sorry for her), but only what you think. I refuse to feel ashamed of my love for you as my marriage was over years before we met. I am a faithful one-man woman and a mother who loves her children to the point of her own unhappiness. I rationalize this is why I feel no guilt or shame and believe even the angels smile on us. Even God did not condemn David for his love of Bathsheba, how could I think He would condemn us. David suffered only because of his cowardly act towards Bathsheba's husband in sending him to the front lines of battle knowing he would be killed. I mention this only because I sensed your concern the night before I left when you mentioned the commandment about not coveting thy neighbor's wife."

I went on to tell him, "No one can know what the future will hold for us, my love...we both realize there are many forces working against us. With you I have found a joy and happiness I never felt before. My love for you is true...true enough to let you go if that is ever your desire."

"I believed you loved me when we were last together.

If this is no longer the way you feel, or if it is, then release me from my confused and agonizing thoughts and write me of your feelings. I will not return to you if that would be against your wishes."

Instead of the usual snow storm, the weather had turned to rain, which only served to add to my depression. I was miserable at home and had only the future goal, still several years away, of being on my own to keep me from going insane.

I couldn't help but fantasize about wanting to spend my life with Ciaran. He would work on fixing up an otherwise broken-down cottage near the sea until I could join him. The living room and bedroom would be the only rooms completed when I arrived. He had handmade the bed frame from a beautiful light colored pine. The mattress was soft enough to sink into with a divan covering the quilts I had earlier sent over. The large glass doors opened to a wooden deck that completely surrounded the ocean side of the house. The lace curtains blew gently into the room from the salt-sea wind. We would use the second bedroom as a guest room, for when our children came to visit. The small coal fireplaces found in each room would keep us warm in the long winter months and we would both live happily ever after...a lovely fantasy that I prayed could somehow come true but in my heart, I knew, it never would...or would it?

Less than a week after I had mailed my last letter, a card from Ciaran arrived. I was elated and sure that the people at the post office must have thought me a nut as I ripped open the envelope, which held no return address, to peak inside to see if it was from him. It was signed "Lots of love, Ciaran, xxx." I read the note as I sat in my car outside the post office. It felt I was in heaven. I knew there would have been no way that he had received my recent letter but, I was undisturbed by its contents as it was written from my heart.

As soon as I walked into the house, I retreated to my bedroom where I called Layla to tell her the good news. She had been so worried about me and the depressed state I was falling into. Our last phone call, just after I had spoke to Rose, was tear-filled. I didn't want to wait to share my blessings to help alleviate her anxiety for me.

"Hey babe, how are things?"

"How are things with you?"

"Wonderful...perfect...never been better."

"You heard then!"

I briefly told her the contents of the letter which had stated that his last correspondence must have crossed mine in the mail...yet I had never received any other letter from him but this. We concluded that I should drop him another line right away lest he think that his letters were being intercepted by Kent. With the joy in both our hearts at my happiness, Layla and I vowed to talk again within the next few weeks.

I made some dinner for Angel as both Kent and Jimmy were out for the evening. As she sat working on her homework, I decided to celebrate my joy through the refuge of a bubble bath. I listed to the music of the Corrs' song, Runaway thinking that it most accurately reflected what I so much wanted to do...runaway with Ciaran...leave my troubles behind and be with the one I love.

After the relaxing half hour in the tub, I pulled Ciaran's card from my purse to read it, once again, in the privacy of the bathroom. Almost immediately I noticed...how could I have been so blind! It wasn't even his handwriting. I re-read and examined each word comparing them to the letters I had received from him in the past. All the a's were different as well as the c's and the signature was obviously not his own. "Why would *he* do this?" I asked myself. "Or *who* would do this?" The writing was in script, not a style he had ever used before. And, a fancy, womanlike script at that. If Rose was responsible then she had done this before I spoke with her on New Year's Day as the postmark from Ireland was in December.

"Is it possible he would have dictated it to someone else," I asked as my head grew dizzy from the never-ending questions. "Is it he or somebody else who would deceive me this way?"

Perhaps he really is illiterate. This was not a new question as I had thought he may not be able to read and write after first meeting him, when he asked Tom to write out his address for me. The thought had remained with me until I had received his letters...but, then perhaps he had someone write those too. On my last visit with him though, I had watched as he read the newspaper in Kevin's living room. But, I was reminded that it was I who had done the road sign reading as we traveled. But, he did map out our route with a pen on my map...not something I believed he could do without being able to read.

I knew it was not Christine or Tom who had written the card as I had samples of their handwriting from the letters they had sent. But, I had nothing of Rose's writing style. Maybe it was Rose's way of securing my return to him as he was in such bad shape at my parting. This thought was not comforting either as my concerns for his well-being and that I was somehow hurting him permanently by our long-distance relationship only increased.

Then again, perhaps I was his game after all. I had done most of the chasing after him. He told me how he hated to write. Was I so caught up in love's blind eye that I missed picking up on the signs of being nothing more than a passing fancy?

I was tormented and was trying to decide on following through with my plans to return to Eire in March. The tickets were non-refundable and non-transferable, "Besides," I concluded, "I must know the truth!"

The only reasonable explanations I would accept from

him would be that either he was unable to write due to a broken hand or an admission that he had fooled me into thinking he could read and write...not an unknown feat for some clever illiterate. It's not that these people are ignorant or unintelligent...it's that they somehow missed learning this basic skill through poorly adapted school systems that simply pushed kids from grade to grade without developing their true potential.   Or, there was always the possibility he was dyslexic.

I made up my mind not to forewarn him by writing to tell of my questions. Rather, I would wait until I was with him in March. I would kindly ask him to write out a post card to Layla for us...if he refused then I would, just as kindly, gently confront him with my suspicions. If he did write out the card I would immediately inspect the writing to see if it compared to his first letters to me. Then, I would, not so kindly, confront him with my misgivings with regard to our relationship and why he would treat my feelings with such inconsiderateness as to have someone else write, and sign, a card to me under his name.

"Yes, there's much Mr. Kelly and I have to talk about," I told myself.

He had more than ample time to have answered my last letter and it was over six weeks since I had written him, and only two weeks until my flight was scheduled. Yet still I had no word from *him*.

I was consumed with having to find the answers to my questions regarding his possible rejection and deceit.   I continued to persuade myself that perhaps he was trying to be the strong one for both of us, knowing things wouldn't work out.   Or, perhaps his feelings had changed about me or perhaps I was just one of the five fs after all. There would be only one way to know for sure. I had to see him one more time. I had to know why. I had to look in his eyes and find the reasons.

I loved him and felt betrayed, confused and hurt beyond anything I had ever known before. I had placed all my trust and dreams in him and now...insecurities or no...something was terribly wrong.

Sweet Isle

I love you, impossible though I know,
If but to ask, with you I'd go.
I alone be held guilty of the crime,
I had to leave, a blink of time.

Love under the sun, the stars, and moon.
I had to leave you all too soon.
Soft kisses and gentle embraces,
circling mind the pain encases.

Sweet God in Heaven forgive I plea,
I'd been lost so long, an endless sea.
But in his arms I felt pretty found.
Now all I want, Ireland bound.

Are thoughts for me or know my plight,
gray-blue eyes, hair dark as night.
Your passing fancy may well you think,
into this muddled mind I sink.

If you love me only and call me yours,
I will venture to your distant shores.
Beckon me home to your sweet isle,
cross me oceans in short a while.

Were you being true when you said you'd wait?
Will mystery lead to heaven's gate?
I'll bare your pain and I'll be your friend,
and be true to sweet or bitter end.

On angel's wings I'll come back to you.
Love me alone and I'll be true.
Emerald Island, I'd call you home,
now and ever, no more to roam.

Chapter 9
What Am I Doing?

"I would be with you forever because I've completely fallen in love with you," I had thought only a short time ago.

I tried to make myself as comfortable as possible for the long plane ride. I wondered if he would use the same lines on Candace from Georgia as he had used on me. No one knew I was still coming as I had sent off a letter to Rose, knowing she would spread the word, saying I may not be able to make the trip after all. Therefore, if I chose to take on my disguise no one should suspect I was in the area. If I chickened out, it would be a pleasant surprise for at least some of them. I had toyed with the idea for over a month and prepared, just in case, by packing a black hair dye rinse along with a complete make up kit, jewelry, and a new style of clothing. In addition, I had shed of an additional fifteen pounds since my last visit. Sleeping pills helped pass the time and I drifted into a deep slumber.

After landing in Shannon, I immediately made my way to Cork, booked a room, made myself up and went to McNamaras where I knew he would show up sooner or later. It was dark and the pub was full when I walked in. He was sitting at one of the bar stools as I walked over, conveniently placing myself next to him as I ordered my drink. He offered me an apple juice; I took him up on it, buying him one in the process. He struck up conversation with Candy as easily as he had with me when we first met. "Hello, I'm Patrick. Who might you be?" He even used the same phoney name. He didn't recognize me at all and continued with his flirtation until the bar shut down. Ushered out the door by Michael, Ciaran, (a.k.a. Patrick), asked me if I'd like to go with him to his place to finish off the cans of juice he had purchased and now had tucked securely in his denim coat pockets. At least he had a place this time. It was as if I were reliving the first time he and I had met, only this time I didn't refuse his advances, but easily joined him in walking to his flat.

He would stop us every now and then telling Candy he "knew it the moment he saw," her and that he loved her. These were the same lines he had used on me and I knew then and there that I had been nothing more than another conquest to him. What an idiot I had been! He toyed with her about the southern accent and commented on how lovely her black hair was. He ran his arms up the sides of her waist catching a feel of the size of her breasts, as he had done with me less than a year before. I told him I felt he should know that I was married, to which he replied that was no problem for him, "I like them married or not," he said, "no difference to me."

I felt the anger welling up inside me and thought I would explode. How would I handle his advances once in his flat? I had so hoped this would not have been our outcome. I had prayed that he was depressed without his Colleen and had some reasonable explanation for his spurious letter to me.

We walked up the steep stairwell to his flat where he opened up a can of cider and offered her a glass. He wasted no time with his advances and I played along for a while, finding myself eventually under his weight on the sofa he used for a bed.

"So you love me?" I asked.

"Why naturally," he told me without stopping his wandering hands from pawing her.

"Then it won't matter to you if I have a small problem," I watched for his response.

"What kind of problem could you possibly have?" He said. "A lovely women like yourself couldn't possibly have any problem."

"I have no protection with me. Do you have any?" I asked.

"No, I don't find it necessary...much too uncomfortable. I'd much rather feel myself inside you naturally." He tried to convince Candy as he started in with his kisses and hands reaching up the front of her blouse. "It's really much nicer without, don't you think?"

So rubbers were for sluts but not for the one you love?

Waiting until we had completed the act I said, "I'm glad it doesn't matter to you about my problem."

He stopped puffing on his fag and sat up straight in the bed and with a new sense of concern written all over his face said, "And what problem might that be? Thought we had taken care of it."

"Just a wee bit of herpes," I told him as the self satisfaction of a revenge filled my heart. "It's not much and I don't think it's active right now. But you'll have to be careful from now on with who you're with."

"Ya don't t'ink." The anger was more than apparent in his eyes as he started pacing around the room like a caged lion. "Ya don't t'ink..."

"...just so long as you enjoyed yourself," I said with a final cocky toss of my hair.

I woke from my dream with a start to the sound of the plane's landing gear. My heart was pounding and I was sweating. It took me several minutes before I realized it had been a dream...nay a nightmare...that could very well come true. After all, he never did write me during this last absence but for the card that someone else sent on his behalf. The only good that came from that was that it convinced me that I must go through with the disguise if I were to ever learn the truth. After all, he had deceived me, didn't he? Revenge may have been in my unconscious mind, but it was not in my heart...only a unquenchable desire to know the truth.

The plane landed on time. I knew my way around from Shannon, so I boarded the bus to Limerick. I would need to prepare myself, therefore I found a simple bed and breakfast to spend the night before continuing on to Cork. My evening was filled with perfecting my costume. I had styled my hair differently while still in the States, parted down the middle rather than the side part with bangs he had gotten to know. I poured the mixture over my blonde hair, dried it thoroughly, and gazed with amazement at the new person who now stood looking back at me from the mirror. "I hardly recognize myself," I thought with greatest self-satisfaction.

My early years in theater helped me create the effect I needed. I practiced applying make up and strategically placed highlights, narrowing my nose and enhancing my eyes. I felt confident that he wouldn't know who I was and I would, at a minimum, be able to put an end to my tormented thoughts.

I left early without anyone seeing the stranger who had spent the night in their home. The bus arrived in Cork on Monday at three in the afternoon. A bitterness seemed to start filling me and I knew exactly where he would be, McNamaras or Jackies, spending his unemployment check, quickly emptying his pockets so he would be broke again by midnight. I waited for darkness to help perfect my deception. Feeling it prudent to try out my facade on someone who had dealt with me on my past trips, I checked into the King's Inn where Aiden was tending the bar.

"Hello," I chirped in my best southern accent. "Do you have a room available?"

"Why yes," he answered with not even a hint of recognition. "Would you like a room en suite?"

"That would be very nice, thank you," I said enjoying the way he doted over me.

"Your first time in Ireland," he asked as he handed me the registration slip.

"No, I was here once some time ago," polishing both my story and southern accent I planned on using the upcoming evening. "But I spent most of my time up north visiting relatives. This is my first time to Cork. Is there anywhere special you'd recommend?"

As he carried my luggage to the room, he told me about Blarney Castle, the various churches and how to get to

Cobh. He even offered to take me for a ride around the following day if I would like. "That's very nice of you," I covered, "but I'm married and I don't think it would be a very good idea, do you?" The last thing I wanted, for the rest of my life, was to ever fall victim to a man's counterfeit affections again. I'd rather live out my life alone than to open myself up to the ultimate hurt and humiliation ever, ever again. Perhaps my young girl's impressions were right after all...love is just another four letter word for fuck!

Aiden backed down immediately with a look of disappointment in his eyes. Handing me the key he added, "If you change your mind, I'd be glad to escort you, married or not. I promise I would treat you with the utmost respect." I thanked him for his hospitality, feeling completely full of myself as I closed the door and dove upon the bed with the knowledge that my disguise would provide complete secrecy.

After a few minutes, I heard voices whirling around in my head. "What are you doing? Why are you doing this?" I reviewed the justification to both these questions that had tormented me since I first arrived at the decision to deceive. Why...I was seeking out truth the only way I could think of, because my restless and broken heart had grown a barb-wired fence around it. I had to be able to control my heart, which was again growing cold as stone and bitter with disillusion. Yet, I wanted so much to be proved wrong and maintain the softer, gentler spirit he created in me. "No, I was not going to talk myself into being old Miss Trudy Prudy. I had come a long way and I must follow through. After all, I already committed myself by committing adultery in his arms, what difference would what I was doing now make," I cynically told myself.

Touching up my hair with a light spritz of hair spray, I readied myself for the coming evening. I slipped on a camasol, suit jacket and black hose. I chose to wear a skirt -- he had never seen me in one before. My disguise had worked on Aiden whom I had seen on several occasions when last here. Would it work on the others who knew me better?

It was after nine when I walked into McNamaras. The Crowd busied itself spending the Monday checks. The pub was full as I had expected it to be. I didn't enter without being noticed but to my joy, unrecognized. I saw Tom sitting with Ed at the bar. There was Rose sitting at the same bench where I left her last October. There was no sign of Ciaran, so I sauntered up to where Tom and Ed were sitting. Tom and Ed both fawned over me without a clue as to who I was. Tom had risen from his seat offering it up to me and telling me about all the possible choices for a pint. When he got to the Buhlmer's cider I told him, with my ever thickening southern accent, that it sounded charming but would try a Guinness instead.

Ed started in right away with his old antics of taking my hand and kissing the knuckles one by one while singing his favorite Sinatra song, New York, New York. "Some things don't change," I told myself.

"Where are you from in the States," Tom asked.

"Near Atlanta, Georgia," I told them.

Rose called Tom over to where she was sitting and after a short discussion he returned with her to where I was.

"I understand you're from America," she remarked.

"Yes, Georgia. I've never been to Cork before," I told her. "Do you live around here?" I was at first concerned she had seen through the lipstick and rouge and would give me away at any moment. But, it became increasingly clear she was simply curious about the newcomer.

"Just down the road," she told me.

"I hope it's not improper for a lady to enter a pub here on her own."

"Oh, no, no problem at all. I often come here by myself," she assured me. "Would you care to come join us at the table?"

"That would be very nice, thank you."

"It was working, now hold on to yourself Colleen," I assured myself, "you can do this." Ten o'clock was fast approaching when Ciaran walked in. He looked even leaner than when I last saw him and I felt my heart stuck in my throat as my eyes followed him to where he walked up to the bar. He was with another man who I later learned to be his new room-mate, Paddy. They spent time saying hello to Tom and the others, glancing quickly to and away from me. "He hadn't a clue," I told myself then turned to Rose and asked, "Who's that?"

"Oh, the tall one's Ciaran and the other is Paddy," she answered. "Some of the regulars here." She picked up on my interest in Ciaran immediately when I asked her if she would introduce me. Tom looked somewhat dejected that my interests had focused on this newcomer to the pub rather than him as Rose called Ciaran over. "Ciaran, come over to us here"

"Maintain, maintain," I kept telling myself.

"A moment Rose, let me put down me pint first," Ciaran answered.

His first pint went down in less than sixty seconds and it wasn't until after he finished a second, and received his third that he came over to where we were sitting. Rose placed him sandwiched between us. "Ciaran, you must meet this lady from the States," then turning to me said, "What is your name, dear, I forgot to ask?"

I reached out my hand to Ciaran and with all my best flirtation skills emanating said, "Why, hello, my name is Candace, but my friends call me Candy." He hadn't recognized me at all. He even seemed distant and uninterested. Maybe the southern accent wasn't a good idea after all.

"It's lovely to make your acquaintance," he politely answered as he quickly shook my hand leaving it to dangle midair.

Mary entered the pub and immediately focused her attention on Ciaran. "So... perhaps this was the cause of my rejection," I thought. But the thought rapidly dissolved as Ciaran avoided her conversational advances. "Sorry, didn't realize you were with a new slut," she said as she retreated to one of the other tables with a look of hurt and disgust.

"Pay her no mind," Ciaran told me, "She's like that when she's been at the drink. Don't mean a t'ing."

I found it difficult to gain Ciaran's attention for any more than a minute or two at a time. Rose seemed to be enjoying playing match maker and continued to try to draw his conversation. She would whisper in his ear from time to time and he would then turn to look at me asking questions about my home and if I had ever been to Cork before. "Where are you staying?"

"Just down the street at the King's Inn," I answered. He grimaced noticeably and I asked, "Is it a bad place?"

"No, of course not, just too close to the guarda station for my taste," he said then excused himself from the table.

"You're not leaving," I asked reaching my hand out to take his elbow.

"No, be back in a minute," he answered while patting my hand to reassure me.

I turned to Rose and quietly asked her, "Is he available?"

"Yes, dear."

"He doesn't seem very interested, perhaps I should just go ahead and leave now."

"No, dear, you don't understand," she started. "He's just been to much to himself for a while. It would be good for him to get to know you better. Don't be too concerned, he'll come around I'm sure. Why, he's already told me how attractive he finds you."

"Well, I'm not looking for a big romance or anything

like that. But, I must admit I find him a very handsome man. Is he married or engaged which makes him act so distant?"

"The woman he was last involved with is far away. I think you may remind him of her as she was from America also...but, she's been out of the picture for quite some time and I don't expect he'll ever see her again."

"Why's that?"

"Well, I don't like to talk about such things but, since you're asking, it was because she was married. He's completely over her now...just a bit rusty is all. Why don't you ask him to walk you to your place," she said.

"That's a wonderful idea...I will."

Seizing an opportunity to get a sample of her handwriting I asked, "Rose, would you please write down your name and address for me so I can send you a card when I get back home?"

Handing her a piece of paper and a pen she easily agreed. I watched as she wrote the words. The "c" in Cork was not the same "c" that was used in writing my name on the Christmas card. The mystery continued.

Paddy was very friendly and before long wanted to exchange addresses with me so he could have a new "pen-pal" in America. As soon as I saw him write out his and Ciaran's name I knew he was the one who had written the letters.

There was no doubt, the fancy circling tail that started and ended was his! I tucked the paper in my pocket and got up to leave. "Why would he have done this?" I wondered.

Michael was making one of his last calls when I asked if Ciaran if he would walk me home.

"Oh, I'm sure Tom would be happy to escort you," he told me.

"Look," I said, "I realize I'm being quite forward but I'd really prefer if you walked me to my room. I'd like to get to know you better."

He smiled and agreed, seeming to be more than open to my advances now. After all he was a man with a man's needs, not to mention at least seven pints of Guinness in him. Michael and Maggie finished escorting the crowd out the main door, placing Ciaran and I, joined by Tom and Paddy, together outside where we started our walk downtown. Near the stairs I knew Tom would need to take to his home, I conveniently fell back with him a moment and asked if he would leave me alone with Ciaran as Paddy had already made his exit. Tom graciously, but somewhat reluctantly, agreed and bid us goodnight at the base of the stairway.

"Would you mind very much if we stopped off at my place," Ciaran asked right after Tom's departure. I told him that would be fine with me. He then took me by the hand and with his long legs walked quickly towards his flat which he kept telling me was "just a little bit up the road." He stopped us occasionally just long enough to kiss me, catching the feel of the sides of my breasts along his arms. He was working me to his bedroom to fill himself with a night of sensuality. I was relieved he didn't use the same lines on Candy as he had on me. There was no, 'I knew it the first time I saw you,' or words of loving me without knowing me.

His flat was neat and clean and with no signs of Paddy, he walked me to his room. The bed was made and the television had been left on, tuned into international news of America.

I resisted his initial seduction in order to get a closer look at how he lived. On a table near the bed I saw the picture of us I had sent him. As I continued to wander, my eyes caught glimpses of the gifts I had given him, tapes, photographs, and even the handcuffs I left behind were set on the entertainment center.

"Who's this?" I asked pointing at a second picture of us placed next to the cuffs.

"No matter to you who it is," he snapped. He was

sitting on his bed now gesturing for me to join him.

"I don't mean to pry, but Rose was saying you had a girlfriend in the States," I pressed. "Is that her?"

"Don't be paying any attention to Rose." He didn't bite, but insisted by patting his hand upon the mattress, "Now why don't you come sit next to me here." When I hesitated he added, "I thought you were into the craic and wanting to be with me tonight."

"Now, sugar," I said, "don't be like that, why she even looks familiar to me.   What's her name."   Ignoring my persistence he offered to walk me home. "Oh, no darlin' that won't be necessary."

Here I was with the man I loved, deep in disguise and feeling justified because of his deception towards me. He took my arm and pulled me to him on the bed. His lips avoided mine but rather descended down my neck to the low frontal opening of my camasol. He pulled out a condom and placed it in my hand. "Oh, that won't be necessary," I told him. "I'm on the pill."

"But you don't even know me!" He said as he pushed the package into Candy's hand. "And I don't know you. We'd best not go on if you're unwilling to use it." I was elated. I was falling in love with him all over again but still could not understand why he hadn't taken time to write me himself. He had been turning out to be all I had thought him to be. It was good he saw Candy as the slut she was. How would I break it to him that I was who I was and not this southern floozie who was eagerly being seduced.

"You seem quite anxious," I told him as he made his ascent up my blouse with his large slender hands. It was unlike the touch I had experienced with him. This was a new, less gentle Ciaran that lay before me.   He started to persistently move my face towards his penis. This too was new. I had volunteered this service to him in the past without any prompting or pushing from him. This man who lay under me was a stranger and I was thrilled he treated her so dissimilarly from me. Now I must come up with something to jar him awake to my facade before things went any further and pray he would forgive me for my actions...and that I could forgive him!

"Let's just say it's been a long time." he said as he pulled his pants further down his thighs with one hand while pushing my mouth to lower on him with the other.

I had to break this off. I jolted up demanding as myself, "What's my name?"

He looked at me oddly as I spoke the words. "What's my name?" I demanded again.

He didn't say a word as he stared at me. These had been the same words I spoke to him our first night together kissing outside McNamaras.

"What's my name?" I repeated in a softer tone.

"Jesus Christ! No it couldn't be. My mind is going." He said as he jumped from the bed and began pacing around the room.

I got up from the bed. He was looking out the window and without recognizing I was Colleen, not Candy, said, "It'd be best to take you to the King's Inn now."

I slowly turned him around, placing my hands strategically on his neck and stroked his hair along the side of his ears with my fingers. He quickly pulled my hand away.

"It's a lovely ear." I told him, running my hand down his chest. He continued to look at me as if he knew the answer, but refused to admit to it. After a brief period of silence I confessed, "Look past the makeup and hair color and you'll see that it's me, Ciaran Kelly."

At first I thought he was going to collapse as he began to fall back but caught himself on the window ledge. He then suddenly reached forward and snatched me up in his arms.

"What the fuck are you doing Colleen?" he sternly asked as he started to push me away from him.

I wasn't going to allow him an upper emotional hand and immediately inundated him with my interrogation. "Why didn't you write, Ciaran? What happened to us? You left me no choice but to try and find out what was going on. This was the only way I could think of." The rambling that had gone through my mind for the past six months came out in a waterfall of emotions and inquiries. "I thought I was going to lose my mind without you. Please forgive me for this deception, but try to understand I have to know. Why, Ciaran, Why!"

He seemed to quickly resign himself to my deception and without any anger left in him said, "Why couldn't you leave well enough alone."

"Ciaran, what are you talking about?" I grew increasingly anxious for the answers. "I thought you loved me...or have I been merely a game for you? I apologize for the disguise but it was the only way I could think of to try to get at the truth."

I sat down on the edge of the bed with tear-filled eyes while he sat in the chair that was, in this small room, butted up against the foot rail. "Please Ciaran, tell me why, without any explanation, you have chosen to reject me."

"Colleen, Colleen. It's not you, it's me." He began. "You've been no game and you shouldn't be thinking that way. It's all my fault. I'm no good for you, can't you see that? I haven't worked steady in years, my settlement has never come in and I don't know when it will. I can't provide for you, and...it would be better you had just forgotten me."

"How could I ever forget you?" I asked. "I love you as I have never loved anyone before. I believed you thought bad of me being a married woman and throwing myself at you the way I did. Do you really think these things make a difference to me. We can make this work Ciaran...if you want it to. Together we can do anything, I'm sure of it!" The tears were flowing down my face freely now as he got up from the chair and joined me on the bed.

"Don't cry, Colleen. I should've handled this differently," he said as he placed his arm around my shoulder to console me. "I didn't mean to hurt you. I do love you but it won't work, can't you see that?"

"No, I don't see that," I whimpered. "You say that you love me -- then prove it by believing in yourself as I believe in you Ciaran. Besides, if I wasn't just a game to you then why the Christmas card?"

"What card?"

"The Christmas card you had Paddy write me for you."

"I had him do no such thing," he insisted.

I pulled the card from my backpack and showed it to him. "I know nothing of this," he said. "I chose not to write at all hoping you would become angry and forget me. What makes you think Paddy did this?"

In answer to his question, I removed the piece of paper he had written out earlier that night and showed it to him. "Compare the writing."

After a brief inspection, he concurred with my findings. "I don't understand why he...but that he knows how much I love you and that I couldn't write expecting you to want me Colleen. I'm no good..."

"I'm sure he only meant right by it, Ciaran," I told him as a sense of relief and total forgiveness flooded my heart. "And no more of that "no good" talk from you. I take you the way you are. I love you Ciaran, with all my heart and soul." Then I asked, "The letters I received before were from you?"

"Of course!"

"I can't tell you how happy that makes me," I exclaimed, thankful my thoughts of his illiteracy were unfounded. Not that it would have mattered to me if he were; but, at least now I knew the words were private between us two as he would not have needed any assistance in proclaiming his love to me.

I looked deep into his eyes and he into mine. The temptation to jump him was beyond measure and he clearly felt the same as we both fell into our deepest desires and back onto the blankets, where he wrapped me neatly and comfortably in his arms. Words couldn't describe the elation I felt as he made his way slowly, methodically, his familiar path up my skirt. Working his way down my stockings and up again, ever so gently, rhythmically to the throbbing of my heart. We didn't speak but to proclaim our love during our first two rounds of love-making that night. At the third round I started blackharding him. I had fetched a bowl of warm water and soap and proceeded to massage him with the sudsy liquid. He knew from past experience that this would lead me to gentle tongue probing of his cherished area. Finishing with his bath, I placed the bowl next to the bed and began to run my lips and tongue down his naked body starting at his neck, then slowly down his hairy chest, to the area that would most appreciate my attention.

I began to kiss him in that shadowy place which sent him immediately into ecstasy's delight, I stopped, looked up at him and asked, as I had the first time a year before when I performed this same act, "You'll hold your flow back?"

"Of course," he barely had the answer out of his mouth as I continued my tongue search of his palpitating mass.

Stopping again and with a glimmer of a grin on my face, I remarked, "You're sure."

"You know me better," he said.

I ran up and down with the tip of my tongue slowly making my way to the orifice which quivered with delight. I stopped abruptly once again and, hardly able to hold back my laughter said, "You're absolutely sure now, I wouldn't want to be compromising your enjoyment."

He thrust his head back upon the pillow laughing with

frustration as he said, "Just get on with it will you? Fuckin' woman driving me mad! Ya tease!"

"Just don't be pushing on my head like that slut you started out the evening with!" I was not going to let him off too easily.

"Ah, yes, what was her name...Sugar or Sweetie...something like that. Yes, she was a jewel of innocence," he said baiting me.

We both laughed and I went on with my massage more seriously now, wrapping my lips securely around him, I rotated my tongue around, then worked my way down, then up, then down, then up.

He reached down to me, tugging me farther up on the bed, turning me on my stomach as he did so. Spreading my thighs ever so gently, he nuzzled himself near to me.

"I want to feel you inside of me," I pleaded.

It didn't take much encouragement for him as he sweetly penetrated me more gently than ever before. "I love you," he repeated the words. "You're a crazy woman, but I love you, right!"

The weight and motion of his body against my buttocks rocked me softly into the mattress. He reached his hand around to the front of me, fulfilling both our climactic energies with his gentle thrusts and exploring fingers. My hands grabbed at the pillows next to us, allowing me to dig in my nails from the overwhelming rapture he filled me with. He did not stop even after I felt the warm fluid flowing freely between us. He continued to stroke my most sacred place until I reached a height of orgasmic ecstasy that went beyond words of human expression or comprehension -- still he did not stop. He slowly pulled himself from me only long enough to roll me on to my back. As he gently penetrated me again, I was left breathless yet completely immersed in his wondrous seductions. Still he did not stop. He rolled over onto his back, never disengaging from his primary position. I sat up in order to straddle him, rocking him gently between my thighs while contracting the muscles of my sacred secondary lips to pull him even deeper inside. Beads of sweat descended from my heaving breasts and he pulled them to his waiting kiss, gently massaging my nipples with his native tongue. And, still it was not at an end. Once again, he placed me on my back reviewing his repeated and rapid thrusts of passion. We went on for hours, not wanting it to end. Finally, after a final propulsion, he gently collapsed on top of me in exhausted euphoria, nuzzling his lips to my neck while stroking gently the outer regions of my breasts. He whispered, "I'm sorry Colleen, I have never loved anyone...never before you. Please forgive me, mo grah..."

"I love when you speak Gaelic to me, my love." I told him, "it rolls off your tongue with the ringing sound of romance."

"Mo grah, means my love," he whispered. "And you already know that "cor tu solas I mo speir" means you are the light in my sky...and you are my light, my love, my life."

We rose to watch the sun rising over the tops of the buildings of Cork City. He stroked my black hair saying, "you look quite the different women I must admit."

"Do you like it then?"

"I like you whatever way you look, you know that, right." Then after a short pause, "How shall we let the gang know who you are?"

"Some will probably not be as understanding of my charade love, as you have been. It may be better for the rinse to wear off before I show myself there again and act as if I had just shown up. What do you think?" I inquired.

"We may have a bit of a craic with it," he told me. "How long will that stuff in your hair last?"

I explained that it should fade out after just a few days and he said he wouldn't mind showing the gang that he was over Colleen now by having latched on to the southern filly,

Candy.

"It may be fun at that to see how Tom and Ed will react. I'm sure they'll have many a 'tear into her' quotes ringing out." I reminisced. "Even Rose, who was, after all, quite anxious for you to spend the night with Candy to help you get over me. I wonder what she'll tell Colleen when I show up in a few days?"

"Let's do it then, no one will ever know and no one will be hurt." He concluded. "But we'll need to stay clear of the pub until you look more yourself."

"Once my hair is back to blonde and the makeup off, I think they will only be able to draw one conclusion."

We spent the next two days off by ourselves. I charged (even though I could ill afford anymore on my credit card) a rental car and we drove to Killarney, then explored the outreaching areas we had missed on our previous sojourn to the Ring of Kerry.

He was over his feelings of inferiority now. How could I possibly hold anything against him as my insecurities had ruled my life for so many years I could easily relate to his. We thoroughly enjoyed our days together and found a lovely field where, in the middle of a heavy rain, made love.

Lay Me Down In The Paddock

In the green of the paddock lay me down,
gentle breeze surround me, heather my crown.

Take me in your arms day and night,
call me sweet to you tame twilight.

Give me the soft dream and I say so,
clouds for our bed, ribbons and bow.

I will love you by evening and all the day long.
Lovers envy our promise yet lift it in song.

And the lorries make music as fly they by,
luring you from me...deepening sigh.

And I'll wait in the paddock, purples and green.
Return beloved to me in shadows unseen.

****

We made our plans for returning to Cork. I would suddenly show up at McNamaras, suitcase in hand, looking for him and watch the reaction of our friends having not seen him since he left with the fluffy Candy girl.

To my delight, Rose was sitting at the bar when I walked in. I wished I had my camera ready to forever freeze the look of shock on her face. "Why Colleen, what are you doing here?" She nervously asked. "I thought you weren't coming."

"The tickets were non-refundable...didn't want to throw them away. Besides, I wanted to surprise Ciaran. I haven't heard from him for a very long time, do you think he'll be pleased?"

I thought she was going to choke on the words, "Why of course he'll be happy to see you. He's been a miserable sight since you left, as I told you when we talked."

Ciaran wasted no time in joining me inside to observe the reactions of those around the pub. He acted at first as if he didn't even notice me when I called out his name. He then walked over to us, hugged me, and said, "Why Colleen, what are you doing here?"

"I hope you're pleased," I told him as I noticed Rose nervously expecting Candy to walk in behind him. "Have you been behaving yourself?"

"Of course!"

I excused myself to the ladies room giving Rose her opportunity to help him cover his ass in case the seductive Candy were still lingering around in the shadows. "Where's the one from the other night?" She asked him.

"Well away by now, I hope," he told her. "She was good enough for a night." He told me later how happy she was at the thought of his tearing into Candy and enjoying himself. I knew Rose's loyalties lay with him and not me.

When I returned from the ladies room, I found Rose whispering in his ear and thought I would have some fun as I could easily tell she was trying to come up with a story to help him out if he needed it. "So what's this I hear about some dark haired American you were seen with the other night?"

"Now who'd be telling you a t'ing like that? Why, has been no one but you, now isn't that true Rose?"

She backed him up completely. She told me how he had been with no one since I left six months earlier and couldn't believe that someone would say such a thing.

"Not that I'd have much problem with it, anyway, Ciaran." I said while trying to hold back the grin. "After all, I told you I would hold you to nothing, with my being so far from you, to keep up with your needs. I do hope she was clean and you took care of things, if you know what I mean. Just so long as you've saved some for me!"

I thought Rose was going to have a cardiac. She couldn't comprehend how I could be so understanding and hold no grudge or acts of jealousy. Ciaran ate it up. "That's one of the t'ings I love 'bout ya." he said.

Tom and Ed walked into the pub at that moment with jaws hanging wide as they saw me standing next to Ciaran.

"Why Colleen," they chorused, "how nice to see you back with us."

Tom had walked right up to Ciaran pulling him to the

side to ask where Candy was. Ciaran told him he wasn't sure. He told Tom that Candy was a good time for a day or two and nothing more and how he just had a knack for picking up the married ones and told Tom, "you know me Tom, find 'em, feel 'em, fillet 'em, fuck 'em, and forget 'em."

Ciaran and I continued with our ruse with us privately exchanging smiling glances of our inner knowledge from time to time.

Our friends sat back and accepted my return with occasional glances to the front door expecting Candy to walk in and start a fight at any moment. I thought I would further the fun and said, "You know, my cousin was due to meet me here but I'm not sure if she's made it yet. Has anyone stopped by looking for me?"

They all said no one had been looking for me when I added, "Her name is Candy and she's from the Southern United States so her accent would be much different from my own."

Now I thought I was going to have to perform CPR on several of them at once and watched as Ed almost fell off his barstool. "Don't recall having seen anyone like that," he said.

I thought Ciaran was going to burst out laughing, but instead played the almost-caught lover giving glances of apprehension to those around us.

It was not even closing time when we retreated from the pub with my suitcase in hand. "We had quite the time didn't we." He retorted.

"Yes, but I admit I feel bad, though not too bad, at our deception."

"Oh, but it was alright for you to deceive me," he laughingly said as he slapped me on the butt during our ascent of the stairway to his flat, "You should've been an actress."

We stayed mostly to ourselves the next several days with only occasional visits to McNamaras to watch the increasingly amazed crowd enjoy our banter and signals of love.

We had several conversations about my impending divorce and the possibilities of our future together. I told him he best write me as he had promised in the past so as to not have me come back a redhead next time. He said even if the worst came, he would be sure that I knew what was happening. He had been successful so far in stopping Jane from selling the house and had been trying every legal possibility to keep the children in Cork. He didn't seem at all confident that the final result would be what he hoped for, but I tried my best to encourage him.

Lover's can be so strange in their devotion for the other. He was willing to give me up, the woman he clearly cared for, rather than have me tied to the loser he felt himself to be. For me, I wanted answers and dressed in costume to get to the bottom of the situation.

If the old concerns of age, religion, distance, and lifestyle posed any apprehension in my mind, they all disappeared as we frolicked in the noontime mist, making our plans for the future. When he received his settlement and I my portion from the divorce, we would put the money down on a cottage. We would rent a portion of the house as boarding rooms to help pay for the mortgage allowing us more time together. We developed our dreams for a glorious future together.

I explained I wanted nothing elaborate and that we could live quite simply; in fact, "I long for a simpler life," I told him. We could both work part time and with the boarding rooms rented, could well afford for our children to come stay with us for summers. He knew how difficult it was for me to think about leaving my kids and how selfish I felt...even if they would be of a more mature age by the time of the divorce. Ciaran reassured me we would have the children with us as often as possible and I would certainly visit them in the States any time I wished.

We filled our days and nights embracing and relishing every moment with each other. Just another year or so, we told ourselves. Certainly we could deal with that. He would arrange a trip to meet me in Pennsylvania this fall. We'd stay at Layla's for a while, then he would return to Ireland to purchase the house.

Our joy was unending, but our time together was not. My flight left in just two more short days and we set out to make the most of them.

He had borrowed a car from a friend and drove us to Derry, Northern Ireland. It was a pleasant town, but I longed for the coastal roads, so we made our route by way of Dromore and Killary Harbor, then along our familiar way to Galway, then back to Cork.

We looked at houses along the way, talking about where we would like to settle.

I no longer felt lonely as Ciaran made me feel like a rejuvenated woman -- not a mom -- not a wife. A woman with passions and desires boiling up inside, ready to spill over...and only with him.

"With anyone else it would be just sex," he reassured me, "and you have spoiled me forever in that regard. Why do you think I had waited so long to even entertain the thought. After all, it was a beautiful stranger who seduced me. All her fault, I'm as innocent as a new born lamb," he chided. "No, I'll never make love to anyone but you again."

"Just be sure to make friends with 'Mr. Righty' then, and stay clear of any other beautiful strangers," I joked, "Remember, it may not turn out to be me in disguise next time."

We wrestled playfully and fell into each other's embrace our last night together.

My first trip, we met and feelings inside grew into massive insecurities which I overcame to return to him. During my second trip, we fell in love and his insecurities almost forced our goodbye. On this, my third trip, we fell even deeper in love and in so doing felt all our insecurities disappear and our spirits filled with contentment.

Mo Muirneach

As Autumn approaches I again will see,
my beloved smile down his light on me.
And speak sweet Gaelic to my face,
mo muirneach touches tender place.

Then take my hand and draw me near,
and lay to rest my childish fear.
To feel his warmth against my chest,
in his strong arms I take my rest.

The answers to questions that I once sought,
seem pointless now and bring to naught.
Mo muirneach, dwell where you belong,
and chant anew with devoted song.

Under crescent moon with a longing heart,
with you I will all my love impart.
And I will dote over you with such a fuss,
as wings of angels brush next to us.

Chapter 10
Pennsylvania

My life was not without event as the months passed. As a firefighter/EMT, I had responded to several incidents involving fatalities. The first was within weeks of my return and involved two fifteen year old girls who were hit head-on by a drunk driver. One of the girls died a week later, leaving the other behind with a life now changed forever. The second, even more traumatic, and located almost at the identical place where the girls' accident was, involved two vehicles. Again, a drunk driver at four o'clock in the afternoon. His pick-up truck hit head-on with a compact car, killing that driver instantly -- his wife followed him within a half hour.

Both incidents were particularly stressful for my guys. The first, not only due to the senselessness of the drunk driver, but because the girls were so young and we knew their families.

I had been working dispatch during the second collision and again found myself stuck behind a radio when I wished to have been out in the field working the scene. After the initial influx of 911 calls and dispatching applicable agencies, I quickly phoned home to check on my children's whereabouts. I heard over the radio that one of the cars was a small white compact. Jimmy had a small white compact car and this was the main stretch of highway we all traveled to get in and out of the capital city. I was relieved when he answered the phone -- I knew he was safe. I found out later that Jimmy had been just a few vehicles ahead of the accident when it occurred and I thanked God he was not involved.

There's a cold professionalism that kicks in when we work a scene. My guys were exceptional in their ability to hold back personal emotion until after care was completed. The husband, who was terribly mangled by the impact, the wife who had also been killed, in addition to the female passenger in the pick up truck who was airlifted to a larger hospital due to her extensive injuries, were personal friends of the responders. No one other than those of us who work in this field can understand how impossibly frustrating it feels to work on someone you know only to place them in a body bag. It's the least pleasant way to say goodbye.

A Critical Incident Stress Debriefing, otherwise known as CISD, was called by my department. CISD involves all emergency responders who meet to discuss the incident. CISD is not held for each incident, but only those that are particularly horrific or personally stressful for the responders. The debriefings I attended in the past revealed the emotions of many a strong willed person breaking into tears discussing what they felt, saw and did during the scene and after. This venting allowed us to express our feelings without any repercussions, since anything said was held in strictest confidentiality. Although I was invited to attend as the dispatcher for the incident, I was unable to make this session as I was still on shift.

I heard the debriefing went extremely well. Preserving the confidentiality of the meeting and only speaking in general terms, one of the officers told me he never saw a more open group of people, in touch with their feelings as well as those around them, in all his career as those of my department.

I organized a CISD a year earlier with my department's membership and personally witnessed this group of men filled with heart and soul. I hadn't a problem dealing with the scene and rode in with the burn victim to the hospital. I watched as his skin peeled off in my hands and could do little to help other than render psychological support. While the paramedic applied an intravenous line, I talked with the twenty-eight year old newlywed, jokingly, and tried as much as possible to keep his mind from what his body was going through. A furnace had blown up on him, leaving a fiery hot black coal mixture embedded into his face and neck.

His chest, arms and legs had also sustained second and third degree burns. He was burned over eighty percent of his body. Somehow I knew he'd pull through against what most saw as impossible odds.

Several of the guys called me later that evening and said they were having difficulty dealing with the incident due to their personal acquaintance with the victim. The Chief was out of town and I was asked to organize the CISD for the next evening, which naturally I did.

The debriefing lasted only two hours with police, ambulance, and our department's responders in attendance. I listened as the men spoke about their impressions. I watched as tears welled up in their eyes and eventually could not hold back my own from falling. It wasn't that I felt any problem with this particular scene, but, from the pride I felt at being part of this wonderful brotherhood. They helped me to maintain a sense that not all mankind was evil and uncaring.

I felt positive about the victim's pending outcome and wouldn't have asked for CISD for myself. Besides, this incident had helped in getting me over the one call that had almost ended my career...the fatal fire I had dispatched only a month before. It had almost broke me and I spent almost every night since that call up until this one thinking that it would be best for me to get out of emergency services all together.

It was knowing now that I could handle an on-scene situation, coupled with my continuous dissection of the dispatch tapes of the fatal fire, that helped me gain control over myself. I thought I'd never be of help to anyone after feeling so helpless behind the radio, while two children died in the raging inferno. It was pointed out to me now that it was because I was an action person that allowed me to be so calm and professional in the field, while feeling helpless when dispatching. Still, I knew that being a dispatcher also was an integral part to emergency services and was proud of my work there. Injured children are the toughest to get over. Luckily, the worst we had to handle lately was nothing more than a broken arm from falling off the monkey bars at school.

After these last two accidents, teaching multiple medical classes, and serving on various department committees, I felt I was reaching my burn-out point. I've heard that most people serving as medical technicians burn out after five years...so it was also said of dispatchers...and of firefighters. Here I was doing all three on top of teaching, working full-time, running a household and waiting for an impending divorce. Perhaps all this, coupled with my mind being preoccupied by thoughts of Ciaran, made me realize I couldn't keep up at the current pace any longer. I had perfect attendance to every meeting and drill of the department but now I began to pull back from making them. I declined several overtime shifts at dispatch and decided that I wouldn't schedule any more medical classes for the next year. While I had attained the greatest satisfaction from the life I chose, now all I wanted was to be with Ciaran.

He had promised to meet me at Layla's Pennsylvania home in October and I looked forward to getting away from my stress-filled life. He would love it there during this time of year, seeing the leaves turning into countless autumn colors. Since Layla and her boyfriend lived primarily in New York City, we would have the place to ourselves. She told me she would loan us one of her cars so we could further explore our freedom, giving me an opportunity to show him part of America.

Ciaran had increased the frequency of his letters, as he had promised, and I read each one with growing anticipation of our next time together. I had noticed a tone of something bothering him in the words he wrote but, had decided it best not to question him about it until we could speak in person. It was now September in Montana. It had been a busy summer for the state with all the publicity attached to the

Unabomber, the Freemen and the Militia. Granted, Montana certainly has it's share of fanatics and hideaways, but the fine people far out numbered the rest. Montana's pristine beauty boasted places like Flathead Lake, Yellowstone and Glacier Parks and was known as the Big Sky Country and the Last Best Place. Still, many jokes had been told, especially since the Unabomber was apprehended and held in the jail where I dispatched. I enjoyed the humor and always felt that laughing at ourselves was the first step to healing and moving on.

The weather was beautiful and I just hung up the phone to make my reservations to fly into Kennedy Airport when Kent walked in the door. I don't even remember how it began but we argued about everything. "I thought this was decided," I said.

"Sure, if you hadn't yelled at the kids when they were little," He bellowed.

He entered into his most beloved argument knowing my lack of self-control in yelling at the kids had always been a thorn in my own side. I had stopped it years ago, but it didn't seem to matter since he enjoyed pushing the thorn further into my heart. "I told you before, I won't fall for your setting me up for all the blame. I haven't been perfect, but neither have you and I refuse to get into this any further!"

"So what are you going to do, move to Ireland or maybe New York with Layla? Just tell me when are you leaving."

"When the time is right for the kids," I replied. "We'll put the house up for sale as soon as Angel graduates eighth grade in June, like we agreed, okay!"

"It'll be good to be done with you," with his added, "you're not just filled with Satan, you are Satan!"

I did all I could to hold back in view of his latest tirade.

Unfortunately, near the end of our angry discussion, I noticed Angel walk in the back door. She had heard the whole vicious argument. She ran, crying, to her room.

I poked my head inside her bedroom door and asked if she were all right. She asked me to come in.

"Please don't leave Mommy."

My heart was breaking. Kent could only have guessed at my deep desire to move away. Confronted by my daughter's unhappiness, how could I possibly go through with any plans for moving to Ireland anytime in the near future. This was the time when daughters needed their moms the most.   My feelings of selfish abandonment became overwhelming. Although I knew I'd have to continue with the impending divorce, I also knew I would have to stay in Montana until she could be more accepting of my move out of the country. I knew that could very well take years. My children were my life and Ciaran was my life, but the children's lives were just beginning and I felt like mine was over. I knew also his children were too young for him to leave Ireland.

I promised I wouldn't leave her and tried to explain about her father and me splitting up. She seemed to accept the splitting up portion of the conversation, but was concerned I would leave and she would never see me again. "No, I'm only going for a visit to see Layla in New York," I reassured her.

****

I knew before I landed at Kennedy International that I'd have to tell Ciaran of my decision to stay in Montana. I wouldn't tell him our first night together, but wait until Layla returned to her apartment in New York, leaving us to be alone. She was meeting me at the airport with her boyfriend, Paul. Ciaran was not due in until the next day, which would give me an opportunity to cry on her shoulder. I hadn't had a chance to tell her what was going on. Our lives had grown increasingly busy and but for the quick phone call to tell her when my arrival would be, we had not talked of much else the prior month.

It was good to see her shining face. She stood about five foot six, always several inches taller than me. Her face was beautiful, olive skin with dark brown eyes and hair; I always thought she resembled Elizabeth Taylor, only prettier and more sensuous. Paul was waiting outside so we, as quickly as one could at Kennedy, retrieved my bags and went to the car to meet him.

It was near dinner time and, after dropping my bags at the Milford Plaza Hotel, where I would spend the one night, we went downstairs to Mama Leones to enjoy fine Italian cuisine. Layla and I always made a point to eat there at least once when I was in town. It was especially enjoyable to have Paul join us. We listened as the waiters sang opera and musically went about their taking care of the customers.

Paul himself was quite an accomplished singer and joined in, to the enjoyment of everyone, with a medley of music from Man of LaMancha.

After dinner we went to the Stagedoor Canteen located on the other side of the building. One thing about being in New York is you don't need to travel far to cover all the bases. We sat at one of the many tables and ordered ourselves a round. Paul knew nothing of my relationship with Ciaran so, when he left the table for a minute, Layla took the opportunity to ask me if Ciaran would arrive as planned the next day so we could pick him up and drive to Pennsylvania. "I'll just be spending one night so you two can be alone."

She was such a dear friend. Always willing to go out of her way for me. In the beginning she had been skeptical of this lover of mine and the possibilities of me being hurt; later she grew to see the love as permanent...at all times she was supportive. I had reassured her our love was real and how happy I was with the possibilities of starting a new life with him in Ireland. Now, I'd have to tell her my sad news.

I spotted Paul approaching the table and asked if there was any way she could stay the night with me at the hotel to give us a chance to talk. She agreed and informed him a while later; he had no objections.

Settled in the room a few hours later, I confessed my decision to remain with my daughter. "Jesus Christ, Colleen," she scolded me, "When are you going to start thinking of yourself!"

I explained that if she had children she would understand why I had to do this. "Of course I love him and I've never been happier. But what happiness could we hope to have knowing that Angel felt alone and abandoned, and me thousands of miles away. Please try to understand. This is, of course, not easy for me."

She naturally accepted my decision after a while. Yet she still tried to convince me I was making a big mistake and that kids were adaptable. "Angel will be fine in the end," she said, "Go to him Colleen, and be happy."

Though sad, my mind was made up. I could only hope and pray Ciaran would understand. Something in my heart knew he would, however reluctant. I'd set him free to find someone closer to home that could satisfy his needs.

Layla took my heart break to be her own; we passed the evening both filled with tears.

****

She waited in the car at the airport. I saw him stepping through the custom doors, standing well above most of the crowd, obviously searching for me. "Ciaran," I waved, "over here."

He took me tenderly into his arms placing a slow sensuous kiss on my lips while saying, "I've missed you."

We walked along the polished terrazzo floors making

our way to the parking ramps. We easily found Layla, who was eagerly waiting to meet my mystery man. He had talked to her only once on the phone from Ireland and she had sent him a card occasionally, telling him how welcome he would be in Pennsylvania and how happily in love with him I was. Feeling like old friends, they embraced briefly.

We drove directly to Pennsylvania. I watched as his eyes grew large in wonderment at the enormity of the City that changed into mountainous roads then farm land. Layla and Paul had remodeled an old school house into a beautiful suburban dream home, filled with Paul's antique treasures including a full set of armor placed strategically near the entryway.

Except for photographs, it was the first time I had seen the place and Layla was more than proud and happy to give us both the grand tour.

After washing up, we joined her in the spacious living room to sit on the velvet covered Victorian sofa. I watched as she poured drinks and was excited to be able to offer Ciaran a can of Guinness. "I'm sure it won't be near as good as in Ireland," she told him as she placed the brew into his waiting hand, "but I hope you'll enjoy it all the same."

"Lovely, lovely. And very t'oughtful of you. Thanks!"

We lounged in the overstuffed chairs as Ciaran stretched out on the sofa while Layla and I reminisced about our times growing up together. "Now don't you be telling him how dodgy I was growing up," I jokingly told her.

Ciaran thoroughly enjoyed our revelry and the stroll down memory lane.

We laughed, telling him how, when we were just eight and ten years old, used to trek to New York City from our Jersey side to 1960s Greenwich Village to watch all the hippies, and palm readers. How at the same age we would sneak down to Palisades Amusement Park which was less than a mile away to spend the day. "Many people would think we were pretty wild, even by today's standards. But, really we were just a couple of kids out for the craic." I told him. He enjoyed my use of the word 'craic' in that some of Ireland remained in my mannerisms and talk.

"We were a perfect team," Layla stated as we high-fived each other.

"Yeah, you always had the money and I always helped you to spend it!" I joked. "She took good care of me. We were, are, like sisters. Her dad was my dad and her mom was my mom."

We talked until the wee hours of the morning before turning in for the night. Ciaran looked very tired, yet never once complained. He simply sat back, soaked up all our stories until I noticed his drooping eyes and helped escort him off to our room. "Good night, Layla," he called out to her, "Thank you."

Our room was beautiful, as I knew it would be. Dotted with antiques throughout with lace and velvet curtains covering the large bay-styled picture window.

Ciaran wasted no time scooping me up in his arms. I could see the fatigue in his eyes and told him, "Ciaran, we can wait until tomorrow. You look like you could use some rest."

"Not likely," he said paying no attention to me. Soon he was unsnapping my shirt and I returned the favor.

The moon shone through the skylight over our bed as we made love well into what was left of the night.

I heard Layla get up. It was already eight in the morning. Ciaran lay in a deep sleep, so I quietly made my way in to greet Layla, who would soon be on her way back to the City. "Good morning," I said. "Aren't you tired?"

"Well, I didn't have the distractions of a good looking man in my bed to keep me up. He's wonderful, Colleen. Everything you said and more. It's obvious he loves you. I could see it with every glance last night. He couldn't take his eyes off you. Are you sure you're doing the right thing? I so much want to see you happy at last."

"You know I have no choice Babe," I reiterated. "All I can do is hope he understands. I won't ask him to see me anymore. I think that would be too hard for both of us. Better we just part our ways here so he can get on with his life," I said, lips quivering.

"You know I'm with you no matter what! You can still move here if you want. At least it would be a place in the middle for you both to get together should you change your mind. And it would be easier for the kids to come see you."

"You are my best friend and I love you," I told her. "Do you have to leave so soon? Why not stay for a while and we could all go for a drive this afternoon."

"Three's a crowd, you know that. Besides, I need to get back and answer the business phones. Paul has three jobs lined out for this afternoon. Let's see, today is Tuesday...I'll be back by the weekend to get you. I booked us all some tickets for dinner on a yacht for Sunday."

"What about Paul?"

"Oh, Colleen, he's already figured all this out. He doesn't judge you. After all, I was married to Ben when he and I first got together. Don't worry about it." She told me.

The yacht. What a great idea. It was magnificent. Certainly much larger than just a yacht, more like a ferry that had been remodeled with crystal chandeliers and grand dining rooms. Layla had treated me to it my last trip with her. We sailed around the Hudson River, enjoying being fawned over by the waiters who were more than willing to serve our every need. Ciaran would love it, although I wasn't sure how he would react to such decadence. "We may need to stop off somewhere and pick him up a suit," I thought.

"Call me," Layla said as she closed the front door. "Food's in the fridge."

I made my way to the country-styled kitchen,

rummaging through the refrigerator. She had well stocked it for us. I pulled out some bacon, eggs, and hash browns, determined to cook up a traditional American meal for Ciaran.

I placed the toast on his plate covering it and the rest of the feast with one of the red checkered towels I found. With tray in hand, I walked into our room putting it down on the table along side the sleigh-styled bed. Sitting to his side, I nuzzled up to him, gently stroking his long brown locks. "Wake up love."

He stretched out his arms wrapping me in tender affection. "Not now, you need to eat and I've cooked a lovely breakfast for you. You'll need to eat it while its hot." I propped up the pillows behind him and placed the tray on his lap. As he lazily looked at me without moving I added, "Would you like me to feed you too!"

"I'll be calling you me ma if you do."

"What would you like to do today?"

"I'm at your mercy...you'll need to lead me around these right sided roads."

"And there will be no driving for you!"

I took him on a ride into New York State. It was breathtaking. The leaves on the trees had just begun to turn. We stopped by several parks along the way walking the nature trails. "It's nothing like Muckross," I said. He agreed, but commented on how rich the place was in color and was impressed by the seemingly endless, winding mountain paths.

The weather was still warm. We continued our drive until I spotted a deserted place just off the road. "We'll stop here and picnic by the crick if you like," I told him.

"Crick, crick...what the hell's a crick?"

"Creek...creek, you know, the little river."

"Why didn't you say so...a brook!"

I didn't know how to break my news to him and found myself putting it off at every possible opportunity, trying to enjoy what time we had. He too seemed distant and I kept telling myself it was only jet lag.

As we sat near the water listening to it's babbling sounds cascade over the rocks, I lay in his arms with my back resting against his chest. Under the warmth of the sun, he became frisky and reminded me of our time in the field in Ireland. He twirled me around and with my back to the ground started kissing me. I felt like we were teenagers having found a place at last to be alone and consummate our love for the first time. We made love on the blanket listening to the crinkling of leaves beneath us.

It was sunset when we returned to the quiet retreat at Layla's Pennsylvania home. We first stopped off at a pub nearby where Ciaran naturally became the center of attention. Everyone enjoyed his Irish accent and I noted how much effort he put into losing his Cork accent's sharpness to the sweeter sounding Irish that most Americans are used to hearing.

"Not tonight...I just can't tell him tonight." I told myself justifying holding back by seeing how happy he was.

We folded ourselves beneath the blankets and fell speedily into a deep and restful sleep.

Since he was more rested now, I told him I'd take him to the City. We'd spend the night on the Jersey side, where the motels are more reasonably priced. On the bus into the City, it was my turn to play tour guide and I showed him all the sights of New York. We visited the Empire State Building, Little Italy, Chinatown, and of course, that place Layla and I had earlier spoke of, Greenwich Village. After a quick call to Layla, she met us for lunch at one of her favorite pizza places. "It's not the sushi I like, but something tells me you're not quite ready for that," she said as she rushed off, giving us directions to catch the Circle Line tour of the Hudson River. Ciaran took in all the sights as I had in Ireland. We played the turkeys... gobbling up everything in sight. Exhausted from our long day, we returned to our motel room just after sunset.

The next day, I drove us to the ferry that leaves New Jersey for the Statue of Liberty. I thought he'd enjoy seeing where the Irish immigrants had disembarked. We looked for the "sister statue" of Annie Moore at Ellis Island that I saw in Cobh.

We made an early start back to Pennsylvania. Layla said she'd be by sometime early on Sunday. Still I hadn't told him.

Saturday had come quickly and we'd only have a little more than a week before we had to catch our flights of final separation. I knew I had to tell him tonight, realizing I couldn't put it off any longer.

I popped the manicotti into the oven and prepared the garlic bread for the broiler. Ciaran walked into the kitchen, encircled my waist with his arms and kissed me lightly across the back of my neck and shoulders. With my best Irish accent I scolded him sweetly, "Out with ya', you're only in the way. Get yourself off and watch TV in the other room."

I set the dining-room table in grand style, which wasn't hard to do as Layla had incredibly fine taste in china and crystal. I chose a bottle of wine from the rack, lit candles and called him into the room.

We both sat, eerily quiet, as we finished our meal. He complimented me on my cooking, then helped to clear the table and place the dishes in the washer. Then we both returned to the living room curling up on the sofa watching the fire. I had just built up enough courage to tell him when...

"Colleen," he said.

"Yes Ciaran...what is it?...There's been something bothering you, I can tell."

"I don't know how to begin..."

"You can tell me anything, you know that."

"You remember my troubles with me ex?"

"Of course."

"Colleen, there's no easy way of saying this, so I'll say it all at once. The lawyers say there's not'ing I can do. She can take the kids off anywhere she wants." He paused and I sat in silence waiting to hear more. "I was a fool in not paying attention to what she was doing back when David died. Colleen, I have to go back to her. I don't want to, please believe me, but I'll lose my children forever if I don't."

I sat in a mixture of stunned amazement and shock. She had him where she wanted and there would be nothing anyone could do to stop these wheels from turning.

"Please forgive me Colleen," he pleaded.

"Oh Ciaran, how could I not forgive you. I love you with all my heart and soul. You're doing the right thing and, while I hate it, I understand."

"I don't know that I will ever be able to see you again. She, herself, will make that impossible. It was hard for me to get away to see you now. She doesn't even know I'm here, but believes me to be working in the North."

"I guess it's for the best. I, too, was going to confess to you I couldn't be with you. My daughter is having problems about the divorce and I can't leave. I don't know when I'd be able to be with you. It could be years and I couldn't ask you to wait so long." The well of tears could no longer be held back. "I'll always love you! How I wish things could be different for us."

"Perhaps we can still steal times together somehow," he said, trying to deny what we both knew could never be.

It was out. Both our hearts emptied and were breaking with circumstances that wouldn't make any allowances even for two people so much in love. The gods were not kind to us.

"We'll have to make this final week last us for the rest of our lives," I said, as he wiped the tears from my eyes.

I could see his tears forming in the flickering

candlelight. I turned my back to him resting it again on his burdened chest. We sat in silence, watching the television, not knowing nor caring what the program was about.

Candle Light

When the shadows fall around me,
'tis your eyes I long to see.
When darkness clouds this hazy mind.
your love is all I look to find.

The candle light glows from your heart,
and makes it difficult for me to part.
And yet my spirit groans deeper still,
to fight against my common will.

For in your eyes I have found joy,
glistening sunlight in a child's toy.
You're my summer, winter, spring and fall,
candle in the darkness...you are my all.

Layla came early the next morning. While Ciaran was in the shower, I told her of last evening's heartbreak. She put her arms around me, trying to hug away the pain. "Well then, you must have the most memorable time of your lives this week!" She said. "I've the tickets for the yacht tonight. We'll have a great time! We'll need to swing by and pick up Paul along the way."

Knowing of our impending loneliness, we allowed ourselves the luxury of having a lovely meal with friendly conversation. It would be too late to drive back to Pennsylvania that night and Layla, in all her glory, had arranged a room for Ciaran and I at one of the local swank hotels. It must have cost her a fortune, but she told me there would be nothing but the best for me. There was no talking to her when she was feeling generous, which, bless her heart, was all my life.

The bed was lush and large, with a hot tub just off center of the room. We were both impressed by the enormity of it all and Ciaran was amazed with the hot tub. "Right here in the middle of the room," he remarked. It took little to convince him to lower himself into the bubbling hot water. I soon joined him straddling his legs and lowering myself onto him. "I will always love you, Colleen," he whispered.

The mindless clock was ticking away, still I refused to let the heartache get the best of me and our final hours together. I could see he too held this thought as he ethereally caressed every part of me.

"And I you," I assured him.

The clean sheets felt soft and silky on our warm, bathed bodies.

We spent the next week visiting various tourist attractions. It was as when we first met. Walking the streets, hand in hand, stopping from time to time to embrace and proclaim our love for one another.

The week flew by. Now, back in Layla's living room in Pennsylvania, we didn't want to speak a word about our impending destinies that would start with our morning plane departures.

"I wish..." I told him wrapped securely in his arms.

"What Colleen, what do you wish?"

"I wish what you wish. I want what you want. I guess it was never meant to be for us," the tears again formed in my eyes. "But we both have our obligations and what possible dearer obligation than that of our children."

"I hate her for what she's done," he said in bitter tones.

"Don't, Ciaran. Make the best of the cards that have been dealt and don't forget, I too, had a difficult choice for us...This is not all your doing."

"Will you be all right...with the divorce and all?" His voice grew more concerned now. "He wouldn't hurt you...I swear if he ever lays a hand on you I'll..."

"No, it's not like that. He'd never touch me. I'll be fine, please don't worry about that. I've been on my own before and Layla has offered for me to come here at some point and help me get set up. But, right now I don't know when that might happen."

His embrace was tighter than I had ever felt before as he started to caress my cheek with the back of his hand. "Would've been better, you think, had we never met?"

"No...you mustn't even think such a thing," I said as the tears I had fought back all week started to flow down to meet his hand. "At least we have both known true love...what more can anyone hope for in all their lives. So many go through life never having what we have had mo grah."

"Mo grah," he said, "you remembered."

"Of course I remember. I remember everything you said, did, and have meant to me, my love."

He looked tenderly into my eyes as he started his dear and loving caresses. His large hands massaged my back and reached up under my flannel shirt to unhook my bra strap. The fireplace provided the only light in the room and created a warm, cozy atmosphere. He knelt on one knee in front of me on the plush carpeting and held out his hands gesturing for me to place mine in his. "I'll always love you, Colleen Keating," he said softly. He lowered me to his place on the floor, removing my shirt as he met me with his embrace. Submerged in his eyes, which never left mine, he slowly started to remove his shirt and placed his skin next to mine. We melted back onto the floor, where he unzipped my jeans, placing his slender hand within.

"I want you so much, mo grah," he whispered.

I raised to my knees to work the pants down my legs, fully removing them. I felt no shame in my nakedness with him nor he me as he mimicked my motions with his hands reaching out to assist. I then helped him to remove his garments, gently stroking his tender place with my small, frail hands.

I sighed deeply as he lay me prone upon the soft carpet. From his posterior position he placed both hands to the forepart of my torso to gently knead my breasts. He then descended lower and lower until he reached my eager destination. He continued with his gentle kneading motions against me until I cried out for his infiltration, "now...inside me...now."

He turned me over to again look into his eyes with the weight of his upper body placed fully on his two strong arms. With his familiar gentle thrust, he found his place inside of me. "Deeper...deeper," I pleaded, my eyes rolling back in ecstasy.

His accommodation to my request came quickly with repeated thrusts of desire; he now lay fully on top of me, kissing my neck, eyes and lips with intense passion while never slowing his throbbing mass from it's enchanting duty.

We were melting into one another as we did my last visit with him in Cork. He quickly turned me back onto my stomach, stretching my arms over my head. Then he dropped low onto my body to retrace his steps back up my thighs and buttocks with gentle kissing and probing of my blooming flower.   Then, with a drive of consuming delirium he catapulted us into a place that, even within our prior experiences together, we had never known before.

"You take my breath away...do you know that?" he asked.

"And you took mine a long time ago!"

His plane would take off first the next day.

****

Layla left me to be as alone with him as possible in the middle of this massive airport; regardless, we were completely to ourselves among the crowd as we bid farewell. Before he boarded, we hugged and kissed as if there were no tomorrow, and now we both knew, once and for always, there could not be. I took my cue from our past departures, telling him that I loved him and goodbye. I turned, walked away and could no longer hold back the gasping floodgate of emotion.

I felt two hands grab at the back of my shoulders. Thinking some mad man was about to stab me, I pulled myself free turning around and startled to see him standing there. "Ciaran, oh Ciaran, what are you doing? You'll miss your flight."

"I can't leave you like this Colleen," His kisses swept over my face. "I love you and if I can find my way out of this mess, I'll join you in Montana so you can be close to your daughter.   We can take turns between there and Ireland...somehow I'll work it out. Please Colleen, tell me that you love me and that you want this too."

I fell into his arms and thought my light head would lead me to faint. "I do love you Ciaran, I always will."

Kissing me for the last time, he started back for the gate where the final boarding had already taken place. He called to me as he handed his ticket to the agent, "I'll write you Colleen, I'll write."

Layla had witnessed the episode and consoled me, telling me everything was going to work out in the end. "A man who loves a woman that much won't let himself be held back," she told me.

But, I knew Irish ways were not our ways and his ex would make it as he said, 'impossible' for us to be together. Besides, how many times could we endure the heartbreak that came along with our goodbyes?

Layla sat with me until I boarded my flight a few hours later. Yes, God, I am loved. Everyone should be loved this much once in their lifetime.

Desire

My soul burns with a golden fire,
as consumed I am with heart's desire.
Ring of friendship, loyalty and love,
brush of angel wings from above.

Thoughts of you start each new day,
as in your arms wish I could stay.
When evening comes I name a star,
wandering visions to where you are.

Enchantment overwhelms my dreams,
prance on the water sunlight beams!
With snowdrifts mounting on the banks,
for your devotion I give full thanks.

For as desire burns deep within my soul,
loneliness fled this young new foal.
Soon again wish I could take my rest,
and lay my head on your loving chest.

I have given you all my heart and mind,
and prayed we'd mold this tie to bind.
In my heart you've placed devotion,
and will hold me with your lovers' potion.

Chapter 11
The Beginning

Grandmother moved to the northeastern part of the United States before I was born. She'd often visit us in Montana, then fly me back with her to her small cottage near the sea. My Uncle Jimmy had made a career of the military and was stationed overseas for many years; he and his family joined us in New England as often as possible for the holidays.

One of my fondest memories of childhood was when the family gathered around the Christmas tree which stood in front of the large pane glass window overlooking the ocean.

In the middle of the night I sometimes woke to find my grandmother gazing out at the wave surges from her bedroom balcony and I knew, even in my youth, that there was a special longing in her for the sea. I was only ten years old when she first told me, "Never settle for anything less than true love, and never be afraid to tell someone you love them," -- words she repeatedly told me as I grew into adulthood.

She spoke these same words with even more emphasis when I announced my engagement less than a year ago. "Better to spend your life alone than lonely. Better you become a nun than to be anything less than you are, which is exactly what you'll be if you ever settle for anything short of your true desires in this world. Trust me on this, Caetlin, the Lord won't leave you to be lonely. For you will always be in my prayers and there is a lovely Guardian Angel already watching over you. I've made mistakes and only want to try to spare you the heartache that less than true love brings. Don't allow yourself to become nothing more than a metronome sojourning through this world as a click-clack of monotonous existence. We make our lives what we choose. With God in your heart, make and walk your own destiny mo grah, all I ask is you don't allow your heart to become cold and dull."

Her sincerity and caring sparkled on each word like the fresh morning dew on spring roses. I tried to convince her that my fiancé, Mark, was an exceptional man. He was tall, handsome and well on his way to becoming a successful pediatrician. We had known each other for over three years. When he asked me to marry him I was elated and couldn't understand why she was distressed at my saying, "Yes."

"I just don't think he's the one for you," she told me when I phoned to tell her the news. "Of course, I could be wrong. Only you can know for certain. Be careful not to make him a substitute for the real thing...else you'll both wind up miserable."

"But, Grandma, I do love him!"

There was no anger, only concern in her voice as she told me, "Do you Caetlin? Do you really...be careful, mo grah, for marriage was meant to last forever and it's through our insecurities and the necessities of life that we seem to fall into it more as a convenient circumstance rather than for the right reasons."

"I'm sure. He is a wonderful man. Caring, loyal, responsible..."

"Sounds like he'd make a good lap dog, but may not serve much as a husband. You know I'll stand behind you whatever you do, but I wouldn't sleep well at night if I didn't voice these feelings of mine to you. They are built from years of experience and two bad marriages...I just don't want to see you ever unhappy. Can you honestly say you feel a passion for him? Do your mind's thoughts drift during the day to hold nothing but him? Do your dreams hold only fantasies of his touch and your desires? Or do you merely see a man who can provide for you and possibly give you some happiness through the years? You are as independent as I have been...will he be able to accept that in you? Is he affectionate and romantic enough towards you...if he is now...will it continue, do you think? I don't pretend to know all the answers Caetlin...only you can look deep within your heart for the truth."

I found myself wondering if she had ever known the true love she so often spoke of. I was sure she hadn't found it with my grandfather, nor her first husband either, although she cared a great deal about both of them but more in the way of a friendship. Perhaps with one of the other men that were in and out of her life, although I could never recall a time when I saw her with a man other than as a friend.

As the only woman firefighter, she was surrounded by men. But she never spoke of any of them with anything more than "sisterly" love.

I had recognized a compelling desire in her for Ireland some time ago, but she never indicated to me, in all our many talks, that there was some special "one" there, either.

Still, I never saw the look in her eyes as when she gazed at the photos of her trips to Europe. I remember her talking with unique fondness of her driving escapades throughout Ireland...the gardens...what did she say about the gardens?

She looked so frail lying in her bed. Even though she was only in her sixties, I knew she had lived the life of excitement that many people would never dream possible, even if they lived twice her years. I held her hand in mine as life slowly drained from her. The scent of her perfume circled my senses.

"I'm so very glad you came, Caetlin," she said. "Don't look so unhappy dear, death is a natural process freeing us from this temporal life to a more glorious one, full of love and forgiveness...you know how much I believe in life."

Her words did little to comfort me as I knew she would soon be gone. She had insisted on remaining in her New England home to die and had sent for us just days before.

"Angel, darling, try and understand, I'll not be dying in a hospital!" she had told my mother. "Hooked up to a bunch of tubes, with nurses in and out...wouldn't give me a moment's rest. And to what purpose? The inevitable is inevitable and not to be feared nor prolonged. Best to die in my bed where my dreams and the sounds of the sea surround me undisturbed."

"Your wedding is only a few months away."

"Yes, grandmother."

"I still believe he's not the man for you."

"Mark really is a good man," I said trying to convince her of the match. I didn't want to argue with her now.

"Sometimes, 'good' is not enough, Caetlin. All I ask is you be careful with the choices you make. You'll have to live with them all your life." She continued, "I know you must make your own mistakes and commandeer your own path through this life. I'm an old woman, riddled with cancer, and close to death's door...your life is just beginning...don't worry about me, for before the night is over I'll be singing with the angels. The last thoughts I leave you are not unlike what I have been telling you all your life...Never be afraid to tell someone you love them...Don't worry about playing the fool, as the Lord will shine His endearments on you and heap coals of fire on the heads of those that purposely hurt and wreak destruction on others. You'll be their better and can walk with your head held high. Don't risk someone passing through this life without your having spoken the words. But, remember, there are many different forms of love...you know the old cliche' it's better to have loved and lost than never to have loved at all?"

"Why of course, I've heard it many times," I told her.

"Love only with your whole heart, Caetlin, and remember, never settle for anything less! Friends and lovers may come and go, but true love never dies...it endures for, nay, even beyond a lifetime."

She had excited herself trying to assure that I understood. I soothed her by gently rubbing her forehead only to have her move my hand away saying, "No time to be fawning over me child, for there are only moments left." There was an urgency in her voice as she pointed at the old oak vanity sitting cris-cross in the corner. She was barely able to raise her arm, and, with ever laboring breaths asked me to retrieve a wooden box that was neatly tucked beneath her bits of lace and linens. I handed it to her, laying it in her lap as she gestured me to do, when she said, "Caetlin, you're so very dear to me and the others so far away, or perhaps it's because I see so much of myself in you that I want to give you something that tells my heart's deepest thoughts and desires. It's a book of poems I've written over the years. I'm entrusting them to you."

"What would you like me to do with them grandma?"

"When the time comes, do with them what seems right...you'll know."

I had seen only two of her poems over the years, as she always held them a private part of herself and didn't share them freely. I was honored at her gift. I was also amazed at the thickness of the journal she placed in my hands as it must surely have contained her life's work. "Take good care of them for me Caetlin," she entreated, "and don't think too harshly of me as you read them."

"How could I ever think harshly of you," I said as I looked into her green-hazel eyes with wonderment. Here was the woman who held the greatest influence over my life, yet I felt I had barely known her. "I love you Grandma!"

"I know that dear...love, true love, knows deep within the soul when it is requited. I hold myself fortunate indeed to have been loved in my life and I cherish your love so very, very much." With these final words, she breathed her last breath as I dropped my head to her chest, groaning out my loss of her.

****

    She had wanted to be buried back in Montana and had made all the arrangements with the assistance of her attorney well ahead of time so no one in the family need be burdened. The funeral, complete with an Irish wake in Montana, was now over and I was busy preparing myself for the return to the New England cottage she had left me.

    In the privacy of my old room, I curled up in the window box to read the treasure she had given me. A light hint of snow began to fall, more typical for this time of year here than the rain, mixed with intermittent sunshine, which fell earlier that day.

    The pages fell open to a poem marked with an old, dried-out flower and was dated June 5, 1995.

Ireland

Fresh heather, kind clouds, and spring rain,
Emerald isle, green waters, with eyes gray-blue.
Leaving you ferries me to both heartache and pain.
Trapped in the mist of my thoughts for you.

Dark hair, gentle locks, and brightest smile,
"Tear into her" and "I say so", you said beaming.
Still seizing more of my heart all the while.
Wanting you again I went home heeding.

Soft shadows, sweet words, and evening glory.
Stealing, then winning, my affections.
Could what you said fly away on wheels of lorries?
Or be spoken to another upon reflections?

And I wonder, do you think of me ever?
And I ponder, and I the fool for loving you?
Then I thunder, was our love truly forever?
Though seemingly impossible through and through.

Surrounded by soft kisses and warmth I long to be,
wrapped by you in the moon and starshine.
When I close my eyes 'tis only you I see.
Sheathed within your strength and arms entwined.

Sweet Ireland, my love, how I long to be back,
safe within your caress and shielding care.
Let's not goodbye but have another craic,
for 'tis only adieu until into you again I tear.

For it is written on the winds, ignore our foes,
then once again with you I can be true.
God will not be too unkind as He well knows,
you have touched my soul forever...I love you.

As I continued to read through the pages tattered and worn from years of handling, I began to see a fire and passion unknown to me before. Her poems told how she must have fallen in love when in Ireland. The man's name was not mentioned in any of them and that point seemed unimportant to me now...still I marveled at their devotion to one another. I devoured the contents as colored prisms of sunbeams cascaded through the stained glass window, falling on the pages of the open book.

Another was dated September 25, 1995. I immediately knew the meaning of the Gaelic title for she had used it as an endearment to me through the years, "Mo grah", my love.

Mo grah

"Mo grah", I'll whisper in your ear,
and give to you my love so dear.
And try to fill your yearning heart,
on gypsy wagons and farmers cart.

"Mo grah", you'll say in sweet reply,
as wipe old teardrops from my eye.
And hold me tight in endless embrace,
before Cupid we lay our sweetheart's case.

"Mo grah", I'll state to you once more,
and touch you deeply to your core.
For I feel myself grow weak of knee,
as your piercing eyes look down on me.

"Mo grah", you'll clutch me to your chest,
and give to me your cherished best.
My heart forever yours, we stand combined,
beloved vision we're now assigned.

Her poems loomed up at me, pulling me ever deeper into her weave. Oh, Grandma Colleen," I thought, "you both gave up so much. How unselfish, how beautiful your love for each other." The final poem was incomplete and spoke kindly of her affection for him and how they had to part due to family obligations and some darkness that came between them. Even though it was obvious to me that she had fallen in love with him while still married to my grandfather, it didn't seem to matter. "A lover can become your friend...and while not always true, it can prove a great mistake for a friend to become a lover," she told me with regard to her relationship with my grandfather.

The journal slipped from my hands and fell to the

wood floor. An envelope, hidden deep within its sleeves, fell out. Picking it up, I immediately recognized her writing and removed the perfume scented stationary from within. "Mo grah," it began. "How I yearn for you and the tender way only you could touch my heart. So much time has passed without word between us and I have spent these years looking out over the ocean to my Eire with longing thoughts of our love. We promised we would respect our decision and I do knowing it was your unselfish nature that forced us to part. We overcame so many of the differences that could have eventually broke our spirits. But, we could not overcome the loving obligations we held for our children. I want you to know that I believe with all sincerity that your feelings have remained the same towards me all these years. Be assured that I have never stopped thinking about or believing in you and your innocence. I realize I need not write the words as you already know my heart. Yet, I am compelled to say once again that I have and will remain always, deeply, passionately, and completely yours. Until I see you again in paradise...ta me I ngra leat, now and always. Colleen."

The letter was without name or address to give away her secret lover.

The Promise

Promises made in heat of night,
while lovers' passions fire.
State the pledge then take our flight.
Lost in our intense desire.

An island unto ourselves we flee,
as morning brings its light.
The harsh cruel voice of reality,
now sadly in our sight.

Now kiss goodbye and sweet assure,
love's ambitions in vault be kept.
Who knew what fate would have in store,
first joyous then silent tears be wept.

Now I understood the urgency in her plea for me to know true love, since she had found it only after other sad relationships. I felt I had just finished reading the finest romance novel of all time...and it was all true and personal, which made it that much more special to me.

Sealing it with a tender kiss of affection, I placed it back in the hope chest she had given me as a wedding gift. She had known for some time her end was near and wanted to make sure she had attended to this detail, giving me the cedar chest that at one time held all her personal memorabilia. I remember the day she cleaned it out, watching as she threw all it's contents into her small fireplace, telling me, "There comes a time that a woman wants her private life kept private to all but a very few. Only God can judge the heart. Use the chest for your most valuable possessions, Caetlin. And, I don't mean blankets and the like that are merely temporal. This is a chest for keepsakes of the heart. These letters that I toss in the fire were my keepsakes, but now the memories contained within these cards and letters from a lifetime are forever cast well within my soul."

Even though she disapproved of my marrying Mark, she would never have abandoned me, just as she hadn't abandoned my mother and Uncle.

I found myself dreaming restlessly over the love story she had revealed to me. I held a vision wherein I saw her walking barefoot on the clouds. She was a young woman again with her dark golden locks cascading down her back and wafting gently in the breeze. She turned, looked at me, smiled and said, "Do you know it now, mo muirneach? My Ireland...my Eire...my longing heart...my one true love...my

Ciaran."

"Of course!" I should have known...the way he looked at the albums at the funeral...now her words seemed obvious to me even before she spoke them.

"Do you understand now what you must do?"

The dream held too much reality for me not to see it as a vision from beyond and therefore I naturally wanted to respect her request. "But how will I find him?" I asked.

No sooner had I thought the words than her voice, speaking with the clarity of fine crystal, spoke to my spirit, "he's leaving on this morning's flight. You can catch him if you hurry."

Even though the airport was small, when I arrived, I frantically rushed around looking for him with no success. Then, after I was close to giving up my quest, I caught a glimpse of him about to enter the boarding area. "Mr. Kelly...Ciaran...please wait."

"Why Caetlin, how nice to see you." He said smiling. "What brings you here?"

"My grandmother wanted you to have this," I explained as I handed him the entire journal. "There's a letter inside to you and I know she wanted you to have it." I opened the journal handing him the letter and was glad he didn't wait to read it but opened it there with a look of great anticipation. I watched as a tear formed in his eye then slowly made it's way down his cheek dropping to the floor.

"T'ank you," he said reaching down to give me a hug. "T'ank you so very much." Neither of us spoke another word as I watched him turn away from me. Before he started back through the gate, he stopped, wrote something out and handed me a piece of paper with his address on it and said, "Come visit me sometime...I'll show you Muckross and the other places Colleen and I went...she'd like that."

"How did you know about her passing?" I inquired.

"Why, Layla, of course," he told me.

He walked through the gate for the last time and I watched as he disappeared from my sight, just as I knew my grandmother must have done so many years before.

****

Months later, the charges of her poetry were still fresh in my mind as I approached the alter to take my vows. Not until this late date did I acknowledge I was about the make the biggest blunder of my life. I turned to Mark telling him it would be the biggest mistake of our lives to go through with it. I then reeled around, looked at the crowd, apologized to the hundred and fifty guests neatly tucked away in their pews, pulled my long train over my arm and ran down the flower lined aisle throwing my bouquet behind me.

I couldn't hold back the giddy laughter as I lunged out the tall oak church doors to freedom. "Thank you Grandma," I thought, "thank you. I really understand now and I promise you I'll never settle for anything less than you found with Ciaran!"

His Love Is A Beacon

I will sail me the sea with the wind in my face,
set myself proudly as in love run the race.
I am crowned in his splendid and glorious eyes,
a new world beholds me as my old orbit dies.

He encompassed my thoughts and all of my dreams,
and laid in me fires of sweet passions it seems.
His love is as a beacon in a mid-winter storm,
as wrapped himself 'round me in original form.

He took my heart in his hand speaking sweetly his charm,
his honored protection assured I would never know harm.
As the angels play their harps he played me his song.
And made his sweet love to me all the day long.

Read the continuing story of Colleen Keating in Book 2 - *Irish Hearts - Beyond The Tears*...coming soon to a book store near you.

****

IRISH HEARTS - Beyond The Tears

Successful in backing him off I retreated to the comfort of my bed after taking a nice long hot bubble bath. As I lay back running the silky foam over my legs and breasts I found myself mixed with emotion. I don't remember ever experiencing a panic attack before but I was sure I was having one now. The thoughts whirled around my mind, Alex, Jake, Kent...all these men who were complicating my mind...wanting something from me I was unable to give...wanting to possess my soul if I'd let them. Then one calming vision came into my being, filling my heart and soothing my inner child...Ciaran. "Sweet Lord, will I ever be able to move on?" I thought to myself. Even these sweet thoughts turned to torment when I started to think, "where is he now? Is he still with Jane? Does he ever think about me? Would he still want me even if it were possible?" The floodgate of insecure thoughts opened wide. It must be this new attraction I seemed to feel for Alex that triggered these newly confused and agonizing thoughts.

Look for Ms. Thomas' sequel
Irish Hearts - Beyond The Tears
coming soon to a book store near you.

****

Use This page to order additional copies of
Irish Hearts - Caress Across the Ocean.

ISBN 0-9667714-0-0 ** $12.00 US/$16.50 CAN

Send to: Blaze Books
               P.O. Box 766
               East Helena, Montana 59635

Please send me ___ copies of Irish Hearts - Caress Across
The Ocean at $12.00 each. I am enclosing $_____ plus
$3.00 for the first book (plus $1.50 each additional book) to
cover postage and handling for a total of $_____. Please
send check or money order, no cash or COD's.

Your Name: _____
Address: _____
City/State: _____ Zip: _____
E-Mail: _____

PLEASE TYPE OR PRINT

Please allow four to six weeks for delivery. Prices and availability
subject to change without notice.